SUMMONED

BOOKS BY DANA REDFIELD

EZEKIEL'S CHARIOT

LUCY BLUE AND THE DAUGHTERS OF LIGHT

SUMMONED

encounters with alien intelligence

dana redfield

HAMPTON ROADS
PUBLISHING COMPANY, INC.
for the evolving human spirit

Cover design by Grace Pedalino
Cover painting by Giselle Gautreau

For information write:
Hampton Roads Publishing Company, Inc.
134 Burgess Lane
Charlottesville, VA 22902

Or call: 804-296-2772
FAX: 804-296-5096

e-mail: hrpc@hrpub.com
Web site: http://www.hrpub.com

If you are unable to order this book from your local
bookseller, you may order directly from the publisher.
Quantity discounts for organizations are available.
Call 1-800-766-8009, toll-free.

Library of Congress Catalog Card Number: 98-73905

ISBN 1-57174-126-7

10 9 8 7 6 5 4 3 2 1

Printed on acid-free recycled paper in the United States of America

DEDICATION

for Many   ⊕   Feathers . . .
Thank you for remembering, friend.
There is nothing quite like the balm
of knowing another knows,
and cares.

Jesus said,

If you bring forth what is within you,
what you bring forth will save you.
If you do not bring forth what is within you,
what you do not bring forth will destroy you. "

Gospel According to Thomas,
The Gnostic Gospels, Elaine Pagels

ACKNOWLEDGMENTS

Thank you, Thomas Jefferson, for the Declaration of Independence; and thanks to the framers and defenders of the Constitution of the United States, and the Amendments, without which protections I might have been burned at the stake for heresy, or some such.

Thank you, Jesus Christ, shepherd of my heart;

Albert Einstein, model mind; and Carl Jung, master cartographer of the human spirit.

Heartfelt gratitude for everyone who helped me survive "the business":

Frank DeMarco, lion heart, king of minds, keen of sight, brave soul, friend *extraordinaire*; thank you for caring, Frank, for never doubting, for always expecting more than best.

Robert Friedman, one of the quiet greats in publishing, stalwart in the uplifting of the evolving human spirit; thank you, Bob, for your patience and generosity.

Ginna Colburn, gentle spirit, fiery mind, universal heart; thank you, Ginna, for faith and support, and . . .

to everyone else at Hampton Roads, thanks for loving me through the darkness into the light.

Dave Wallis and Leslie France, Bruce Moen and Pharon, and friends on the mountain, thanks.

I am indebted to Linda Moulton Howe for her gift of care, time, energy, and insight. Thank you, Linda.

Colin Wilson, thank you for your gracious gift of time and wisdom.

Love and gratitude for my parents Nolan and Yvonne Morse, for enduring love, and support in all ways.

Michelle Tomburello, wise, precious daughter;

And dear friends who were there as usual with love, patience and laughter:

Ann Dekker, Sue Laramie, Eileen Dow, and Larry Schmitt; special thanks to Keith Montgomery for many hours of caring and listening, and Jacki for sharing; and for the healing love of friends, Bill McGann, Connie and Ed Mills, Michael Carlyle, and the gang at the Trinity House; and other friends appreciated, Nolan Neilson, Anne Whitcomb, Dan Star, Al MacLeod, Kathryn Kemp, Ila Lee Swanburg, Paul and Aggie Evans, and Roman Vodacek.

Special thanks to more than friends, Connie Isle, Beverly Carter, Don Worley, Dr. Karla Turner, Carla Rueckert, James McCarty, Dr. Helen V. Walker, Dr. Ruth Hover, Kris Garrett, Father Ken, Dr. Joe Lewels, and Katharina Wilson.

And those who were light on the path: Dr. John Mack, Budd Hopkins, Dr. Jacques Vallee, Zecharia Sitchin, Whitley Strieber, Stanton Friedman, Raymond Fowler, Betty Andreasson Luca, Zack Van Eyck, Dr. Leo Sprinkle, Dr. David Jacobs, Dr. James Harder, Travis Walton, members of MUFON, and all of the many experiencers for courage in sharing their stories, along with the pioneering spirits of researchers and investigators, worldwide, who have given so much in time, energy and expense, often at risk to careers or reputations to bring to light these controversial truths.

Special thanks to a dream team of professionals who helped polish the rough edges:

Frank DeMarco, chief editor
Larry Schmitt, copy editor
Rebecca Williamson, managing editor
Anne Meador, proofreader

Last, but hardly least . . . thanks to the Servants of El, and all who uphold the Law of One.
Adonai.

TABLE OF CONTENTS

FOREWORD

Dana Redfield is a talented and perceptive writer who says what she means. So, I asked her about the word "summoned" in this book title. She told me the verb focused on the emotional residue that has remained with her after five years of interactions with entities she sometimes thinks are extraterrestrials and other times wonders if they might be angels and demons. But she cautions that her inability to distinguish is probably a limitation of her human perspective. Whatever the entities are, Dana feels that non-humans literally aroused her from normal human day-to-day routine and summoned her to write down their telepathic communications. She is not alone. Dozens of other people in what has come to be known as the "human abduction syndrome" have also been provoked to write what each perceives to be "downloads of alien telepathic thought."

Dana wrote more than a thousand pages over five years and wonders,

> *"Why should I be given so much, if not to share? That is one of the mysteries that confounded me. My head must explain. So, I say that it was all some sort of schooling to prepare me to write this book, even though that really makes no sense, because this is not so much a book that informs, as it is one that questions as if to provoke a stirring in another's heart of the secrets written there, as they are in all hearts.*
>
> *"I have experienced what it feels like to encounter someone who can see behind my eyes, every thought and feeling. That is the omniscient eye of the alien . . . as it probes and sees all at once, everything you have thought and done but cannot hold in conscious awareness. Thus, the devastating feeling of someone knowing more about you than you do."*

A major theme in *Summoned* is that advanced alien intelligences made several species of humans and put them on Earth to live out dramas for the education of souls. If *Homo sapiens* is in fact the deliberate product of DNA manipulation in already-evolving primates, is it correct to call our makers "alien?" When I asked Dana, she said:

*"You have to add 'intelligences' to the word alien—**alien intelligences**—alien to my everyday consciousness. Outside myself, I can't identify it and sometimes it's almost like an assault or harassment out of my control. The alien intelligence communications are like being on a phone with somebody, but there's no phone and it's thoughts instead of a voice you hear with your ears. Also, the word 'alien' is now interchangeable in the general audience's mind with the concept of non-humans. If I had to get more specific, it becomes very complicated and beyond a single generic word. Summoned is about those complications."*

Questions about other intelligences interacting with earth and what their agendas might be first surfaced in my work the fall of 1979. I was director of special projects at the CBS affiliate in Denver, Colorado. After graduating from Stanford University with a masters degree in communications, I produced TV programs and documentary films about science, medicine and environmental issues. It was in that context that I produced a 1980 documentary entitled *A Strange Harvest* in which I explored the facts and eyewitnesses of the mystery known as "animal mutilations."

For decades, sheriffs, deputies, police, ranchers, and others have reported seeing glowing discs, beams of light, and sometimes non-human entities and even animals raised or lowered in light beams. Flattened circles of grass have also been found in pastures and backyards. The same patterns of tissue have been excised from the head, genitals, and rectum of animals around the world. In my television documentary, I investigated the mystery which led also to people who complained about finding small scoop marks where tissue was removed from legs, arms, chests, backs, and other body areas after vague memories of interactions with glowing discs, beams of light or haunting bedroom intruders. A major difference is that the humans are returned to their lives—often with hours of time missing—but the animals are left dead with no tracks around them, not even their own.

Both animal mutilations and the human abduction syndrome have been linked by ex-military and intelligence agents to a non-human intelligence interacting with earth life since at least the 1950s. Army Lt. Col. Philip J. Corso (now deceased) stated in his 1997 book *The Day After Roswell*: "In the Pentagon from 1961 to 1963, I reviewed field reports from local and state police agencies about the discoveries of dead cattle whose carcasses looked as though they had been systematically mutilated and reports from people who claimed to have been abducted by aliens and experimented on.

> ". . . I also remembered that both civilian and military intelligence personnel attached to the staffs of individuals who worked for the Hillenkoetter (first CIA director) and Twining (Nathan F., chairman of the Joint Chiefs of Staff, 1957-1960) working group on UFOs in the 1950s were actively engaging in research into the kinds of surgical methods that would produce 'crime scene evidence' like this. . . . We had irrefutable evidence that EBEs (extraterrestrial biological entities) were landing on farms, harvesting vital organs from livestock, and then just leaving the carcasses on the ground because they knew we couldn't do anything about it."

People are repulsed by the animal mutilations, yet fascinated by the beautiful, glowing discs. The fact that there is a link between them is readily dismissed by most because no one wants it to be true. And when the media and public are presented with eyewitness testimonies about interaction with what is *inside* those discs, the common response has also been disbelief and ridicule. But U.S. government insiders *do* know about all this, have tried to cover it up, and Dana Redfield thinks have even cooperated.

> ". . . some portion of the government has known about the aliens for years. There are rumors from high places that the 'black government' made a deal with the aliens to pretend ignorance of abductions in exchange for technologies. If true, who knows what the aliens told those in power to secure their cooperation? Maybe the deal-makers thought their decision was for the survival of our species. The few are sacrificed for the many. Maybe the aliens convinced the government some catastrophe was on the horizon that would soon drastically reduce our population."

Since my 1980 documentary investigation, I have interviewed several hundred people who have claimed encounters with alien life forms, even in broad daylight. Many are convinced that the reason tissue is taken from humans and animals is a genetic harvest. One possible use of those genes, abductees say, is to create another hybrid species that is part human and part alien. Dana Redfield agrees that some kind of hybrid mix is evolving on, or from, our planet. Its original alien source and destiny, though, are not always clear as Dana struggles to understand the complex alien thoughts that demand her attention. She wonders if the entire phenomenon is a non-human theatrical production to wake people up at the end of the 20th century.

> *"Or maybe I'm too smart for my own good. Maybe we are being invaded, soon to be supplanted by heartless but intellectually superior aliens who have been marauding us all along, keeping us in the dark with their powerful, unnatural hive mind.*
>
> *"Or maybe both are true . . . If myth-makers themselves had orchestrated these events, they couldn't have done better in setting the stage in this millennial change to reflect a host of prophesies that foretell the end of the world as we know the world.*
>
> *"But where in our myths comes the story of ETs on the scene at such an important time in history? Whisking away ordinary citizens, up into mother ships to extract eggs and sperm, to create those freakish half-breeds. Well, God provided an ark for Noah and company before the Big Flood, didn't He? Why not a complex gene bank befitting our science-minds before the Big Fire?"*

Big Fire means Armageddon to Redfield. In addition to physical examinations and tissue scoops, human abductees like Dana are often shown three-dimensional images of environmental destruction in the Earth's future.

So, in addition to telepathic downloads, holographic images and three-dimensional symbols seem to be used "to teach" abductees as if the alien intelligence itself struggles to find a communication interface. Dana Redfield has been shown symbols reminiscent of a Florida abductee named Jim Sparks who described a telepathic, 3-D education in his conscious encounters with gray-skinned, large-eyed beings in my 1998 book *Glimpses of Other Realities, Vol. II: High Strangeness*. Sparks said he was forced to learn what he calls "commonground symbols between us humans and the aliens." Raymond Fowler's investigation of an abductee named Betty Andreasson also involved symbol training. In several books, Fowler and Andreasson detailed her experiences in an alien world in which Betty saw her own daughter, Becky, sitting before a console tracing odd symbols very similar to the "school room" Jim Sparks described. Betty was also shown a mysterious and holographic-looking image of a phoenix bird rising from ashes without clear explanation.

Debating in her own mind what path the Earth's future might take, Redfield says,

> ". . . I'm a little nervous about the Armageddon and extinction scenarios, I confess, but the professor in me can make no sense of them in light of so much information given that indicates that we are going to bypass the Awful Probability."

The problem we all have, investigators and experiencers together, is what exactly *is* the truth? Dana Redfield, Jim Sparks, Betty Andreasson and others cannot *prove* their experiences. Further, the current global paradigm rejects the human abduction syndrome as not credible and therefore not worth reporting.

Thus, Dana Redfield adds her poignant voice to a growing human chorus over the decades who have largely been ignored, but who persist in trying to share information each perceives is communicated from other beings in other worlds. The reader's challenge is to view the material with a curious, open mind and at least one question: what is behind the worldwide reports in the last half of the 20th century of similar types of non-human beings, craft and technologies which interact with Earth life and human minds and dreams?

Linda Moulton Howe

Author of *Glimpses of Other Realities, Vol. II—High Strangeness;*
Glimpses of Other Realities, Vol. I—Facts & Eyewitnesses;
An Alien Harvest—Further Evidence Linking Animal Mutilation and Human Abductions to Alien Life Forms.
Producer of documentary videos *Strange Harvest* 1993 and *Earth Mysteries: Alien Life Forms. Strange Harvest* won an Emmy.

PREFACE

GETTING REAL

"Get real," we are fond of saying. "I don't think so!" I often responded during the past few years. But there is nothing quite like an editor to change an author's mind. When Frank DeMarco called, in January 1997, expressing interest in my book-in-progress, I tried to "get real"; but even writing the first draft of *Summoned* seemed a dangerous thing to do, and the thought of publication gave me serious jitters.

When Frank asked to read what I'd written so far, the fears triggered were like lions, with big mouths, flying at you in a corner, where you have not so much as a wooden chair. If I couldn't get past the cats to even *talk* real with Frank, how was I to muster the courage to complete the book?

"Yes, yes," he said on the phone, responding to my intellectual stumbling around, trying to explain my problem, "but how do you *feel* about all this?"

Good question. But one very hard to answer, because I stay in my head a lot, afraid to know what is in my heart. I resorted to the language I know best: story. In chapter 14, "Getting Serious," I refer to the allegory below to help in discussion of the communication problems between the head and the heart. Much of the alien abduction phenomenon can only be understood by the heart, especially concerning the very real barriers an abductee encounters in the way of disbelief and skepticism.

Here is what I sent to my editor:

February 28, 1997 (letter):

Dear Frank,

You ask me how I feel. Like a peasant come to town weighed down by a burden of hay. . . .

This allegory is full of literary problems, but something works here for me, so you're getting as it came, with no editing.

Now imagine . . . I must pass through this certain country town on my way to . . . I will think where later. This is the only safe way. Other ways I will encounter wild animals or rapists or some other danger. The town is the only way. But it is a hard way, and dangerous, too. Some who enter this town do not make it through. Now it is hard to imagine, but try . . . the townspeople have strong emotions and opinions about hay. Never mind why . . . something happened in this town a long time ago that created this attitude towards hay. I will think of it later. As I will think of why it is so important that I pack this hay through this town. Possibly because my horses will die if . . .

Whatever, I must pass through this town where people hate hay. If I could, I would keep to the shadows, and hurry through, undetected. But I am a comely peasant, so someone is bound to notice, for comeliness is a powerful draw, even when the comely one is packing hay. If I were larger or stronger, I would stomp through this town with a threatening glare in my eye. Maybe I would carry whips, and fondle them as I stomped, angry of eye. But the best I can do is to walk swiftly with an air of calm, hoping people will receive me with a modicum of respect, though I know to expect at least snickers, snide smiles, hoots, or flares of anger at someone so bold as to dare walk through this town with a bundle of hay in the light of day.

As I pass, there are jeers, and jokes. Someone kicks. Someone tries to trip. Someone throws a stone. Someone demands to know the reason I am doing something so loathsome as to parade hay in sight of decent people.

When first I came through this town, I tried to explain the reason I was packing hay, and why I needed to come this way. But it made no impression on these people, for they had lost all reason as pertains to hay. Next I tried to be friendly, pretending that their opinions did not bother me as I moved as a good sport, swiftly past the glares.

Finally I knew it best to just move swiftly.

Then one day . . . let's say that an old woman follows me in the shadows. She is smiling in a peculiar way. I am not sure what to think. Maybe she means to lure me to pause, then she will spit in my face. I hurry on.

The old woman moves out of the shadows to confront me. My heart leaps in my chest. But she does not spit. She beckons me over to a maple tree that is ablaze in autumn gold, away from the attention of other townspeople.

The old woman grasps my arm. Her face is wrinkled; her eyes, electric blue. "I have watched you come this way, packing hay," she says gently. Then she says, as if to strike lightning at my feet, "*Why?*"

The word startles me so, I almost laugh. *Why?* Someone wants to know why I pack hay through this town? My relief is profound. Maybe I am a fool for trusting her so quickly to be genuinely curious, but I am so starved for human kindness, her question is like a great kettle of savory stew.

The sad story of what I must endure to get hay to my horses spills out of my mouth like a child howling a dissonant song.

"Ah . . ." she says, rolling her eyes, a smile brightening her face. "I *remember* now, I do! *Hay* . . . food for horses! That's what it is—that's what it *always* was! Oh . . . and to make the walls of a house sturdier, I remember that, too, now. And to spread upon the floor to catch the droppings . . . and to bundle for a bed . . .

"Ahhh . . . !" She leans back her head, a most particular twinkle in her eyes. "And a place for lovers in the loft!" But then a shadow falls over her eyes. "Oh, yes," she says, now her words less sure. "That's when it all began."

"What?" I respond in a small voice I hope will not scare away the wisdom she knows.

"A *baby* was born in the hay!" she whispers harshly. She looks quickly to the left, to the right, then bows her head, and heaves a sigh that startles the apron across her bosom.

That's all? I ask with my eyes.

"The baby that began it all." She nods her head.

She leads me closer to the tree, and there proceeds to tell me in fast cadence of the baby, the hay, and the cause for the taunts that had chased me through this town.

The baby was born to young lovers unmarried, though their sin was not the cause for the fear of hay, for they were a couple loved, and all was forgiven. It was the baby itself—not the baby—the man he grew to be. He was one who saw behind every eye, every thought of every man, woman, and child. And though he was kind, and most loving by nature, it was a thing the people could not abide, for he saw in them what they could not see themselves. But that was a lie, he would point out gently, for if they did not see also, how did they know to feel ashamed?

He tried to teach the people his way of seeing; he tried to teach them not to be afraid, to look . . . for, he said . . . when you look, your eyes are torches that burn away the darkness. But most refused to believe him for the discomfort they felt when he looked. He tried to tell them that if they would but look, *together* they would see beyond the darkness to the light in one another, and become a true community. But still the people could not abide what he taught.

"But why not?" I ask.

The old woman answers in a tone of sadness, "Because if all is in the light, who has advantage over another?"

"Oh," I say, as if I understand. "Oh," I say, understanding. "Oh," I say, my tone now as sad.

Yes!" she hisses. "It is true!"

"But the hay . . ." I say, desperately.

"The hay *reminds* them, you foolish girl!"

"Reminds them of . . . Of . . ."

"Of what they killed to have their way!"

"Him!" The word burst from my lips. Suddenly I am so overcome with thirst, I feel faint.

The old woman grabs both my arms.

"But . . . But . . ." Tears fall from my eyes, as if to answer the thirst in my mouth. "So . . . they *hate hay*?"

My astonishment could not be greater if I had discovered the meaning of a secret that had long mystified sages.

"Yeesss . . ." she says, the word like a rusty gate creaking open when the key of truth releases, ". . . they are quite insane."

If not for her eyes, her calm would ice my heart. She looks at me, and I look at her, and light passes between us. "You had better get along," she says, glancing toward the sun on the horizon. "When you come again, I will be waiting," she adds, just to speak, for she need not say another word. Her embrace is enough, the look that passes between us, the light it makes, the truth we share.

As I set toward the rosy glow of the sun, I wonder if it will be different when I come this way again. Yes and no, I decide. Yes, for Mary (she told me her name before we parted); no, for the people who hate the hay for the man who came this way before me.

Could I say anything to them, to persuade away the veils over their eyes? Nay. They hate the hay for what it reminds, the very thing I would say. Will my burden feel any lighter? Nay. Heavier, I think, for what I learned in the light that passed between my eyes and the electric blue in Mary's.

Will I bear the burden easier for the truth I now know? Aye. For now there is another, the one from whom I learned the truth, the one who bore her heart to me. But what did I learn this day more than the terrible truth the townspeople hide beneath their hatred of hay? That if even two share a truth, if a terrible truth, the heart is made lighter, though the burden remains heavy; and for that truth, surely all my steps shall come easier.

How do I feel? That it is best to move swiftly.

Summoned is more than a personal rendering of experience with beings commonly called aliens; it is a story about me, you, us, them—humankind and alienkind; how we are related, and the bearing that relationship has on our evolution.

Readers of *Ezekiel's Chariot* and *Lucy Blue and the Daughters of Light* know me by my signature of humor. I confess that during the intensity of contact and encounters, in the words of Mindy—I almost "croaked of terminal seriousness." But my sense of humor is returning, if like a cautious child treated too sternly, peering around a corner at laughing children, wondering if it's safe to come out and play now.

I do play in this book, using fable, allegory, parable, or poem, when discussing things the heart comprehends easier than the head. Later I will tell you another story, "Brother Brain and Sister Soul," to help in discussion of my suspicion that all this abduction business may point to a "merging" of the cerebral hemispheres, or activation of a hidden potential in our brains. While my experiences were very real and physical, in light of a leap in conscious awareness, the word "real" is just too small now to hold all that has happened, all I learned, and what I now see. Perhaps meta-reality better describes my view since "the Breach" (when the aliens got up-close and personal). Meta- is a Greek derivative of *metabole*, meaning change, and means now in this context, beyond and transcending. Reality for me *has* changed, and transcended the consensus view I accepted without question before these extraordinary experiences.

Most often we have heard from those who are working on the "nuts and bolts" aspects of the UFO phenomenon. If science were able to address every facet of our being and reality, there would be no call for a book like this one. In the relating of my experiences, I will explore several theories, but the one that provokes me the most is an element of the phenomenon that may herald something far grander than the stories we hear about cosmic kidnappings for the sole purpose of creating hybrids to bolster an alien species at an evolutionary dead end, or to supplant us. If indeed a new human-alien prototype is in the making—and I have reason to believe it may be true—it is being conducted by means of the creative principles of nature that govern Earth's web of life. How could it be otherwise? Everything that happens on Earth, or in the dimensional vicinity that interpenetrates our manifest world, is natural and real.

The gift in writing this book was that it helped me focus more clearly on the "big picture" in a way impossible, just thinking or talking about it; or driving myself nuts reviewing all of the seeming disparate parts of a very complicated puzzle.

On the surface, and even deep into its tunnels, the alien abduction phenomenon can be very scary. But there are elements that give rise to hope. Maybe in the shadows of what appears to be a nefarious plot to invade and supplant, a new kind of human being is in the making—not a freakish, robotic, emotionally-challenged hybrid—but a "humaniel,"[1] a being as close to an angel as can be in human form on this plane; a being capable of fulfilling our legacy of humane guardianship of this sphere we call Earth.

That's my brightest vision, but there is much dark territory to cross before I can show credence for such a glowing speculation.

---

1   In ancient times, the suffix "iel" or "ael" signified either an angelic being, such as Gabriel, Zadkiel, or Raphael, or a human being such as Ezekiel or Daniel of Biblical record who had earned the divine designation. The literal meaning of *iel* means "of angels or of El" (see chapter 10, ELOHIM, for more about El).

1

WHO AM I?

I can neither speak nor write precisely of the mysteries in my heart. What I know belongs to a knowing too large for any one heart to contain, as my head cannot process the consciousness of all of the information given to me in a way that can be rendered intelligible to minds unprepared.

Why I would be given so much, if not to share, is one of the mysteries that confounds. My head must explain. So I say that it was all some sort of schooling to prepare me to write this book, even though that really makes no sense, because this is not so much a book that informs, as it is one that questions, if to provoke a stirring in another's heart of the secrets written there, as they are in all hearts.

I am female, eldest of seven, ex-Mormon, ex-wife, mother, daughter, sister, friend, late-bloomer, violinist, poet, artist, wanderer, God-seeker, Aquarian, INFJ type, author . . . and alien abductee?

The key, I said one morning, is to shuck the label alien abductee, along with all the rest. After all, what we appear to be are moths to the butterflies we really are. Whoever, whatever I am, I'm just passing through. Everything I create here, including my "identity"—based on beliefs uninformed of truth—will die with the moth; dust to dust. What I am, in truth, will endure. The rest is human costume and drama.

If only we could write off the challenges of human life so easily . . .

In 1980, when I accepted employment at an aerospace company in Denver, Colorado, for the second time in my life I had to qualify for a Top Secret clearance. Eventually I was interviewed for five hours by two squinty-eyed Department of Defense agents. They said I had the longest personal history they had ever investigated. At the conclusion of the interview, they required that I place my right hand on a Bible and swear that all that I had confessed was the complete truth. No problem. I honestly told them everything. That's why I had the longest personal history they'd ever seen. After all that has happened, and all the rumors about cover-ups or possible government mind-control experiments, I could only wonder, in hindsight, if the five-hour interview with the D.O.D. agents was for the reason they claimed.

Some believe that all true alien abductees are "military-connected." In 1964 I was employed as a clerk typist at the Nevada Test Site, flying to work each day on a DC-3 Gooney Bird to a site called the Paiute Mesa, 120 miles north of Las Vegas. The Paiute Mesa is on the way to Area 51, "Dreamland." Once when our transport was grounded for repairs, our crew was flown to work on an Area 51 Gooney Bird with passenger windows painted black.

The G-Men could have got me then!

Another government connection was at Hill Air Force Base in Ogden, Utah, in 1943. When I was conceived, my mother worked in the cafeteria there, and my father was an officer in the Army Air Corps. Could this relate to the numerous times I was missing as a child in Vernal, Utah? Vernal is a UFO-sighting hot spot, from past to present. Details were documented in a book (now out of print) titled *Utah UFO Display,* by Frank Salisbury, Ph.D., professor at Utah State University in Logan. On June 30, 1996, Zack Van Eyck, staff writer for the *Deseret News* (Salt Lake City), wrote a lengthy Sunday feature article about UFO activities in the region of Vernal (Duchesne/Unitah Counties). Van Eyck called me for input; some of my story appeared in his article.

A person of my experience can feel paranoid sometimes. The facts are: I do have a long and complicated personal history; twice I was employed by Department of Defense subcontractors; and my parents were working at an Air Force base when I was conceived.

If government is responsible for my phenomenal experiences, we have severely underestimated these people. If the rumors are true, someone in the government is very interested in our spiritual development. Someone is interested in our souls. Someone in the government is calling us to remember that love is the only force by which we survive in community, or as sovereign individuals. Does this sound like a message government agents would send in a mind-control experiment?

I can twist it around to make it sound believable. Fiction was my business before I was summoned to do this work. (Summoned by celestial ancestors? I have come to believe, yes. But belief is not knowledge. Belief is a kind of bridge I choose to walk in faith.)

Among my peers, in the 80s, it was standard fare to joke about having alien origins. To my knowledge, none of us ever considered it to be more than an interesting intellectual possibility. Frequently we debated the four "RE's"—Religion, Reincarnation, Reason, and Reality, never fully agreeing on anything, of course, but that was the point. Who really knew? Do we spend hours, years, lifetimes debating whether or not the sun is hot, the ground is hard, water is wet, trees grow, flowers bloom, babies laugh, eagles fly, and the Earth is flat? Before Christopher Columbus set sail, there were a lot of people who knew for certain the Earth was flat. Any fool could see that. We don't debate facts.

Life might have been dull if not for friends who were eager to debate the imponderables with me. But there was one subject that these lively thinkers were not interested in: Are we being visited by extraterrestrials? Are spaceships real? Do people get abducted by aliens? I don't remember when I became enthralled with the idea that the rumors we'd heard about spaceship activity might be based in truth, but the fact that most of my friends were not interested stands out in memory.

"Don't you realize what this would mean if true?" I asked them. "It'll blow religion right out of the water! Our whole system will collapse! Scientists will go mad! The stock market will plummet! Politicians will run for the hills! Think of it—something *higher* than us! Not a fuzzy God idea—*real aliens*!"

The term "get a life" was not in vogue in the early 80s, but that describes the looks I got. Pats on my head, grins, eye-rolls. For my friends, it was all the stuff of science fiction. Even back then, I felt alone with a Big Secret. It wasn't that I knew UFOs were heralds of my future; nonetheless it was with me, in me; I couldn't shake it . . . the *feeling* it was true.

My upbringing in the Mormon church ought to excuse me from insults hurled at "true believers." I never saw any science fiction movies in the 40s and 50s (such films, and even sci-fi comic books, were forbidden), but my church taught me that other planets are inhabited, and God is a super-physical being who lives on a planet called Kolob. In the opinion of some ufologists, Joseph Smith, founder of the Mormon church, was an alien contactee.

Before I left the church, at the age of eighteen, I never heard prophesy that our space neighbors were going to pay us a visit. Jesus was going to return, of course, to kick butt, and usher in the Millennium. Mormons, of course, would be the elect who would govern the whole affair (maybe warming up with the Olympics in 2002).

The "who-am-I" question has to include these root teachings as possibly influencing my perceptions of my extraordinary experiences. Another possibility is that I was selected/targeted/used (take your pick) *because* of my roots in Mormonism. Either way, it seems more than coincidental that the essence of some of the information imparted to me links with some of what Joseph Smith was told. This awareness did not penetrate until I was deep into the mystery, when I was jolted to discover that one of my sources—Elohim—purportedly also communicated with Joseph Smith.

For all I know, Smith and I, and everyone else reporting these things, are experiencing some sort of evolution in consciousness no one comprehends yet. If true, naturally there would be similarities among all participants. Naturally, stories would vary in details all over the globe, because who among us is not biased by cultural or religious programming? Naturally some would be instant true believers of whatever perception possessed them. Naturally some would build whole cosmologies upon their assumptions, as did the Hale-Bopp crew who committed suicide, believing their bodies to be mere containers. Naturally, some would eschew all religious references and concentrate on the mechanics of the phenomenon. And, naturally, scientists would be the last to take seriously such reports. To thoroughly study this business, a man or woman of science would have to depart from both lab and established methods. But if he or she did that—would that be scientific?

Who am I? One who has had her thinking re-circuited. Did my predisposition to beliefs about extraterrestrial life churn in my mind along with a vivid imagination to a point of manifestation in my physical environment? If so, why don't I see, hear, and experience manifestation of all of my passionate beliefs, and *everything* I powerfully imagine?

The most celebrated accounts of alien abduction are of the spectacular kind: unwitting humans beamed up into spaceships, to the amazement of credible witnesses. But information shared across the planet indicates that most cases are of the "bedroom" kind. A silver disc in the sky that resembles a human-produced construct is easier to accept as "real" than is something we do not readily recognize as conforming to established beliefs about the nature of manifest reality. The proposition that Others exist who have mastered the ability to summon and fetch us at will, directly from our homes, through walls or windows, is subject to the demand to show or explain the science behind such claims before the case is even considered as possibly valid. My perception of the interconnectedness of all, including events and purposes, is cause for me to wonder if the resistance to serious investigation of such activities serves as a cover that modulates awareness of radical changes occurring among humankind, on a time-table of controlled preparation for revelation.

Like many experiencers, my history includes missing time episodes in early childhood, suspicious phenomenal events throughout my life, evidences of insertion of devices into my body, and indications of an orchestration of events that prepared me for realization of the "alien presence" in my life.

My extraordinary experiences are summarized below, to provide grounding for coming chapters where I interrupt the flow of the personal narrative to share information by way of alien intelligence.

STAGE ONE—Birth to 1984, then . . .

STAGE TWO—1984 to 1992: August 22, 1986 is the day I awoke to find evidence of implants in both of my hands (details later).

Almost immediately following this event, I was compelled to study quantum physics, strange for someone of an artistic temperament. But I did not "connect the dots" from the evidence of implants to this new interest. I was also drawn to study ancient history, genetics, mythology, and related subjects.

During this phase, I began to become aware of the holistic nature of life on Earth. I was surprised one night when tears filled my eyes as I watched a documentary about whales. And watching the movie *Abyss*, when the actors encountered the under-water aliens, I burst out sobbing . . . which was *almost*, but not quite, an inner admission of my "secret life." In my "upstairs" consciousness, I was so bothered by this emotional reaction, I rented the movie a few months later to see if it affected me differently. Again, the tears flowed. I rented that movie twice more, each time feeling the same depth of emotion. I could admit that I was somehow connected to aliens, but still the idea of abduction was abhorrent, and I had a list of reasons why that could not be true. Unpleasantly, these changes in my interests and awareness marked a divergence in paths in my marriage. The more I moved—or was moved—toward disclosure of my involvement with aliens, the wider the gap in interests, values, and goals with my husband. Divorce was the outcome in 1992.

STAGE 3—1993: Indications that I was in contact with extraterrestrials were strong, but I was still resistant to the idea that I could be an abductee. In the latter months of 1993, I was compelled to begin work with letters and numbers, *kaballah*-like exercises that I would later interpret as a kind of schooling that prepared me for all that has happened since.

STAGE 4—1994-1997: The Breach is shorthand for the time in May and June of 1994 when suddenly there was an acceleration of phenomena in my physical environment, namely light displays, sound announcements, and a range of physical symptoms that precede abduction events. There were electrical disturbances in my home, discoveries of new scars on my body, or marks such as claw-like streaks on my legs after abduction events. My special Zoom pen disappeared, to reappear in plain sight a few days later. Such "cosmic displacements" are common among abductees.

At this stage, the terror I felt derived from a serious "knowing" that this was a passage, or initiation, that I might *not* survive. Some don't.

During these three years, every aspect of my life, on all levels, underwent radical change. The sense of alienation I experienced among friends and family was profound; not to mention the ridicule one sees, hears, and feels from the usual sources. But throughout, there always was a "double reference," which I now feel is indicative that I am among many "forerunners" of a new kind of human species, which theory I discuss throughout the book.

Although my experiences were not spectacular, I doubt that many abductees kept records as thorough and meticulous as I share in the appendix. The record shows a great deal of "high strangeness" that other experiencers should readily recognize. I moved details to the appendix to reduce the "re-living factor" as I wrote. I can still feel overwhelmed and spooked, just reviewing the record.

Is Stage Four the end? I'm afraid this is only the beginning. First, a lifetime of suspicious events; second, preparation; third, The Breach and acceleration of phenomena impossible to suppress or control; fourth, relief from the intensity; fifth . . . sixth . . . seventeenth? When does it end?

We don't end. The human experience is but one dynamic of our beingness. Don't let the stories of "invasion" or supplantation by sickly, robotic hybrids influence what you know to be true of the indomitable human spirit.

2

BEFORE THE BREACH

We are all one, they said. (If true, who are alien?) *All you judge as Other*. (Foreign words to my learning.) *All die*, they said, *some to rest in tombs of time, some to rise anew, some to shuck cocoons nigh before the portal closes*. (Gobbly-gook to ears deaf to the heralds of memory.)

In the months preceding the Breach (when the "Others" got up-close and personal in my physical environment), I'd never been happier. My life had been hard, but now in the autumn of my years, I could see across troubled waters to the shores of my content.

Emotional crises brought me to Moab in May, 1992. Here I would recover after the collapse of my only true marriage. Here, near my parents in retirement; here where my polygamist ancestors rest in the soil in smug Mormon peace.

I cried for three months, wiped my face, then moved into a modest home on Moenkopi Street and got to work on finishing my novel-in-progress: *Lucy Blue and the Daughters of Light*. I had suffered a great loss, but I was still able to write!

By spring '93, I had begun another novel when Dr. Helen Walker in Denver called and invited me to present a writers' workshop at the Rocky Mountain Seth Conference to be held in September at Winter Park, Colorado. I told her I'd be delighted.

Creative writing can't be taught, I believe, so I fished for a way to inspire people who wanted to write but lacked confidence. Recently I had become fascinated with certain patterns of letters in certain names. Words were meaningful . . . were letters? I had thought of letters as no more than the mechanics of language—levers, cogs, wheels. The patterns that had caught my attention hinted of hidden meanings in letters. If I could get my mind around the concept, maybe I could use it to convey something of the mystery of creative writing.

My love for writing was seated in my love for words, which may have originated before I was two years old, when my grandmother taught me to read the alphabet. Soon I would realize that this hook I was biting was on a line submerged in deep waters.

This seems a good place to mention the "generational factor." Most abduction researchers say that "where there is an abductee, there is a family, or lineage of abduction." If anyone else in my family is an abductee, it is well hidden. But my grandmother was an unusual woman. As a child, during a prayer session over a premature baby, she saw, outdoors, three men dressed in Biblical clothes, watching. The baby lived.

Like me, Grandma was precognitive, and was something of a mystic. Once she wrote and submitted a piece on intelligence, and was told by the publisher, "No one understands intelligence." Grandma was my primary caretaker during my first three years, while Mother worked to support us.

Excited about the speaking engagement, I got to work on a presentation of the topic of my interest.

On flip charts, I showed some of the peculiarities I had spotted in letter sequences, for instance, in my mother's name, relative to three significant men in her life:

YVONNE	SORENSEN	Mother's name
JOE	MOORE	My birth father's name
ROD	JONES	A man Mother almost married
NOLAN	MORSE	Her husband for over fifty years; my dad

In my own personal lexicon I saw these patterns: I was born Moore, adopted by Morse, raised Mormon, lived in Moab on Moenkopi Street, and my best friend at present was Montgomery. MO seemed to be my "M-O." Another pattern, just as an example: In the 70s I married a man named Kerry Mikkelson, who was born in October 1955; his mother was Irish, his father Finnish. In 1993, I met a man named Michael Keeney who looked enough like Mikkelson to be his brother. Michael (same root as Mikkelson) was born May 12, 1955 (the day and month I married Mikkelson); Michael Keeney's father was Irish, his mother, Finnish. Here's how it looked on the chart:

KERRY MIKKELSON	Born: Oct 1955	Mother: Irish	Father: Finnish
MICHAEL KEENEY	Born: May 1955	Mother: Finnish	Father: Irish

I might have dismissed it all as coincidence if I had not met, soon afterward, *six other Michaels, all born in September or October 1955*.

Something seemed to be showing me Something. Was there an "alphabetological" influence in our lives, like astrology and numerology? My interest quickly surpassed this superficial question. The coincidences in the letter patterns had hooked my curiosity, but upon closer inspection I noticed something that captured my attention more.

I was no longer looking at mere letters; I was seeing geometric shapes that I intuitively felt had been designed to attract or direct energies. Or *something* like that. Suddenly the Bible verse in *John* about the "Word being made Flesh" pressed upon my mind, as did Yahweh's pronouncement, "Let there be light." Maybe *sound* was the first principle; not light, after all, God first spoke; then creation, light, appeared at His command. Was I touching the hem of *Logos*?

By the time I left the conference, I was obsessed to know intimately each letter of our alphabet.

The novel I had started remained on the shelf, never to be completed. I cleared off my writing table and began an odyssey to break the letter-number codes. Little did I realize the impact this work would have on me, and my life.

After tracing the history of each letter down through Medieval, Roman, Greek, Etruscan, Phoenician, Semitic to Egyptian hieroglyphics at 3000 B.C., I moved on to study the geometrics of each, and then the relationships of one letter to another, from every angle I could conceive. Each letter related to a number in each chart, graph, or formula I created. Soon I was deep into an alpha-numeric language that underlies familiar meanings. One chart, entitled "Structure = Energy Crystallized," showed relationships between letters, numbers, and musical notes; another was a mandala called a "Sciosis" that revealed portals on a kind of map that symbolizes this plane of existence. A "house" similar to the Jewish Tree of Life came to me in a vision, and work on this mystified me for hours and days on end. The charts, graphs, symbols, and formulas gave way to pictures, as I probed concepts too large to describe with words.

Magda, a friend, suggested I was "into *kabbalah*." I didn't know *kabbalah* from cabbage. To educate myself, I bought *The Book of Letters* and *Honey From the Rock* by Rabbi Lawrence Kushner, and was astonished to learn that *he* knew what I had discovered about letters, at my kitchen table.

> *"In each letter and each line and each crownlet of each letter are entrances to worlds of awareness."*
>
> *—Tanhuma Bereshet I*

> *"There is not a word or even so much as a letter of what the Holy One has given that does not contain precious mysteries."*
>
> *—Zohar III*

Honey from the Rock, Lawrence Kushner
Jewish Lights Publishing, Woodstock, Vermont, 1992

The familiarity I felt scanning these and another book about *kabbalah* suggested I had come to this work more than a novice. It felt like I was retrieving remnants of knowledge from my deep past, or a collective well of memories.

Immediately, embarking on the quest, I experienced Guidance in a profound ways. It was as if an intelligent being stood over my shoulder, telepathically directing, as I worked. But the instant I would mentally salute awareness of this Guidance, it would cease. I learned to work in a state of "split consciousness." Several times while I was drawing, I literally felt a force moving my hand and pen. At one level of consciousness I gaped, amazed, while at the level of focus, I acknowledged the "automatic drawing," as if this were an everyday occurrence.

Guidance steered me into the Bible to fetch the names of the twelve sons and one daughter of Israel, and the seven churches addressed in the *Book of Revelations*. Formal names of angels were added to the picture taking shape, along with appellations of planets and star systems. These were puzzle pieces I shifted from one construct to another, as Guidance continued to instruct. Some of what I was shown personified the physics I had studied, which opened gateways in my mind for a glimpse of a Great Design behind all we perceive and experience as random, disparate, or coincidental. Finally I was shown how to create a cipher that was personally meaningful to me and my life.

Now I knew that our lives were knit together in a maze of interconnecting events and elements that made our linear perception of time and our distortions of spacial separation seem like checkers to chess. Interconnection was no longer merely a concept; I knew it to be a fundamental principle of life.

A common stumbling block in Religion is to fixate on a finger that points at God. I suspect that Science may have fallen into a similar trap. Mathematical formulae are as much fingers pointing to reality as Holy Scriptures point to the Divine. There are profound differences between symbols (words, numbers) and the realities they represent. In the lexicon of Religion, fixation on symbols is a form of idol worship; illusions, in Mystical terms; and signs of default to a technical mind-set among the high priests of Science called to lead us into the Cosmic Age.

Pearls are not given without price. Concurrent with the mysteries unfolding at my kitchen table, telepathic communications quickly reached a new level of impact.

I did not aspire to be a channeler, a messenger, or anything of the sort. My belief was, this contact business was all mystical experience that would fuel my next novel. I was willing to convey the essence of the information transmitted to me in fiction—and that's all—and the transmitters seemed to agree this would be sufficient.

Some of the material coming across the transom definitely had an extraterrestrial signature . . . but was this a screen? Jubilant as I felt about the mysteries unfolding, I felt cautious about the communications. I felt from my sources a deep sense of familiarity, trust, and even love—but could I be tricked into feeling this way? I was no Pollyanna to the subject of deceit, mind control, and deception. My first two novels, written in '85 and '86, read like cover stories for covert alien abduction. This I realized later, as I would later admit that I had always lived a "double-life," detectable only after phenomenal evidence directed me to examine my life through the lens of suspicion that I was one who had been taken and schooled young. I often say it all began in June 1994, but that's just when the phenomena intensified and accelerated. Throughout my life there were signs of preparation.

On the night of November 9, 1993, awakening from a dream about the *kabbalah*-like house I had created, I saw across the room a man I had dreamt about before. Because he resembled an old friend, Tucker, I called him that.

"Tucker . . . is that you?" I was sitting up, foggy and flabbergasted that I was seeing him . . . *in my room*. The light was dim, but I could see that he was wearing a body-suit. His hair, or skull cap, was black, and widow-peaked. I will never forget his dark, penetrating eyes. How could I see his face so clearly? Mysteries, mysteries.

He said in a stern, precise voice, "I am not Tucker. I am Los Angelos [sic]."

I don't know what happened after that. I woke the next morning feeling physically "whacked," and haunted by the event.

Four years later, January 5, 1997, on a show called "UFOs Down to Earth" on the Discovery Channel, there was a drawing of "Los Angelos" on the screen. The drawing was made by an English policeman, Alan Godfrey, who was reporting on an abduction into a spaceship where he had encountered this being. Apparently Los Angelos gets around.

Similarly, I was jarred several months earlier, reading Linda Moulton Howe's book, *Glimpses of Other Realities, Volume I: Facts and Eyewitnesses*. There on page 275 were drawings of beings with widow-peaked hair, or skull caps. Other features—slanted, cat-like eyes, and very tall bodies that taper significantly from shoulders to feet—reminded me of Rowah, my childhood "imaginary playmate."

Dream, vision, visitation, hallucination—I did not interpret the "appearance" of Los Angelos as an indication of alien abduction, nor did I want to court association between extraterrestrial contact and abduction . . . never mind the evidence of implantation, and all the other arrows indicative of alien high-jinx.

In the fall of 1993, I was soaring on a mystical cloud, my feet rarely touching ground.

3

CONTACT

If alien abduction were not controversial enough, I bear the added burden—or gift, depending on the view—of "contact" with intelligences I call alien only because they don't sit down with me and chat, face-to-face, with coffee and cakes, in my primary reality. If not for this added burden-gift, I would not have written *Summoned*, because there are already many excellent books by and about abductees.

As a member of MUFON (Mutual UFO Network), I am well aware of the skeptical attitude toward telepathic communications in the public, and among UFO investigators and researchers who are working to gain the respect of the scientific community through presentation of "hard facts." There is hardly an article written, or show aired on TV, that does not include apologetic remarks about the "lunatic fringe." Sometimes such comments are directed at anyone who claims contact with "meta-terrestrials." In the 50s, fantastic stories of contact were plentiful, and the cloud over the most ridiculous still hangs in the air, to be pointed out, in case you might be one of the gullible who needs to be told what to heed, or ignore, by people too smart to be fooled.

Like it or not, and mostly I did not, I was one who was schooled, and physically prepared, to convey certain information. I had a choice. In choosing to write *Summoned*, I trusted that readers would be savvy enough to judge for themselves the merits and authenticity of anything I share, about myself, or under the alien signature. Because I have no way of confirming the actual identity of my sources, or their motives, each person must discern for him- or herself the truth, or distortion of any given message.

Contact occurred the first time in 1989. It never seemed like what people described as channeling, or automatic writing. There was always a sense of a telepathic link. This will probably sound nuts to non-experiencers, but abductees will understand. Because of the bell-like tones, hums, vibrations, and zings in my ears that seem like audio punctuation marks at significant times (and trouble I've had with my jaws), I am suspicious there are implants inside my head.

In 1989, contact made me nervous, and I did not pursue it. When it began to happen again in 1993, I was more curious, and cooperative. *Something* intelligent was communicating, and would even answer some of my questions . . . but who? And why?

Well, they told me why, but I just had trouble accepting it. I told myself something like, "This sure sounds like ETs, but what if it's just a bunch of discarnate juvenile delinquents playing a game? I know this happens all the time, and a lot of the stuff people say while channeling bores the heck out of me, so what's the point? Okay . . . I'll just go along for awhile and see what develops. . . ."

Well, the information coming through was not boring me. It had me sitting on pins and needles. I was told a lot of stuff that I later learned others had likewise been told. This proves nothing to you, but for me it was one way I could confirm I was not "making up" the information.

Most of it was like a kind of home-study course in something that might be called the "physics of spirituality, or consciousness." I never received information on "Earth changes," but plenty about the creation of a new or hybrid species.

Certain sources communicate in a kind of "natural-ese," using examples of how nature works to explain spiritual laws and concepts. You will see what I mean later, for instance in the message I named "Make a Baby Form."

Some of the stuff I recorded is "quasi-technical." For instance, I was told about travel from one dimension to the other, utilizing principles of "tetrahedron physics." Sometimes simple symbols are communicated to illustrate.

Before I stopped recording information in 1997, I filled up about 100 thick spiral notebooks.

Regarding translations of information from my energy fields: in 1993 I was told: "You are *encoded*." Though I had not the foggiest notion what that meant, it rang true. A word, a phrase, a thought that

I write down is sometimes like a bottlecap popped, and out pours information I clearly know I am not "creating."

In 1997, I was told, "We [aliens] are speaking of an 'infusion' of energy-intelligence into the human being at the fetal stage. The child is then monitored and schooled in secret. . . ." (More on this in chapter thirteen.)

Because it is virtually impossible to share all that I was given, I have to wonder if, in part, the "translation" process had something to do with changing the nature of my consciousness, and maybe even the neurology of my brain.

But my primary interest was in the content of the messages. For instance, in August 1993 I was told not to be surprised if some government *staged* a phony UFO landing for their own purposes. So many people are expecting a real "mass landing" event, or the like, it wouldn't be difficult to deceive a good portion of the population with a simulation. Do I think this will happen? Maybe the communicators meant to encourage me to *question everything*. I keep in mind that our present-day technologies are so sophisticated, almost anything can be "staged" to appear to be real.

It was my special torment to have to select from the overwhelming number of messages what to include in *Summoned*. A few messages, such as *The History of Humankind in Summary* (chapter eleven) were meant for this book, but the rest was up to me.

The following telepathic communication, recorded before I knew I was an abductee, is a kind of teaching about the "principle of probabilities." In the form of it, you will see something of how a telepathic communication "happens," where they "insert" with imagery that somehow I convert into words. Perhaps you can imagine how fast my pen was moving to get it all.

For a long time I had a good grasp of the principle of probabilities in the *abstract*, but it took a while before it became "real" for me in a way that I could act on it. Eventually I realized that my frequent precognitions were precise examples of what the transmitters are talking about. Glimpses of future events are a look at "gaps in comprehension" of that which is already in motion or in progress. The more aware we become of the reality of this principle, the more we can exercise our will to reduce "surprises," and actually transform our experiences. This I found to be true about my perception of the abduction phenomenon, and I'm actively working to use the principle in my everyday life. It works . . . but for me it *takes work*. Just because I have the ability to record telepathically communicated information doesn't mean I'm quick to comprehend it, or put it to use in my own life.

Don't worry if it sounds like "gobbly-gook" at the first or even the second reading. Some of this stuff takes thought. That's what it's for. I beg your pardon for the "roughness." I was new at this in 1994.

Recorded January 30, 1994:
"Simultaneous Time/Staged Events"

First, my notes:
Regarding the idea that time is not linear, but all is happening simultaneously . . . but we can only *observe* and *experience* one event at a time . . . (They) say events are already in motion, "happening," like temporary static . . . waiting for activation . . . the "waiting" a way to describe this "differentiation" we experience as moving through linear time . . .

So I begin to glimpse a vision of the placement of events . . . not "out there" in future, but sort of stacked around, to be slipped into place at points of activation. . . .

[Next, "they" insert. Often they begin with the word "Now."]
Now. Delays . . . or the experience of delays . . . lapses waiting for comprehension . . . or conscious choice . . . to catch up . . . see wave movements . . . energies at different frequencies and speeds . . . holding in check . . . like a holding pattern . . . the aircraft is circling but does not land until conditions are right. But it is in motion at all times . . . not *en route*, not landed, but holding.

Idea of simultaneous time allowing in the *arrangement* of events for all stages in an infinitude of correspondences to "pass through" the consciousness of the experiencer(s) of the event. . . . All events interlocked into a weave that is so "loosely knit" it extends over a vast "space". . . the "spaces" between threads being experienced as time . . . when in actuality they are like air space over an airport where aircraft circle in holding patterns until all threads are aligned in proper sequence . . . not a "do this, then that, then that sequence," but more a chain reaction, each participant from the smallest units of energy composing matter to the largest visible complexes, interacting in symphony—but un-aware for the most part at this juncture of the score or the conductors . . . both of which are the "rest of the story" . . . or the "other side of the equation," or the flip side, underbelly, in essence, that which consciousness projected into form cannot comprehend beyond the veils imposed in the brain.

To see it, to be conscious of score and conductor . . . as if one listening to a CD play and hearing the music, could at the same time, be present the "space-moment" the music is played and recorded . . . would be equivalent to a turtle with head tucked inside shell being able at the same time to study the pattern on the top of his shell.

Simply, you are a species specializing in focus . . . requiring the screening out of all data that would interfere with intense study of your immediate environment . . . and providing for an electri-fying sensual experience . . . i.e., you are so close to what you study, your interactions are so closely woven, you can "feel" the dance of life more vividly than if a "space removed" . . . i.e., parallel realities . . . on *one* level of experience. On other levels, this "other" reality is intermeshed with yours . . . so that it depends on your "position" what you perceive and experience. Like a hand accordion that is stretched and closed, each position producing different sounds . . . so is the nature of "simultaneous time" arrangements in space that accommodate the grosser aspects of matter and the "pauses" of energy between that which you perceive to be "empty space" or "delays in time."

[Me]: And how does choice fit in? As opposed to pre-destination . . . probabilities being most likely events to be activated—stages set, waiting for activation . . . and suddenly the actor changes her mind? Suddenly, a perception. When a seemingly sudden change of mind occurs, the stage is set already (for the new choice) . . . the suddenness of the actor's realization she has absentmindedly arrived at the wrong studio!

This describes the sometimes sluggish apprehension of the design . . . the mind is confused by fixations or wrongly interpreted data or signals . . . which is why sometimes on the way to a set, an actress may "experience" all sorts of mishaps. But she *will* arrive where she belongs. As she gets better at recognizing and interpret-ing cues, less mishaps occur and then life seems to "fall into place."

The results are the same, the show is played, but how the show is perceived might be the difference between a B-version of the story, as compared to what Spielberg or DeMille would do with the same script. In *any* event, the essence is experienced at a level of richness or dullness, depending on a complexity of interactions and connections around the staging and playing out of the event.

In other words, the play could go on "without you" . . . on a level where you were fixated by other events. . . . In other words, in one probability, Steven Spielberg directs, Julia Roberts plays Mindy . . . but if your belief *screens* this out, you will perceive some other set of circumstances that will play out on "another set" simultaneously, one "event" being no more or less "real" than the other.

[*The rest of the recording was personal.*]

4

HOW CAN THIS BE TRUE?

THE BREACH

Working on a novel I call *Jonah: a Millennial Tale*, I felt confident that I could "fulfill my task" in fiction, without having to disclose my secret life. No matter the phenomenal activities, *Summoned* was not so much as a twinkle in my eye during the next two years. My focus was on finishing *Jonah . . . and on economic survival*.

A subscriber of *Publishers Weekly*, I had seen a review of a book about alien abduction, and ordered it from the local bookstore, Back of Beyond. The book arrived in mid-May 1994: *ABDUCTION: Human Encounters with Aliens,* by Harvard psychiatrist John E. Mack. Something nagged at the back of my mind that maybe I shouldn't be reading a book like this while engaged in writing the novel. Shut-up, I told Nag. *Jonah* was not about alien abduction . . . exactly.

After Mack's compelling introduction, I heard no warning bells as I began reading the first case history. There may have been a low drum rumble, but my declarations of innocence about abduction had made me dull of hearing.

Halfway through the book, feeling angry and threatened, I commanded myself to shut this book for good. But I couldn't. These people were speaking of things I recognized—scores of details I had no way of knowing about, unless . . . but how could it be? Because of my near obsession with UFOs, I had been alert for signs I might be an abductee—but I wasn't! Couldn't be! No missing time! (Forgotten.) And I'd never even seen a UFO! (In plain sight—yet.) I was just a scribe . . . taking notes for the next humankind. Then . . . why did I identify so strongly with these people? I had tagged so many pages in Mack's book, to mark information relevant to my own experiences and knowledge, hardly a page was free of a tag. I was angry, threatened, spooked, disoriented, chilled to my bones.

I dashed off a letter to Mack, practically cussing the man for writing such a revelatory book, as if it were his fault I was shaking apart inside. (As a result, I was invited to participate in a research project, conducted by PEER, which I did over the next few years.)

So far I had managed to rationalize every suspicion of abduction, every glitch—except the evidences of implants, which I had neatly filed away in memory. But now I was remembering the incident, vividly.

Waking the morning of August 22, 1986, I found, on both of my hands in the fleshy regions near my thumbs, two places where the skin had been scraped away, leaving bloody, triangular marks about the size of pointed pencil erasers. There was no pain, no itch, no sting. I could see, and feel, a small spherical object beneath the topskin of my left hand. By flexing my fingers, I could move the ball up and down from knuckles to wrist. My husband photographed these curiosities, and I showed them to my doctor.

"Probably a calcium deposit," he said of the ball under my skin. He was bored.

"Showing up the same time I find these?" I indicated the marks on my hands. He shrugged. How easily we dismiss things we cannot explain.

Why did I not request X-rays? First, I did not want to risk being seen as a fool if the ball was something natural; and second, if it *wasn't* . . . *I wasn't ready to face that.*

At home, I thoroughly examined my bedroom scene. There was nothing sharp within arm-moving range, and the fact of identical cuts on both hands in identical places made it hard to guess how this could have happened accidentally. My husband was a excellent close-up photographer, but of course the photos came back blurred. Never mind; photos are not proof. Photos are photos. The proof was visible on my hands. But proof of *what*? The scrapes quickly healed, and the ball disappeared—into my system? Or dissolved?

Abduction as a cause did cross my mind; I just couldn't see how it was possible. A UFO hovered over my house in southwest Denver and swooped me up, without alerting the neighbors? *Nothing* escaped the eyes of my neighbors to the north. If an owl had landed on our roof at midnight, Nada Zawodsky would have seen the bugger.

For days I was haunted by the episode, but I just couldn't believe . . .. Soon afterward (not associating this with signs of possible implantation) I was compelled to study quantum physics. Conveniently, books for laymen on the subject were amply available. Strange fare for an artistic type, but then my husband was an aerospace engineer, so maybe I was just going to become more interesting company for him. It's easy to explain away glitches in one's ordinary life. I was a master at it.

Later, another reason for the obsession with the subject of quantum physics came to light: I needed a fundamental understanding of new physics in order to channel some of the information that would come over the transom.

I might have managed to explain away my powerful identification with Mack's abductees if not for the courtship, in lights and sounds, that began almost immediately after I finished reading his book. This I call the "Breach." Betrayal is what I felt.

They came as naturally as rain, snowflakes, sunrays penetrating glass. As naturally as the wind that howls down the red rock canyons around this funky little town they came, making their sounds and shining their lights with the insouciance of circus performers invited to entertain.

I don't remember inviting them. You create your own reality, say metaphysicians, looking me squarely in the eyes. Oh, yeah?

One day I wrote a letter to Dr. Karla Turner, complaining that sometimes I felt like we were their pets. That night, a clearly audible male voice said, "Here, Kitty, Kitty . . ." Figures I would get smart-aleck aliens.

Soon after the light displays and sound announcements began (details in appendix), came the physical effects . . ."pins-and-needles" tingling in my feet, and "sweeps" of energy pulsations all over my body, as if a wand were being passed over me. Next came the "Oz factor," named by Jenny Randles, British UFO investigator. Often I heard bee-buzzing sounds as I felt myself coming apart, floating, dissolving. I would wake up later feeling whacked, angry, and terrified, with fragmented memories of UFO-related incidents.

The physically sensational phenomena sometimes lasted for hours because I could not relax and go to sleep. I was determined to "catch them in the act." Hyper-alertness made for detailed recordings of these events in my journals.

The energy pulsations sometimes were so powerful, the bed beneath me vibrated (as I was vibrating). To spite disbelievers, I would sit up, snap on the lamp and press my hand firmly down on the mattress to prove I wasn't hallucinating. The damn bed vibrated under my hand. I could see, and feel it vibrating. Sometimes I got up and left the room; ate something; drew; read; wrote; meditated. The moment I lay down on the bed again, the business would start up where it had left off. I had a choice: I could let go and let the thing happen, or keep resisting until I could no longer hold my eyes open. I learned early: if they want me, I am going. It seemed I had no choice in going or not—only *when* I went.

What do I mean—"going?" I don't know! Out-of-body? I've heard the litany of popular explanations. I just don't know. But I know what *doesn't* happen. Some skeptics harp on "paralysis" as proof that people like me suffer from some sort of sleep disorder. The only time I have ever experienced paralysis was by means of a saddle-block when I gave birth to my daughter in 1968. A few months after this business began, on the night of November 2, 1994, I prayed earnestly that God help me stay awake enough to determine what in the blazes was happening to me. Sometimes we get what we pray for—sort of.

All doubts I was an abductee were put to rest that night.

After the usual phenomenal, sensational preparations, suddenly there was a change in the air. *This is it*! I thought in panic. *Stay awake! Remember!*

I did not see any intruders in my house. I wonder if such events can be triggered by some sort of "come command."

This event happened while I was still awake, though I felt extremely disoriented. I was "flown," my body in a dog-paddle position, down the hall, lightning-swift. Then up to the window in the kitchen door, where everything "disassembled" into a kind of energetic, prismatic, multi-colored blur.

How the hell does one describe such a thing? Somehow you are rearranged, shifted into a different atomic structure, so you can be whisked through walls or windows, on the way up, over, down . . . to a place just west of Hell. Why wasn't a window in my bedroom used? No idea. The kitchen door faced the back yard to the north.

After the "dissembling," the next moment remembered, I was sitting hunched over in gloomy light, still feeling extremely disoriented. The impression was, I was naked.[2] A small being was at my side, seeming to help me sit up. My focus was a narrow beam; clearly I could see his thin flesh-colored arm around my waist. I probed the arm with my hand. *Oh, shit!* I thought. *This is real!*

Before I could focus on anything else, I felt a needle stab into a muscle in my back, and cold fluid entering me. I blanked out. The next conscious recall was of waking up, spitting mad, feeling as though I'd been roughed up by a gang of thugs.

During a hypnotic regression, nine months after the abduction event, I probed my memory for details (more about hypnotic regressions in chapter 5). I saw myself in a huge dome of a place with the feel of a mausoleum. Barely discernible in the strange, gloomy light was a tall, thin being I can only describe as insectile. "She" I knew and trusted. In her presence, I felt an insect to her intelligence. I felt absolute awe, and respect. I was there to receive an "infusion" of information. During the hypnotic regression, I discussed the particulars of this strange process of collecting information in my energy fields, and bringing it back for translation.

As for the needle and fluid sensations, I spoke of receiving some sort of treatment that had to do with the balancing of amino acids. Possibly the sensations I reported were the best my brain could do in translation of something for which I have no words to describe accurately.

---

2   (Information gleaned during hypnotic regression is cause to wonder if the sense of nudity was a screen impression for my altered state of being. Veteran OBE travelers say we have a "second body" imperceivable by the primary senses. As I understand it, somehow we detach from our dense "shell bodies," *l*eaving them in the bed while we travel in our more flexible second bodies (a silver cord connects the two bodies) to environments much less dense. This would constitute the "between world" locations mentioned in information given me about how and where we meet with entities who reside at other levels or in other dimensions.)

The soul knows what the mind barely perceives.

Translation of "infused energetic information" can leave me feeling debilitated. Sometimes after recording, I was unable to sustain walking or sitting. I would fall upon the bed, dizzy, famished, exhausted. Instantly, the electrical-like pulsations would begin sweeping over my body. These "treatments," I call them, might last up to an hour. To this day, I continue to experience such energetic treatments. I am somehow replenished by them.

Months before the remembered abduction, in the first couple of weeks in June 1994, I had only hinted to my mother that I was having strange experiences. We didn't keep secrets, but I didn't know how I was going to tell her what was happening—if I mustered the courage.

Daily we lunched together at the Golden Stake, a local restaurant. One day, the fear I was holding inside manifested as inability to swallow food or drink. Mom insisted I go to the emergency room at the hospital. Tests revealed an abnormality in my blood that the M.D. said could be evidence of blood clots. I could die suddenly if the condition were not treated. The next day, I drove to Grand Junction, Colorado, for additional testing. No blood clots. But I came away with a bill for $1,500 for a diagnosis of hyperventilation. Fear is expensive! It was time to 'fess up.

Tears flowed down my face as I tried to explain to Mom what had been happening. We were in the Golden Stake again; mercifully no one was sitting close by. Telling her about the phenomena wasn't so hard . . . it was the painful wad of emotion in my chest coming out in sobs and whispers when I spoke of how horrible I felt for *betraying them*. Mom could make no sense of what I was saying. I could make no sense of it—it was pure emotion garbled in words I was loath to give to my angst. I was not aware of this taboo "not to tell" until the moment I began confessing. There was the confounding feeling I was betraying "them," complicated by the feeling that I had been betrayed by guides who should have warned me that my world was on the brink of shaking apart.

The second confession was to a friend, and happened in similar fashion—triggered by an incident that alarmed me, as had the expensive bout of hyperventilation. I had sent off for information from one of those "discreet help for abductees" post office boxes. The brochure sent was helpful; the inside scoop on the light and dark of the abduction phenomenon. But, irrationally, I was instantly *enraged* when I read that "all abductees are military connected."

"That is TOTAL BULLSHIT!" I exclaimed out loud. Furiously I began a letter to this reckless helper of abductees. Down the page I stopped, remembering that twice I had worked for Defense Department subcontractors, and that my parents were military-connected at my inception. I had military connections.

A terrible pain shot through my head. There is no logic to this reaction. I'd heard about government conspiracies, never feeling terror at the prospect. But that's what I was feeling now, stark terror. I doubled over on the floor, and clutched my head. Colored squiggles of light obscured my vision.

Get to your bed, was the only thought that penetrated the terror. I don't remember how I got to the bedroom. I lay down on the bed, on my back. *Go deep, very deep, where they cannot touch you. If you die, it's okay . . . you'll be fine . . . just rest . . .*

These words were not thoughts but instructional feelings. I was temporarily incapable of thought. All I knew was, if I moved so much as an eyelash, I was going to die. It was as if something was issuing the death message below the clear instruction to "go deep." I was truly incapacitated. I lost all sense of time, space or place, but did not sleep.

No idea how long I lay that way. When I began to come out of it, I glanced at the clock, alarmed. It was dark outside. Past the time for the fellowship meeting I normally attended on Saturday nights. I made for the bathroom, showered, dressed, and flew out the door, arriving at the fellowship hall just as the meeting was adjourning. My friend Keith saw me and came over.

"You okay?" He could see I was not.

"I'm anemic!" I spurted. I knew I had to tell him what was going on, but I was so used to covering up such things, I honestly felt maybe I *was* anemic—maybe that explained all!

Keith indulged me a trip to City Market to buy some liver. Home, frying it up with onions, still hoping I was anemic, I began haltingly telling him about what had set all this into motion. Keith is an archeologist. His down-to-earth scientific mind was respite from my wild fears. He listened to me attentively, and believed me. He knew me well. He knew I would not concoct such a story, nor was I prone to hysteria.

Over the summer, I continued working on *Jonah*. And the phenomena continued. I had to face this business. Was I truly an abductee? No one knew what that really meant! Did my life show evidences other than possible implantation, contact with "intelligences," and now these lights, sounds, and sensations?

The first place I looked was in my journals where I had recorded dreams and paranormal experiences since 1985. In my customary analytical style, I made up charts and graphs to study the particulars. It was exhausting work because of the threat I felt, discovering record of so many UFO-related dreams, some with accompanying sound or light phenomena I'd forgotten about. (See Appendix.)

Now even my medical history looked suspicious. The hysterectomy, the sudden onset of new allergies, the trouble with my jaw. All these correlated to "dreams" of surgeries performed on me by "Asian" doctors and nurses; dreams about pregnancies; dreams of caring for strange-looking, highly intelligent babies who communicated telepathically; many classroom dreams, and gatherings in underground facilities, some including military personnel; and quite a number of dreams that featured vivid UFOs, or abduction dramas.

The day I realized I did have missing time was another blow to my sense of well-being. At the age of five, in Vernal, Utah, I was missing so often my parents finally withdrew me from kindergarten to put a stop to these errant episodes.

"So, where was I?" I asked my mother. (All my adult life I had joked about getting kicked out of kindergarten. I wasn't laughing now.)

"You told us you were visiting friends," she reminded me.

Did my parents ever confirm? Ever talk to my teacher? Ever meet any of these friends? No, no, no. A very delicate subject. Was I insinuating my parents had been neglectful? Quite the opposite; they were strict.

If you are knowledgeable of the confounding aspects of abduction, it is not hard to fathom something like multiple missing time events getting swept under the carpet of conscious awareness. We had our stories. Mine was that I was visiting with school friends. My parents' story was that I was rebellious and stubborn, willing to suffer scoldings and spankings to have my way. With so much upheaval—scoldings, spankings, withdrawal from school—why couldn't I remember one time going home with friends? I only remember getting spanked once for coming home late . . . but no recall of where I'd been.

The day my mother decided enough was enough, I had come home four hours late from school, by way of a dirt road. That was my last day in kindergarten.

There were other suspicious signs. In middle childhood, seeing "sparky eyes" in the night, and the life-long "fat-hand syndrome." Sometimes the experiences we call abductions are preceded by sensations that feel like the hands are growing to enormous proportions, while at the same time a tremendous pressure is felt, bearing down on them.

Through the lens of abduction, my whole life began to look different—look *programmed*. My life had been out of the ordinary; now it looked to be *purposefully* out of the ordinary.

In 1995 when I probed these and other events using hypnotic regression, I would have felt relieved to find I really had been with peers during the missing time episodes in childhood. Eliminating indications of a lifelong pattern, I could have concentrated on finding an explanation for this business other than alien abduction. That I was missing often in an area well documented as a UFO sighting hot zone did not encourage the "other explanation" hope. But I was not interested in believing I was an abductee if it wasn't true. I hated not knowing for sure. But how does one verify such a thing, short of a spectacular event as happened to Travis Walton? (Walton's abduction was witnessed by six co-workers—"the best documented case of alien abduction ever recorded," says the front cover of his book, *Fire in the Sky* [Marlowe and Company, New York, 1979, 1996.] The book was basis for a movie of the same name.)

But even he is not certain he was taken by aliens. Like me, he is a careful analyzer who sticks to actual experience and memories. Memories retrieved under hypnosis, and the feelings we have about such things may very well point to truth—but feelings and memories are feelings and memories, not proofs. I can't even prove I was born. Birth certificates can be forged . . . and I'm sure by now some even know how to fabricate foot- or fingerprints.

Challenged to search for answers, in late June 1994, I bought another book of case histories, *Taken: Inside the Alien-Human Abduction Agenda* by Karla Turner, Ph.D. On July 4, I had a UFO-related dream that was precognitive of something I would read in Turner's book the next day.

In brief, the dream shows an odd, grounded spacecraft that opens out into classroom platforms. It is a place for people to gather, converse, and eat. I am seeking an old friend, John. I spot him eating with some people behind the classroom platforms. I wave and call his name. He picks up his tray of food, and walks over. He's no one I recognize in my "real life," but my dream self knows him well. Medium build, bald, blue-eyed, and wears glasses. He comes over, smiling. "Watch closely," he says. His face transforms. Suddenly it is covered with light-colored fur. At this moment the dream seems more a virtual reality scenario. I reach up to touch his furry face. That instant, I wake up . . . and my hand is literally in the air, as was the dreamer's.

I could make no sense of the dream . . . until, later that morning, I read in Turner's *Taken* of a visitation she had experienced. Her visitors had informed her that the story of Jacob and Esau in the Bible was about the genetic alteration of human beings. While working with letters and numbers in recent months, I had reviewed this story, interested in the names of the twelve tribes of Israel. Mention of the Bible story in *Taken* prompted me to review the story of Jacob and Esau.

I came to the part where Isaac (father of Jacob and Esau) reaches up to touch Esau, his firstborn. Instead he touches Jacob, his second-born. Nearly-blind Isaac touches goatskins that Jacob has draped around his neck to deceive his father into believing that he, Jacob, is Esau. (The name Jacob means deceiver.) The instant I read of Isaac touching the goatskins, I flashed on my dream, of touching John's furry face. The dream was a signal to pay attention, here is something important.

Jacob, the second-born son is smooth-skinned, the Bible says. Esau is a hairy man. The story can be interpreted as mythology about two kinds of human beings. Smooth-skinned Jacob receives the blessing of proliferation that had belonged to Esau, who sold his birthright to his brother for a pot of stew, and was told by his father:

> *"Your dwelling will be away from the Earth's richness . . . away from the dew of Heaven above . . . you will live by the sword . . . you will serve your brother . . . But you will grow restless . . . you will throw off his yoke from your neck."*

Genesis 27:39-40
Holy Bible, New International Version

The precognitive dream was cause for me to write to Dr. Turner, which was the beginning of a correspondence between us that lasted until she was too ill to continue. Few were more devoted to helping abductees than Karla Turner. Although for Karla the abduction phenomenon was all dark, it was still a great help to communicate with someone who at least knew that abductions really happened. Corresponding with Karla, I learned a lot about respecting another's viewpoint.

The information I would receive in late 1996—*The History of Humankind in Summary*—tells quite a different story than Karla's visitors conveyed. According to "the servants of El," the genetic alteration was only the beginning. (See chapter eleven.)

5

REMEMBER THE SILVER

In the spring of 1995, a particularly rough nocturnal event I call the "attack dream" convinced me it was time to consider seeking professional help. It was more than a dream. After an entity leapt onto my bed and forcefully grabbed my upper arms, there was an after-effect that lasted for months. A frequent surging of electrical-like vibrations over my lower body, sweeping from waist to feet, was reminder that this business was not "just in my mind."

Despite this and other disturbing events, I still felt I should do nothing as radical as hypnotic regression without a go-ahead from "Guidance." Response to my concerns came telepathically on April 30, 1995. I was encouraged to proceed . . . with caution. Anyone contemplating hypnosis should think well and long before acting on the impulse to get at the truth this way. Hypnotic regression doesn't necessarily help. Sometimes it makes matters worse—any reputable facilitator should warn.

In deciding to go ahead, I named myself solely responsible for interpretation of everything I felt, sensed, or saw during the process. After all, it's *my* mind. Although information accessed with hypnosis is not in and of itself proof of anything, the hypnotized must afterward live with what is "remembered." I think it is very hard to maintain a neutral attitude, but I try.

I chose facilitators carefully, first setting an appointment with Dr. Helen V. Walker in Denver. Dr. Walker had previously facilitated, for me, several explorations into "past lives." (One of the reasons I knew I was not inclined to either "true believing" or confabulation was that even after reviewing nearly a dozen so-called past lives, my internal jury was still out on the question of the reality of reincarnation.)

Before I share excerpts from the regression facilitated in Denver, I need to introduce you to Rowah, my childhood "imaginary playmate," upon whom I bestowed all of my misdeeds, according to my parents. Naturally, an abductee is suspicious of such "unseen friends," so it was the first thing I wanted to look at, under hypnosis. The results were strange—not at all like probes into "past lives," as I had experienced. After difficulty focusing, I finally saw him in my deepest mind's-eye. His face was heart-shaped, his hair, a tawny lion's mane with a widow's peak. His was a familiar face, and I remembered others like him . . . "Sphinx People," I called them. The powerful emotions I felt for Rowah gave credence to his existence—in some reality. But my inability to focus on a setting was unsettling.

I saw him down on his haunches, pointing; saw myself standing beside him, a little girl with long braids. He pointed off in the distance—impossible to describe what I saw—"the future," and something silver in the sky. He told me my life would be hard (it has been), and I was to "remember the silver." This vague detail later shows vividly as a silver seam across the ceiling of a spacecraft.

But what I envisioned of Rowah may have happened before I was born, or so I was told by Guides later. If true, I can wonder if what we pull from "memory" is sometimes cloaked in symbolism or archetypes, as happens in dreams. I don't mean to downgrade hypnotic regression as a valid method of memory retrieval. Even cops use it to solve murder cases, and I used the method myself—sparingly and cautiously—to help expand understanding of the plentitude of phenomena experienced when I was fully awake.

Even though Dr. Walker is an experienced professional, and we had developed a mutual trust from working well as a team before, we encountered trouble. Because hypnotic regression had gone smoothly for me in the past, I was surprised to experience such resistance.

The excerpt below shows what I mean by resistance. Following preliminaries, the questioning begins after I have described to Dr. Walker my childhood companion's "physical" appearance.

July 5, 1995

[Walker]: Does he [Rowah] tell you anything about the experiences you will have when you grow up?

You don't see details. You have to . . . you can see the many places you can get lost and trapped, and there's this silver . . . there's something silver up here, above it all, that you can try to remember . . . and try to take this vision with you . . .

[Walker]: What is this silver?

Like the top of a tunnel, but it's not metal or anything, just some kind of silver light . . . It's just when you think of this, you should remember this . . . It's above, it's above . . .

[Walker]: You follow this silver light?

You don't follow it. You know it's there, you remember it's there, you look up in your mind and it's a focus . . . a memory . . .

[Walker]: Let's focus on that silver light. Focusing on that light, let's go to another time when you sensed that light. I'll count to five . . .

It's on the roof . . . the ceiling of a spacecraft.

[Walker]: What?

On the ceiling of a spacecraft.

[Walker]: On the ceiling of a spacecraft.

Yes.

[Walker]: Are you on the spacecraft?

Yes. I'm looking up.

[Walker]: You're looking up and seeing it.

It's like liquid. It's like liquid.

[Walker]: Liquid.

Yes, it's like . . .

[Walker]: Is it vibrating?

No. It's like mercury, that consistency. And it's . . . now I want to call it a pathway, or entry port, or . . . it's a seam.

[Walker]: Umhmm. Can you describe the spacecraft?

This silver thing, it's like a big seam. I see a lot of panels with lights, but that's kind of . . . I don't see details. This is the top room, the navigation room. This silver seam can completely enfold on itself. It enfolds out of that, and can enfold back into that . . . hmmm . . . (The impression is that the seam is a portal entrancing another dimension, but I don't verbalize this. In this altered state of mind, the "left brain" sometimes has difficulty finding words to describe what is being visualized.)

[Walker]: All right. Do you see . . . are you shown other parts of the spacecraft?

. . . long silence . . .

[Walker]: Are there any individuals there? Are there any people?

I don't know. (Suddenly I am feeling on edge.)

[Walker]: Let's see if we can move forward to August of 1986. You see the marks on your hands, the scrapings on your hands. Your inner mind knows what happened. Let the pictures come forth. What was done to your hands to have those marks on them? What do you sense?

A tube with a . . . a silver tube (with a triangular tip—not verbalized).

[Walker]: You sense anyone there?

Yes, there's somebody doing it, yes. (I see them but don't describe them to Dr. Walker. They are dressed in white body-suits; they have black hair with widow's peaks—or I'm seeing skull caps with V-points at the "third-eye" location.)

[Walker]: When these scrapings were taking place, do they tell you what they're doing?

Well, sure. (I am feeling extremely agitated. Feels like *someone else* is responding *through* me . . . as if I was shoved aside somehow by "someone" very disapproving of these questions, impatient with Dr. Walker—and determined to restrict the information. This is very disorienting. My voice becomes very curt.)

[Walker]: Why do they say they are doing this?

I don't know. I don't have access to that information.

[Walker]: Access to the information . . . ?

Yes. I don't have access to it.

[Walker]: Are they using an instrument to do this?

I see the instrument. It doesn't hurt.

[Walker]: Good. Do they take your memory from this?

They don't take memory. They know how to move it around.

[Walker]: Umhmmm.

They can put it places you don't know where to get it, and there's only certain keys, because there are certain times and keys and events that trigger it if you need it, triggers the memory.

[Walker]: You say there are two individuals doing this?

Did I say that?

(I feel embarrassed at the "superior" tone of my voice. I'm experiencing something like a split in my consciousness, "me" listening from a distance as this "other" voice snaps at Dr. Walker. This is not the state of mind I usually experience when hypnotized! This "other consciousness" is very alert, while "I" am feeling at another level confused, as if drugged.)

[Walker]: You were mentioning two.

Hmmm. There are a lot.

[Walker]: And where are you? Is this on the spaceship?

Yes, but it's another scene. Very bright. Very bright. A lot of metal.

[Walker]: Where do you sense that it is?

On some kind of craft. A laboratory.

[Walker]: On Earth, or is it in space?

Space.

[Walker]: Are you the only one being sampled?

No.

[Walker]: There are others?

We're not being sampled. They put an activator in there.

[Walker]: An activator?

To speed things up.

[Walker]: What is the purpose of the activator?

So you can be more directly taught. More directly guided.

[Walker]: Who is doing the talking³—uh, the teaching and guiding?

They're very businesslike. (How's that for an evasive answer?)

[Walker]: Are these individuals who are implanting and activating the same as those who are going forth with messages, and teaching and guiding?

They're all connected. Different ones have different jobs.

[Walker]: Can you see what the different jobs are?

It's endless. It's complex, or more so than our own civilization, more complex. So when you say other jobs . . . tell me all the jobs on Earth. It's extremely complex.

[Walker]: What are some of the teachings?

It comes to me in bits and pieces, and it all fits together with other pieces.

[Walker]: Do they say why they want to teach you?

---

3   "Who is doing the talking . . . uh . . . " says Dr. Walker. I sense this was a slip; she realizes this was not exactly me speaking. . . .

We're planning something.

[Walker]: What are you planning?

I don't have access to that information.

And no amount of further probing reveals "the plan." Throughout the regression, I felt the same electrical-like pulsations in my feet and legs that precede nocturnal events. When Dr. Walker brought me out of trance, a million small, shimmering gold balls distorted my vision. This had never happened before. A good thirty minutes passed before my vision cleared sufficiently for me to drive my car.

Reflecting on the "silver seam," I can't help but wonder if it might be a metaphor for the division between left and right hemispheres of the brain (more on this theory in chapters eight and fifteen). Or maybe, as reported, it was an in/out portal on the ceiling of an objectively real spacecraft, for "enfolding" from one dimension to another.

Whatever the symbolism or nuts and bolts of these experiences, I am schooled to study the higher view, what I can see of it. The phenomenon we call alien abduction affects the experiencer at all levels—physical, mental, emotional, and spiritual. The attitude that scoffs at a possible spiritual meaning behind the phenomenon may view science and spirituality as incompatible. I think such views illustrate an intellectual disassociation between left and right hemispheres. Because it's important to me to try to mediate between these two spheres of perception, I'm going to tell you another story—the only way I know to address both perceptions, left and right.

This fable is by no means a comprehensive picture of my perception of the UFO phenomenon, or of reality. It took a whole book to weave together a few threads to reveal one small pattern of perception. Alien abduction is serious business. But if we lose our ability to muse, we are goners, in any event.

Remember the Silver . . .
a fable

In the beginning, I could neither speak nor walk, and the sounds I made were constantly misinterpreted by the aliens who looked after me in my pitiful incapacity. They *seemed* intelligent, but *me* they treated like some pet acquired for their amusement. Thank goodness for

Rowah—help from home! I was not alone.

Rowah was invisible to the aliens, but he warned that soon I would be as blind to his appearance as were the creatures who held me in captivity.

"ME? BLIND? WHY?"

Made of light, Rowah could appear in any form he liked. His eyes were blue laser beams, and the hair he made was electrified and danced about his heart-shaped face. Taller than any creature I'd seen in this strange environment, he adorned himself in a shiny, silver body-suit.

In response to my treble thought-tone blasted as strongly as I could send, he communicated, in his usual thinking way, something shocking, though he swore I knew it before I was abducted into this world.

You are now like the ones who care for you, Little Sister, he thought in a matter-of-fact tone.

Hideous!

And he told me things more disturbing. My main communication center was housed inside my crown, and was completely vulnerable to the input of *anyone*. Soon my caretakers would begin programming into my instrument of intelligence their alien agenda!

Remember, Little Sister—your portal is hidden deep within your form.

If I forgot, I would end up a walky-talky doll who would perform for these creatures whatever they desired of me.

I was stunned at this information. "Hidden? Where?" My form was a tiny, blubbery, roundish thing with completely useless append-ages. He pointed at my middle section. Then to make the horrors worse, he said that I would soon become as deaf to his thought-tones as I would be blind to his presence. But though I would cease to hear him, he explained, the *feeling* of his tones would still vibrate deep within me.

It will not be easy, he warned, for my instrument of intelligence contained no program for remembering. *Remember the silver*, he then intoned deep within me. The "silver" was a code having to do with a channel that would be forged through my portal, later—IF I was faithful.

"WHY!"

His response was a fantastic story. As freakish as they seemed, the beings here were not really alien creatures. We were "all of a kind," born into these weird forms, which had been purposefully designed to direct our focus on the unique challenges of existence in this foreign environment. He refused to expound on what these challenges were, because, he claimed, I could only comprehend them by way of experience. If he tried to explain, it would sound like gobbly-gook, for already my understanding was hampered by the instrument housed inside my crown.

Most of our kind, he said, had fallen into a deep sleep; most were spellbound; most had lost awareness of the communication center hidden deep within their forms. It will be my special task, he said, to "remember the silver," and once a channel is forged through my portal (IF I am faithful), my function will be to help others remember their own connections to our celestial ancestors.

My task will seem both perilous and impossible, he said, for in our long, deep sleep, our kind had scattered across this world, and in the diversity of our accomplishments, coupled with our delusion of disconnection, many lived as enemies, with a distorted belief that the "fittest" survived, and all others died.

The fittest of forms, they mean, he added with a happy feeling, as if this amused him. *Few seem to notice that all transforms*! (Which information was to give me hint of the depth of the sleep to which our kind had succumbed.)

It already sounded like gobbly-gook, but I would understand later, Rowah assured—IF (again he toned this word as if a prophesy of my doom) I was faithful to the memory of our connection.

"But why does it have to be this way?" I demanded to know. "Me bound like a prisoner in this form with its dangerous slumber chamber inside this faulty crown. Why don't we just tell everyone the truth? Why this charade—and a perilous one at that!"

AH! he exclaimed, and sparks shimmered off his electric hair. *I'm glad you thought to ask. Though your journey in this form is a perilous one, the prize is worth the danger*.

"What prize?" I said doubtfully, seeing no possible advantage to this set-up.

Compassion! he proclaimed, as if this important word said it all. *And* . . . (he paused, as if to inspire excitement for the real reward for my imprisonment) . . . *transformation*!

"Fiddlesticks!" I declared. "You already said we all transform. Big deal."

A different kind of transformation, he meant—something new for human beings. Much too complex to explain now, and I will barely comprehend it when he reminds me of it later—IF he can. And remember, many will be summoned, each to perform a task, and our joy will depend on the performance of all, as we join and share with one another the information each possesses.

And now I will give you other codes to help all awaken when we begin to beckon you from your sleep. Seek . . . Gather . . . Wait . . . Listen . . . Remember . . . Connect . . . Cross . . . and for each there is a special code, as silver is for you.

And then, as if he had just bestowed upon my crown seven jewels, he fell into a luxury of modest silence, as is characteristic of Siriuns following an act of giving.

"Those codes sound very plain," I complained. "From such plain words we will learn the secrets of this mysterious transformation you boast we will achieve in this awful place in these deformities?"

Plain codes . . . he answered vaguely, for he was beginning to fade.

"Rowah!" I toned with all my force. "Don't leave yet!"

Remember the silver, Little Sister . . . you are never alone . . . we are always here . . . for you to discover . . . when . . . if . . .

He lied! I despaired, for already in the cradle that imprisoned my helpless form, I began to believe only what I perceived with my instruments of sight—two of the jewels in my crown—only what I could hear with the two jewels that were my ears—and smell with the fifth jewel that was my nose—and taste in the sixth jewel that was my mouth . . .

But where was the seventh jewel heralded in the plain codes communicated in such ambiguity?

(You will see . . .)

6

A "WHOLE 'NOTHER WORLD..."

I was intent on trying to find out what had happened to me in Vernal, Utah. If I could confirm that I was visiting *human* children, then I could eliminate myself as a lifelong abductee, and focus on finding out the real source of the ongoing nocturnal ruckus. If nothing came of the regressions, I decided, I would consider consulting a shrink who might show me brass tacks where I had inserted pins with angels dancing atop them.

It took sessions with three different professionals before I was able to access anything in regards to the mystery cloaking my experience in Vernal, Utah. With Dr. Walker, we encountered a block of resistance that could not be penetrated. If I was visiting human friends, why the block? I knew it wasn't because of one common knee-jerk assumption: hidden sexual abuse. There would have been telltale signs in my life, and none existed.

The second try with another facilitator in Denver was slightly more revealing. Regressed to the age of five, I informed Kris Garrett that I could not answer her questions because "I mustn't tell Mother."

"Your mother isn't here, and we won't tell her," Kris suggested.

After more gentle coaxing, I envisioned clearly a round silver craft hidden in the pine trees. But no amount of probing worked to expand the picture. Exhausted and frustrated, I drove back to Moab.

At home I drew a picture of Rowah.

While I am sketching at the round table in my kitchen, I am thinking:

None of this constitutes verifiable data, so it wouldn't be considered in any kind of scientific investigation. But could *it be objectively real?*

Scientists wouldn't waste a thought on the question with no empirical evidence to nudge their curiosity. But I am not so restricted. My curiosity is nudged. This is my life. I'm the one who is seeing lights, hearing sounds and receiving telepathic messages from someone. I'm the one who woke up with cuts on my hands. What the hell do scientists care? They're all busy splitting atoms.

Finished with the sketch of Rowah, I hold it up to the light. Unbidden tears gather in my eyes. I am suddenly filled with emotions I do not understand. My mind cannot grasp it. If I invented Rowah, why the hell am I trembling and crying, and feeling such a deep sense of loss?

Haunted by the image of the spaceship in the trees, and the feelings it stirred in me, I traveled next to Scottsdale, Arizona, to consult with Ph.D. psychologist Ruth Hover, who was said to be an expert in hard cases like mine. Because I was financially strapped, I made the appointment with great trepidation. But as often happens when a person has a real need, and appeals to Higher Guidance for help, a synchronicity opened doors—in this case, literally—to a townhome at a resort, way more luxurious than I'd hoped for. Here, I could spend five comfortable days—if you call probing into the nightmarish realms of abduction comfortable.

Dr. Hover had requested I send her various material about myself to review before we met, and once settled in my plush quarters, the first two days were spent in interview, so she could be sure I was sound of mind and a good candidate for hypnosis, in her professional opinion.

I don't know the reason I could not look at my childhood experiences in Denver but could in Scottsdale. Maybe it had something to do with the facilitator's experience in recognizing and finessing the taboos around abduction memories. Or maybe I just wasn't psychologically ready in Denver. Whatever the case, finally I could look at what I really knew was there all along, but couldn't let myself know consciously. This doesn't mean I accept everything I saw or "remembered" as absolute truth. I still reserve for the possibility of screens, symbols, and archetypes. I give respect to my brain (and all we do not know about our minds, memory, or consciousness), and let my heart decide the essence of what is revealed.

Dr. Hover began by helping me locate myself in the classroom, since we knew that my missing times occurred after school. Skipping a lot of detail here, I envisioned myself walking along a path. I could see a thin silver beam slanting down from the air to my head, as if a "directional" was guiding me into the woods. Certainly as a child I could not have seen from this vantage, even if such a thing could be observed with ordinary sight. After describing the round silver craft and its strange fold-out doors and stairs, once inside, I speak of the interior in five-year-old vernacular,

"It's way bigger [inside] *than what that round thing is* [outside]*."*

There is also a lower level that quarrels with the size the craft seems to be, externally.

Next, in five-year-old astonishment, I describe windows at the back of the vehicle that give the view of a *"whole 'nother world."*

Noticeably there is an absence of adult skepticism. I am five years old. What I see just is.

"It's like another land," I tell Dr. Hover. *"It's like deserts. Past the windows. There's windows inside, and you see a whole 'nother world. But it looks underground, too. I see a ceiling beyond that . . . like a cave, but there's lighting there, too. Looks kind of silvery . . . regular light, too. It goes back, and back, and back . . . "*

On the lower level, I see babies stacked in containers filled with liquid. My alien escort informs that the babies are asleep. This surprises me. I thought they were dead—because in five-year-old logic—how can they be asleep with their eyes open? Absent the repulsion an adult would feel, or the adult fear of what this could mean for humankind, I describe the babies as resembling *"big bugs."*

Throughout the session, Dr. Hover tried to get me to describe the aliens, with little luck.

Excerpt from Hypnotic Regression, August 15, 1995:

This metal . . . I'm going down, down, like a tunnel, walking down into a lower level.

[Hover]: Is she being taken there, or is she going on her own?

No, there's someone there, but this is a place I've been . . . I think we're going to see the babies . . . uh, they're behind glass, you can't really touch them. (I clearly see glass-like containers, stacked one on top of another, babies inside.)

[Hover]: She can see them, though.

Yeah.

[Hover]: Are there many?

A few.

[Hover]: She watches the babies through the glass.

Yeah, they're in a kind of fluid.

[Hover]: Inside the glass.

Yes.

[Hover]: What does she think about all that?

Well, uh, gee, she wonders if they're really okay. They look kind of dead.

[Hover]: Tiny?

Yeah . . . their eyes are open, but they look kind of dead.

[Hover]: You think perhaps she's anxious that they are dead?

They say not, they say they're sleeping . . . but how can they be sleeping when their eyes are open?

[Hover]: And they're in the liquid?

Umhmm.

[Hover]: She's getting explanations from the beings she's with?

Umhmm.

[Hover]: Do they want her to do anything with the babies?

When I get bigger. But not now. Now I'm too young.

[Hover]: When you're older—what will be required?

Then I will train the babies.

[Hover]: Oh.

Teach them something.

[Hover]: Things you already know.

Yeah.

[Hover]: You have some concern and warm feelings for those babies.

Yeah.

[Hover]: Besides their eyes being open and being in liquid—do they look like babies that you know?

Uh-uh, no. They don't look like our babies. Uh-uh.

[Hover]: How do they look?

Well, big eyes. They look like great big bugs, kind of. Like big ants or something.

[Hover]: Looks like you're being prepared for what your task will be later.

Umhmm.

[Hover]: Do you move about after you see the babies? Do you go any place else?

We go back up to where the big window is.

[Hover]: Before you go back to the big window, look very closely at the beings with you—let yourself perceive what they look like.

Hmmm.

[Hover]: Puzzling?

Yeah . . . there's something funny about the nose. It's like I can kind of see what they look like if I'm looking behind or above, but if I look at them straight on, I'm confused.

[Hover]: They probably don't want you staring at them.

Yeah.

[Hover]: They feel okay, though, friendly?

Umhmm, yeah. There's a strange feeling around them.

[Hover]: Strange around them or for you . . .

Yeah, sometimes I feel strange about them, but I . . . it's just like when I look at them, why don't I know when I'm away from them . . . I don't remember them?

[Hover]: Probably don't want even to think about it.

I know. It's so strange.

[Hover]: The strangeness doesn't even occur to you when you're with them.

Hmm. Oh . . . somebody has white hair. Very, very old. White hair.

[Hover]: You know this person, this being?

Umhmm. It's the grandfather kind. Yeah, very old, very wrinkled skin.

[Hover]: Do you feel like you're part of their family?

I belong with them, sure.

[Hover]: So visiting with them feels okay.

Yeah.

(Later, I am escorted out of the vehicle.)

[Hover]: What do you tell your mother when she asks?

I think that I really was with friends.

[Hover]: Is your mom a little angry with you for being home late from school?

Yeah. I'm not supposed to tell them. And Dad gets mad at me.

[Hover]: What do they say to you?

They threaten to take me out of school. "We're going to take you out of school if you can't come home! If you don't stop this . . . "

[Hover]: Is that upsetting to you?

Yeah! I don't understand why I'm punished for going and seeing friends.

If indeed I cavorted with aliens, if I had remembered and confessed with full awareness to avoid the punishments—(including withdrawal from school, which I loved)—I would have been promptly judged to be mentally questionable, and would have missed growing up as a normal child.

Besides the known missing time episodes when I was five, I have memory of something my mother says never happened. Recently I asked her, "Remember that time when we lived in Salt Lake City, and you put me on a bus to go stay with Uncle Tom and Aunt Amelia?"

She shook her head. "They lived right in Salt Lake City. We never put you on a bus to go anywhere."

But I vividly remember lying on their sofa, after riding on a bus to what I thought was their home. I remember there was a "fire bug" in my eye, and my aunt poured scalding hot water in my eye to dislodge it. That's ridiculous! And it is hard to imagine that my parents would put me on a bus to travel anywhere, much less to relatives living in the same town. Not only is this "memory" suspicious in its "facts," but I can't explain why I never *questioned* such imagery as scalding water being poured into my eye to dislodge a fire bug. This is just the sort of "memory" that haunts as a possible screen over alien activities. But I am not inclined to probe further, or deeper. What I uncovered so far is troublesome enough.

7

YOUTH IS ABDUCTION . . .

In Salt Lake City, age five, I am pulling on my mother's skirt, begging her to let me go to church. No one is telling me I should go to church. My parents seldom attend. But my will to attend church is as strong as the desire that drives me later to become an accomplished violinist. Both spring from an unknown source within me. Sometimes I hitch a ride with neighbors to church, other times I walk alone, and sometimes I arrive home late . . . (Because I was visiting with friends? Visiting aunts and uncles? Dawdling? Rowah made me do it.)

The church I nag to attend is the Church of Jesus Christ of Latter Day Saints—Mormons. A peculiar people, and damn proud of it. Latter Day Saints, as I said earlier, live by doctrines that were transmitted in the 1800s to founder Joseph Smith—an alien contactee, so believe some UFO investigators. They interpret the prophet's visions and strange methods of accessing information as mirroring tales of contact and visitation being reported in current times all over the globe by thousands of would-be seers and prophets.

(Well, if I *am* an alien abductee, wouldn't it make sense to belong to an alien church? How else could I expect to get to Alien Heaven?)

In junior high and high schools, I excel in music, English and Latin, compose a poem that is published by the American Poetry Society, and my essay, "Music, the Universal Language" places first in a school contest. In local and state music competitions, I win medals, and play in the pit orchestra when drama students perform operettas such as *Damn Yankees* and *South Pacific*. With other members of the Oklahoma City Junior Symphony, I travel to Kansas City and Chicago to perform.

I am a nerd, a "long hair," and Mormon, a peculiarity in the Bible Belt. Peers write in my year books, "a very religious person." A late-bloomer, too; no lipstick or high heels until I am fourteen. Still, I attract a few boys who do their best to help me overcome my fear of sex. The times I succumb to the passions of petting are followed with fervent prayers, on my knees, that beg God's forgiveness for my wantonness.

Mormons do not say explicitly that sex is dirty. We girls are taught that we must keep ourselves clean, because no man in the priesthood will marry soiled goods. I am shocked to learn that a couple of girls I know are not virgins. I am so modest, showers in gym class are, for me, excruciatingly embarrassing events. Gym is the only class I flunk.

My period begins when I am thirteen, just in time to teach me there is something shameful and essentially wrong with the female body. Girls call menstruation "the curse," and our mothers will hardly discuss it.

I am told, "All men want to do is screw you!" This enlightenment is screamed at me.

If I am chaste and marry in a Mormon temple, I will be issued white garments, which I will be required to wear even while making love with my husband. Men are defenseless against a woman's charms, I am taught. The men I know hate to be reminded they are weak in any way. I hear: If there is sexual transgression, I will be blamed as temptress.

Conversely, society worships the nude female body. I am aware that my body is beautiful. Deep within me, I make a choice. I don't dare test the limits of my dangerous sexuality, but I will not dishonor myself with a belief that my body is something to be ashamed of. Sunsets take my breath; rainstorms stir my soul; babies smile; children laugh; and animals play, all attesting to the essential rightness of life.

But the world is a hotbed of temptations. On maybe two occasions with schoolmates who have access to cars, I experience the customary rites of adolescence—wild rides through drive-in eateries that thrill and terrify me. I experiment with alcohol; drink a half-pint of cherry vodka and a little perfume afterward, to camouflage—(I think)—the smell of the liquor on my breath from my parents. The repercussions are severe. I am grounded from even church social events for longer than my heart can bear. I am daring and rebellious, just enough to learn that the fruits of breaking rules are isolation and ostracism. Still, sometimes I sneak sips from my dad's liquor supply above the refrigerator.

Adolescence is chaos, confusion, and social pressures that baffle me. At church, warnings of all of the ways I can lose my soul are becoming graver.

In the transition from childhood to teens, my free-spirited nature gives way to a serious and troubled outlook on life. The changes in my body are occurring automatically, without my say. I am like a traveler trapped in a vehicle that is undergoing a metamorphosis I am powerless to comprehend, direct, or stop.

The child embarks upon a magical journey, but youth is abduction into a vehicle that is suddenly rocketing toward an unknown destination. A vague sense of betrayal is born, a feeling of not quite belonging, as if a blindfold is being slowly removed to reveal the terrible secret that I am living on foreign soil.

While my Mormon peers are successfully co-mingling with mainstream kids, making plans for college, "missions," and marriage, I am brooding over end-time prophesies, and coming up with questions the adults cannot answer to my satisfaction. In an apocalyptic dream, I see the whole world on fire. In another dream, I see a planet veering close to Earth; people are running and screaming, and sheets of paper (like a book manuscript) are flying in the air. (Realistically, the force of a *planet* veering close to Earth might obliterate us before we could identify the approaching menace. Though as a child my impression was of a planet, I now interpret the mottled surface of the dream sphere remembered as an asteroid.)

Sports and popularity are the primary concerns of schoolmates, but I am most concerned with survival and excellence. I *must* excel. Why? To prove worthy to marry in a temple? If I were excelling in homemaking, maybe. Outwardly, my concerns are more immediate: Will I be asked to the prom? If so, will I survive the gruesome affair? Inwardly, I am serious and morose. It seems important that I fathom infinity; my mind spins out; I pull the bed covers over my head.

Although many Latter Day Saints, in preparation for the coming millennium, are stockpiling, in their basements, enough food and supplies to last them two years, no one seems particularly bothered that we are living in the last days. Why worry? We are the elect. I am taught that ours is God's true church, reestablished purposefully in these times to prepare the world for the return of Jesus Christ.

Mormons are no back-dirt cult. We will save the Constitution, I am told, and ultimately govern these United States. (Joseph Smith ran for the Presidency, and Mormons today are seriously involved in national politics, the FBI, and the CIA.)

Every single person in the world will have a chance to join God's only true church, I am assured. My doubt scares me; doubt is the first step to apostasy. Our missionary force is the largest in the world, but I doubt *every* person can be reached, even if rounded up in audiences of thousands. What about decent people who are not likely candidates for Mormonism? Our way of life is appealing, but I can see that our beliefs about polygamy, human godhood, temple rituals for the dead, and other peculiarities are a hard sell for most.

Other things are beginning to bother me, a lot. The requirements for the Celestial Kingdom are troublesome. It's the only place in Heaven you can hope to be with your loved ones, so it seems important I aim for it. In order to qualify, one must be baptized by a man ordained in the Mormon priesthood. Did that when I was eight. Of course, only a man of the priesthood can enter the "top kingdom," and a woman must be "sealed" to such a man in a temple. This is problematic because my place in *eternity* depends more on marriage than on anything I can be or accomplish on my own. A man qualifying for the Celestial Kingdom can have multiple wives, but a woman has but one ticket to Heaven. . . .

Polygamy seemed a practicality for building up church membership in the early days. No woman need worry about spinsterhood; some man will marry her into his flock. As seems true on Earth, women will apparently outnumber men in Heaven, so even there polygamy makes sense. I try to imagine what it will be like, seeding a whole planet. . . .

Most who claim they are abductees weren't raised Mormon, and almost as many men report being abducted, so I can't make much of the connection to what I was taught about godlike humans creating spirit children to populate other planets, or the women's value being in their procreative abilities . . . but if only Mormon women were reporting abductions, I would be on a psychiatrist's couch tomorrow!

When I am sixteen years old, I receive a "patriarchal blessing." Standard fare for young people in the church. It's a kind of psychic reading given by a patriarch, ordained to divulge information about our destinies. I am told that I will be a mother in Zion. (Sigh.) Everything else I am told is fulfilled by the time I am eighteen . . . as if truly my destiny is to break from the Mormon church.

Thirty-eight years later, while I am in an altered state of mind in a resort setting in Scottsdale, Arizona, Dr. Hover helps me pull on a loose thread, and one of memory's patches unravels to reveal beneath it, (possibly) a more significant event that happened when I was sixteen.

What I saw while hypnotized seemed to come out of left field, because it featured "grays," and there were no signs in my dream life of encounters with this most often reported alien. In my numerous UFO- and alien-related dreams, "Asian types" predominated, along with "Nordics," both human-like in appearance, as are "memories" of the ones I call the Sphinx People (possibly Siriuns). And yet, of the seven events I viewed while hypnotized, the encounter with the grays was the most "life-like," experientially speaking.

I was hypnotized by Ruth Hover, Ph.D., on August 15, 1995. The setting: *Inside a round, metal room; I am lying supine on an examination table. It has a pedestal base, and above me dangles something " . . . like monster dental equipment." The illumination is extremely bright. Several grays are in the room. One is looking at me. His gaze is unbelievably powerful.*

(I had seen depictions of grays on TV, and in various publications, but none were close to capturing the *feel* of them. The fear I felt in their presence was not the kind that causes one to scream out in terror. It is a fear one feels in the face of an unknown you *know* is more powerful than you are. The respect/awe felt dares not show it is afraid. I have seen this kind of fear in the eyes of small, wild animals.)

Transcribed from an audio cassette tape, the following excerpt is verbatim. (italics:Dana; R:Ruth) Missing from the transcription are the emotions I felt. No other encounter was cause for deeper shudders, and nothing about this experience is metaphorically ambiguous.

They're so mechanical, they're just so mechanical. There's like an electrical feeling to them. You just like . . . you just feel buzzed. You just feel buzzed all over.

[R]: Not entirely comfortable.

Their eyes are so liquid . . . you would think if you put your hand on them, it would just like go down a well . . .

[R]: They're mechanical in their movements—are they robots?
There's some kind of intelligence there.
[R]: Do they hurt you?
No . . . I don't think so . . .
[R]: Do they explain to you at all? Give you any idea of what they are doing to you, or for you?
(Big sigh.) *They must tell me something. I know there's something down there.* (In memory.) *I know something is down there.*
[R]: Something they don't want you to know?
They . . . we can't talk about . . . we can't remember—why?
[R]: Well, your conscious mind won't discover it. And that's okay. Let your conscious mind and body remain heavy, and out of this. But let your higher consciousness float over . . . and perceive very acutely, and see if your higher consciousness can discover what it is they don't want you to report.
(Long pause.) *I just want to say a new kind of human being.*
[R]: A new kind of human being. Do you think that new kind of human being is here?
It's like the baby Jesus thing. If some know there's a new human being coming in, they'll kill them, they'll kill all of them, they won't let them live, because they will supplant the other human being, and no human being is going to agree to be supplanted, no animal is ever going to . . . an animal will fight and kill to survive. It has to be protected.
[R]: Makes sense they would keep it very secret.
Yeah, that's . . . as scary as it is, that's why you do it . . . that's why you . . . even if you're afraid it isn't true, even if you're afraid . . .
[R]: And that's why you don't remember it.
But the babies . . .
[R]: Are they here on this ship?
Sometime I saw those babies again. (Ref. the "bug-eyed" babies seen during the earlier regression.)
[R]: Are they still babies, or are they older?
They're not the same babies.
[R]: More babies. They're still not ready for you to teach them?
There are mothers . . . carriers . . . hmmm . . .
[R]: Tell me what you do next after all this has taken place.
I was seeing all the rooms where there are mothers and procedures and this will happen to me someday.

[R]: Does that feel okay to you?

I'm very ambivalent. I want to believe that . . . When I'm not there, it feels like something I should stay away from . . . very frightening.

[R]: But when you're there, it's kind of okay.

Yeah, you kind of . . . you want to believe.

[R]: Umhmm.

Because if you don't believe . . . how can they make you do this?

Of all that was retrieved, this last statement is a most graphic example of the struggle it is to reconcile such memories with consensus reality. But something else disturbs me more. Regarding secrecy, even at the age of sixteen—and I was very protected and by no means worldly—even though I was frightened by these powerful entities, I knew that human beings were really the dangerous ones, who would kill the babies if they knew of their existence.

"It's like the baby Jesus thing," I said.

According to the Bible, when news of the birth of Jesus Christ reached King Herod, he vowed to kill this usurper. Failing to locate the child, Herod ordered that all boys under the age of two in the vicinity of Bethlehem be killed (Matt. 2:13-16).

Was Jesus Christ an actual man, or son of God, whose presence in the world evoked the wrath of humans in power? Or was he a literary personification of a new consciousness that began to herald 2,000 years ago, as savior of the human species? Are prophesies of the return of Jesus Christ being fulfilled in ways no one could have suspected? I don't want to stir the pot of controversy already brewing between Christian factions and new agers, but in my position, I *have* to think about these things.

For me, alien abduction and telepathic communications, though enigmatic, are not theories. I cannot deny awareness of elaborate preparations taking place that foretell unprecedented change for human-kind. If indeed the change is a new kind of human being with the powers of "Christ consciousness," it *has* to be protected from forces that are ruled by the illusion that materiality is the Alpha and Omega of reality.

8

HIVE MIND:

A RADICAL IDEA

When the term "hive mind" landed on the page like a small meteorite during the translation of the *History* (chapter eleven), it sounded at once foreign and familiar. Frank DeMarco asked me to expound on the concept; I told him I didn't know much about it. But maybe I knew more than I cared to admit. . . .

By some quirk of fate I have never been able to put my finger on, at the age of eighteen, I experienced a sudden internal change that resulted in a break from the Mormon church. I still can make no sense of it, except to wonder now if this unexpected fork in my life was alien-influenced, as a step in an "initiation process" that began when I was very young.

Growing up, I never imagined a life different from the religious model programmed into my young mind. I would marry in the temple, have six children, and spend my days as a devoted Latter Day Saint. But something happened to me at Brigham Young University that shattered this vision. The incident that triggered the shattering was petty on the face of it; the unexpected was a sudden "seeing" that the "model" in my mind, which had given meaning to my life, did not match the facts encountered.

The secondary impact of this unexpected insight was that suddenly I was a stranger to myself. Although this was experienced traumatically for awhile, the long effect was that early in life I was set free to search out my own beliefs.

Particularly during my 20s, I perceived myself to be a rebel, doomed to live out the hell promised to anyone who leaves the church. In losing my standing, and having no model to replace the one I'd lost, I made a lot of mistakes in those years, some which carried long and serious repercussions. If I had understood then the workings of hive mind and its purpose and value in community, I could have avoided the troubles I created in angry and reactionary behavior that had, in its expression, not a clue that I had been set free for a reason.

In the *History*, the servants of El ask, "Do you not realize you are biological entities? And that there are biological laws that govern your behavior?"

There exists evidence that hive mind has a biological component. In *The Rebirth of Nature: The Greening of Science and God* (Bantam Books, New York, 1991), on page 115, Ph.D. biochemist Rupert Sheldrake writes about morphogenetic fields:

> *If behavior is indeed governed by morphic [sic] fields, when some members of a species acquire a new pattern of behavior and hence a new behavioral field, for example, by learning a new trick, then others should tend to learn the same thing more quickly, even in the absence of any known means of connection or communication.*

Morphic or morphogenetic fields are a fairly new consideration by scientists, but life experience seems to confirm that our minds/psyches/souls—or morphic fields, perhaps—can be programmed in ways we are not aware. (chapter nine, "Make a Baby Form," contains a more comprehensive discussion of the principles of hive mind, or morphic fields.)

In my 30s, I began to seek a balance between aspects of my childhood model that were worth keeping and the free spirit I was discovering in my make-up. These were the wandering years. Moving frequently, I could keep only what could be crammed into whatever pathetic vehicle I owned—if I had a car at all—as I created a checkerboard resume from a host of jobs and residences that would later give those D.O.D. agents something to ponder. (My life resume also included several short-term marriages that amounted to no more than legalized affairs, and earned me the observation from one old busybody that I was a case of "hot pants and high morals.")

While I must have looked to all the world to be unstable those years, beneath surface appearances I was as serious as ever about things spiritual. When I was about thirty, I reached a crisis point that would return to me something of the faith I'd lost. Because of the traumatic break with the Mormon church, I thought I had lost religion altogether—"and good riddance!" was my attitude. But in crisis I discovered I had a religious soul that called for a new path. The lesson was, the baby need not be cast out with polluted waters. The first leg of this new path was charismatically Christian.

Circumstances had placed me in the home of people we called, in those days, "Jesus freaks." My opinion of them was a mix of revulsion and fascination. Because they were a bit of a laughingstock among my friends, I did not aspire to join them, but at a point of despair, I prayed one night, something like this, "If you will help me, God, I am even willing to believe these people might have it right. . . ."

That night, awakened out of a nightmare, a shimmering shaft of white light fell upon me, bathing me in radiant joy. It was as if in that moment I was transformed. The next morning, I rolled out of bed a total born-again "Jesus freak." Soon I was jumping around like the others, clapping my hands, and singing in tongues. I discovered I could play my violin by ear, which seemed powerful evidence that I had been touched . . . and claimed by the Spirit.

I was baptized again, dunked in a river this time, and for about a year, I thought all this would replace my childhood religion. But the change I had experienced at the age of eighteen, with much less fanfare, went deeper than I'd realized. I could no more adopt the "charismatic model" than I could remain in the Mormon church. Somehow, "hive mind" in any recognizable form, had lost its hold on me. I would be one who would learn from experience; which, in effect, means I often have to do a thing wrong to learn what's right.

The next phase was characterized by Bible studies in my apartment on Josephine Street in Denver. I and other "religious renegades" and "spiritual orphans" called ourselves the Josephinians, and met often with no one in authority to tell us how to interpret Scripture. We had a "cussing jar," into which we plunked quarters for every cuss word uttered during our sessions, which penalty-money paid for the coffee we drank long into the nights as we searched the Word for light.

Musicians and artists all, we formed a group called "the Insuffer-ables," and performed dixieland jazz concerts for people in drug and alcohol rehabilitation facilities, such as the Salvation Army.

1975 was the year . . . the first of many times I was awakened by a sound of "ethereal" chimes. (Though I use the word ethereal to describe such sounds, I assure you these are sounds as clear as any we identify as coming from known sources. I literally heard, with my ears, a ring of chimes in my immediate environment, in the same way that I would later hear, on many occasions, a ringing telephone (not my telephone) from the "ethers," for all I know. The most important element of hearing such sounds is not the wonder of it, or a scientific implausibility to argue. The significance is what the sounds *stir* in me—a sense of reminder, a "pay attention, watch, and listen" feeling—a message to remember something I cannot recall in my conscious mind. There is a sense of announcement of more to come and there is always more. The late Dr. Karla Turner, abductee, investigator/researcher and author, told me that she too had heard chimes in the 70s. There were these subtle prods or reminders all through the 70s, but I considered all of it to be nothing unusual for a sensitive person; nothing to arouse alarm, certainly nothing I associated with rumors of UFO sightings. That suspicion came years later.)

From this rag-tag beginning of a new faith that adhered to no established model, I became something of a spiritual scholar in my quest to go beyond the limits imposed by religion. The nature of my freedom from hive mind, while casting me as a renegade in the eyes of conventional society, cleared the path for easy acceptance of the possibility that the divine beings we called gods, angels, or demons might be highly advanced extraterrestrials.

Having been taught as a child that God was a super-physical being who lived on another planet, announcements of the arrival of space visitors in observable ships did not require—for me—the leap it took for many people to allow such events to be real.

But a mind predisposed to the possibility of the existence of extraterrestrials, divine or otherwise, does not explain the deep con-nection I felt with the whole UFO business from the onset of such announcements, and afterwards. Having become somewhat of a radical thinker, I felt no embarrassment admitting out loud my excitement at the prospect that we were being visited by extraterrestrials. But such declarations were only half the story.

The other half was hidden—all the stuff that would begin to surface once I was more or less forced to face the bone-chilling prospect that the rumored ETs, if real, were more than "visiting," and my interest in them, more than a passing fascination.

Over the course of recording so much in the way of telepathic communications, it made no sense to me that so many ordinary people, like myself, would be the recipients of information about the true nature of reality, and the origins and future of humankind . . . *except* in the context of the understanding that a hive mind exists in multiple forms—not in the abstract, i.e., not as an *idea* about how we relate to one another psychologically—but as a biological reality.

It makes sense that changes in our physical, mental, emotional, or spiritual environment would be first noticed by individuals less influenced by a hive mind. In ancient times, messengers were often shepherds, removed from the hustle-bustle of the marketplace. Today's messengers of change are reporting from fields and hills of a more complex civilization. The shepherd's hill today might simply be the house of someone who lives quietly separate from the hub of hive-minded activities. It's not the location that is important, but where, and on what, our attention is focused.

Much has been written by scholars, scientists, and other cutting-edge thinkers about the havoc that would occur should we discover too suddenly that reality—especially from the religious perspective—is not as we had been taught. History is full of examples of "human-animal" reactions to changes that threaten the status quo. While I don't recall other authors using the term "hive mind" when referring to "mass hysteria" or the "herd mentality," the concept is not really new.

What seems to be new is a global effort, involving many people of many levels of experience and intelligence, to inform and prepare the public for changes that all of the reporters can see from their respective positions and perceptions.

The UFO phenomenon is just one of many heralds of a change in the nature of our consciousness. From my perspective—the UFO perspective, because this is my experience—it appears that the prevailing hive mind is undergoing a metamorphosis.

Earlier I mentioned a silver seam on the ceiling of the spacecraft where I was taken to receive implants that enhanced my ability to communicate with beings of other realms. I tried on, for size, the notion that this could have been a "metaphorical abduction," as in a dream. I have a mind that can associate the spacecraft with the human head, the silver seam as an entry port from one hemisphere of the brain to the other. The events in the navigation room could be interpreted as symbolism for activities in, say, the pineal gland. I could then make the leap that my sudden interest in quantum physics was demonstration of an activation of a new component of consciousness, with all of the dynamics seated in the physical brain. But none of this begins to explain the physical cuts on my hands, the ball beneath my skin, the scars on my body, the electronic disturbances in my home, the disappearance and reappearance of my special pen, and all of the other extraordinary events detailed in the appendix.

If any of this is herald for exclusively a change in consciousness, my experience suggests that real beings are the masterminds and orchestrators of these events.

Reality is not an either/or, black/white proposition. It is not a question of whether these events are physical *or* psychological in nature. They are clearly both. To grasp the concept, one must have some understanding or experience that reality is not, in *essence,* fixed, solid, or hard. (More on this in chapter nine.) This is quantum physics 101. The prevailing hive mind has scientists scurrying to identify a "basic building block," as they persist in the search for a missing link that will prove their theories about the origins and evolution of mankind. In my opinion, both quests are doomed because both are based on false assumptions. Sound/light/energy is the essence of reality, not some infinitesimally tiny bead of a thing that can be slid under a microscope, observed, measured, and categorized. The more powerful our microscopes, the quicker the collapse of the illusion that there is some ultimate "unit" of creation. The deeper we probe inner realties, the more vast the spaces. . . .

It is extremely disorienting, I can attest, to discover that what we consider to be "hard realities" are actually energetic manifestations of inner, or interpenetrating realities that do not behave according to the same laws that govern outer appearances. Take it from one who has passed through walls and windows.

My sources explain that the way to outer space is via inner space. I have a grasp of what they are teaching, but not the words to convey to people who still perceive "form" as the first principle of reality. That's backwards. Forms, or physical appearances, are manifestations of higher or deeper realities that are not composed *of* anything . . . but *are* everything!

If it sounds like I've got all of this figured out, don't believe it. I'm doing my best to communicate my clearest perceptions. The paradox of accelerated consciousness is that one is aware of how much one does not know. I suppose if I were truly humble, I would keep silent. But if I were that humble, I would fail in my function as one of many messengers. The net result of all of our stories and messages is an impact on consciousness meant to inform the prevailing hive mind, so that the human community can make choices based more on reality, and less on the illusions that have resulted in the creation of disharmonious conditions which must be corrected if Earth is to continue as a viable environment for life.

A word here about beliefs that human beings are "fallen" or essentially evil, as is suggested by the ritual of baptism to wash away our sins.

It is my understanding that baptism was originally a ritual symbolizing physical birth, as rebirth (or activation of higher consciousness) was symbolized by the laying of hands upon the head to "receive the Holy Spirit." In some religions, it is believed, no baptism, no Heaven—because the unbaptized are stuck with their sins. How *rituals* come to be considered literal realities is a question to ponder. According to Robert Claiborne, author of *The Roots of English* (Time Books, Random House, 1989), the original root meaning of sin was "what is real." Did we get our wires crossed? Did "knowing too much about reality" (sin) come to mean evil, due to abuses of knowledge? Did the "sin of knowing" mark a beginning of a hive mind that exceeded nature's biological purposes? Would this have anything to do with the global myth of the fall of a tower that confounded all languages, reducing our ability to amass too much knowledge? Could a tower symbolize the brain, or mind? The El provide an alternative viewpoint in chapter eleven. They confirm that something did go wrong in our beginnings . . . but it wasn't sin as most think of sin.

We are getting over the shock of discovering that we are neither the only, nor the most intelligent beings existing in the cosmos. But maybe some of us are still reverberating a bit to learn that beings whom we thought were greatly superior to us—angels and gods—are not perfect, but demonstrate the same ranges of good or ill motives as is true among human beings.

As for the multitude of messages streaming from claimants of contact with ETs who are warning of catastrophic events to come, it is not surprising there would be strong initial negative reactions from a hive mind long conditioned to listen only to designated human authorities. But advances in communication technologies are changing our perception of who is in charge, and why. More and more, people are realizing the wisdom in the counsel to seek the truth *within*, to strengthen our connection with God (or whatever our concept of the Divine). This more than anything will break the bonds of a hive mind which, while perhaps necessary for our development, is also subject to manipulations by forces on- and off-planet; forces vested in keeping us ignorant, and thereby controllable, in service to agendas that benefit the few at the expense of the many.

The El say that many are here to help us cross a new threshold, but *we* are the star performers in this drama. If in fact a new kind of human being is in the making, if we have been faithful to the lessons of love, we will not rush to kill them but will welcome and nurture them as wonder children created to carry on the legacy of the evolving human spirit.

9

MAKE A BABY FORM:

THE NATURE OF HUMAN INTELLIGENCE

In December 1994, after returning from a UFO conference in Mesquite, Nevada, I got back to work on *Jonah*. Fiction, I believed, was the only way I could convey what would otherwise be rejected as ridiculous. I was yet to learn that human logic is not very useful when it comes to fulfilling a task commissioned by intelligences heralding from dimensions where our logic and reason are simple arithmetic compared to the tetrahedron physics of their thinking.

After completing *Jonah*, I spent the last of my monetary reserves on traveling in the summer of 1995, to seek professional help in hypnotic regressions. These trips expanded my education, as did a journey to Woodland Park, Colorado, where I met members of a group of abductees who had moved there, believing that soon a man positioned "near" the government was going to funnel a great deal of money to them so they could establish a "UFO information foundation" that would insure jobs for all of them. This promise looked to me to be a lure to gather abductees in one location so someone in the government could keep an eye on them . . . and what better place than in the backyard of NORAD/Cheyenne Mountain, one of our major defense installations? Sightings of UFOs are common around defense facilities. Would the abductees be bait to draw UFOs closer for study? By the fall of 1995, I believed there was no place safer than Moab. I felt safe nowhere, so I might as well be near family.

The effect of the siege endured while working to finish *Jonah*, the travel to Colorado and Arizona, and the almost nightly phenomena took its toll, physically, emotionally, mentally, and financially. Although UFO-related dreams diminished significantly after the regressions, I was still being "visited" and was still "going." By now it was apparent that the comings and goings related directly to my work as scribe.

My mother was most concerned about my behavior. I was hiding out, writing, and little more.

"*Stop it*," my mother said.

"I *can't* . . . " I tried to explain.

There was no explaining it. I was *pregnant* with information, and the only way to maintain equilibrium was to keep on writing. Surely there would be an end to it someday. Now and then, I would transcribe something I thought would prove to my mother and friends that I wasn't creating this material—obviously it wasn't me—can't you see? They couldn't! It was so baffling to watch eyes glaze over at something I had recorded and thought was clear . . . wisdom. I stopped the "show and tell." It was hurting me more than helping.

"You've got to get a job," my parents said. From their perspective that made perfect sense. For me, it was one more pressure. I was physically debilitated, sleep-deprived, stressed to the max. Fortunately, I was able to work part-time as a copy-editor for my friends, the archaeologists.

Compassion for how hard all this business was on my family and friends came later. I was too out of kilter to see their side; too baffled, too challenged, and I was developing a bad case of the "poor-me's." These were the alien days.

I had a lot of time to think . . . not that thinking helped. I was seeing too much, feeling too much, and knowing more than I could organize in my brain, which now seemed as pitifully inadequate as any machine.

I took refuge in the alphabet again, creating more charts, more graphs, more art. Ironically people were more persuaded to believe that something phenomenal was going on by the strange artwork I was creating than by what I told them of my actual experiences. During these months, the only times I felt centered or peaceful was while working with letters and numbers.

The more I sought refuge in the alphabet work, the less it looked that I would ever function as a normal human being in society again. Scary times.

I was being schooled. My sources continued to deepen in me certain spiritual concepts. But what about the strong impressions that aliens were busy creating hybrids? Messages continued to ring warnings. Mankind was on the brink of unprecedented change. And personal and collective will seemed to be the keys to the puzzle I was trying to solve.

But what were the damn choices?

Preparation is a big word, like a spacious room filled with comfortable furniture; a bed I can crawl into and pull the covers over my head, a rocking chair I can pull close to a cozy fire. Windows give view of a storm brewing. I can pull the drapes if I wish, climb into bed, or curl up in the rocking chair.

Will is the most undeveloped of human powers, I was told. We are so accustomed to making unconscious choices—bed, chair, window—that making decisions in the light of conscious awareness, outside the familiarity of hive mind, can seem, for the novice, as sensible as standing in center field during a thunderstorm.

Against all understanding, against warnings from those who saw only darkness and danger in being a scribe for alien intelligences, I chose to open myself up for deeper contact with those who transmitted, and those who came.

The question I have is: when did I *really* make this choice? Before I was born? That would explain the split-mind I experienced from the onset of the phenomena, one part of me shocked, feeling myself swept on a wave, the other part calm, knowing, and devoted.

My life experience is characterized by "getting back on track." Certain choices I made along the way resulted in experiences and conditions I felt were "off track." But what did I know of "on track?" Something in my heart, something I knew at a feeling level. It was nothing I could define, exactly, but would know in a powerful way when something would spark memory . . . a book, a person, an event, or something as curious as noticing certain patterns in the letters in certain names . . . Such feelings and urges are the soul's messengers. The soul may speak to us in symbols, in dreams, in feelings, while water is running, in sudden recognitions of people or places that cannot be explained.

My life experiences can be described as a kind of fabric, different designs knitted together by the silver threads of the soul weaver who works at an invisible loom. The experience of finding again a connecting thread is sign the voyager is aware that life here is about something other than material concerns and the ambitions of the ego-self.

Beginning in June 1994, my soul's messengers were no longer quiet or subtle. It was as if the fabric of my life was suddenly rent to produce wide gaps in the weave. Would the silver threads woven into the fabric be strong enough to keep me stable as I experienced the shocks of expanding awareness?

Preparation is essential.

How did I end up in a duplex in Moab, Utah, daily recording such material, when all I had wanted was moderate success as a novelist? Our soul's destiny has nothing to do with the things of this world, I am told. I was in the duplex, broke, alone, and deepening contact, because a choice had been made to live by my soul's agenda. The question—when did I make this choice—is as impossible to answer as it is to understand how life is sparked in a fetus. . . .

Translation of the message below wiped me out, physically. After recording it, I was so debilitated all I could do was lie still on the bed and accept with gratitude the powerful electrical-like pulsations that swept over my body for about an hour until my energies were restored.

"Make a Baby Form" is one of the densest and longest messages I've received. Rereading it, I shudder at the memory of the battle conditions I felt at the time. There is a sense of the transmitters working to pound home certain concepts I needed to thoroughly grasp in preparation for coming challenges. In this message are clues in reference to what it is we are becoming. . . .

January 17, 1996:
MAKE A BABY FORM
(*The Nature of Human Intelligence*)

All is spirit, all is physical. It is a matter of density and frequency. See how when the spirit departs the body, the body is said to weigh less. See there was weight to this intelligence, but it is so very much less dense than the form it inhabited.

The body as a habitation. You populate the Earth. And you

yourselves are populated by intelligence. The human form dies and the body is laid to rest in the Earth, dust to dust. And the intelligence that inhabited the body returns to its environment of origin.

See how easily you can see the separate manifestations, when it is a matter of ice to steam. So that the spirit is like steam, the life of a human being like water, and when you crystallize to ice, you die—but see? You promptly melt, returning to your watery state. Does water, too, condense then evaporate? Do we speak of spirit like vapors?

You cannot imagine yourselves beyond your brains. Lacking a brain, how would you *think*? Think of the brain as a complex mechanism designed to facilitate a special way of relating to reality. See how all body functions, including the senses of sight, hearing, taste, smell, and sensation are facilitated through the brain. See the brain as the site where all such experience is facilitated. See the brain as a control center for the body, like the NASA headquarters, with all its computers and message systems.

But what do you know of the intelligence that directs the operations in this headquarters? For all your intelligence, what do you know of the spark of life at the center of every human being?

Think about the marriage of egg and sperm, the coming together of these two genetic carriers. See the genetic material as software. To make a computer work, you plug it into an electrical outlet. What is the nature of the activation of the sperm-egg form? When does the moment of life occur? and how?

We would ask you to consider that there is never a moment or a condition when there is no life. What is life-less-ness? Is anything ever truly dead? Or does dead describe a state of being? And so, then, when is the life-form ever truly not alive? But yes, we must make this distinction, between parents and child. Matter combines to create a new form. Sperm and egg combine deep in the womb and a new life-form is created.

Now, if there is never a moment when there is no life, then one imagines a stream of intelligence from the parental sperm and egg. Now look. If every cell is intelligent, capable of receiving messages from headquarters, the brain, and sperm, and egg are composed of such intelligence; then, when they combine, is there any interruption of intelligence? Are not all cells sites of specialized intelligence, each performing special tasks? And do not cells combine in specialized ways to create sites for more complex functions? Are not the organs and muscles and veins and arteries such sites, where cells are combined to serve in specialized ways?

And so in a moment of ecstasy, the sperm joins the egg, deep in the womb of a woman, and presto! A new site is created, where there follows rapid cell activity as they scurry to respond to the software contained within the DNA. The sperm and egg combine and a message is activated: MAKE A BABY FORM. The response is instantaneous. And in nine months, if the message is carried out perfectly, a squalling child is born into your world, outside the environment of the inner woman.

So again—what is the nature of the intelligence that expresses throughout the human form? What is the origin and can you fathom it, outside, beyond the parameters of human form?

Are you acquainted with intelligence, except as is expressed in human form? Do you imagine that intelligence expressing through the human form is the only expression of intelligence? Are you so conceited?

If intelligence expresses through the human form, why would not all forms be sites of such intelligent expression? Each expressing in unique ways, each composed of elements comparable to human cells, each element a specialized unit, designed for special function.

So why do you imagine some forms are alive and others dead?

Do you not see it is a matter of density and frequency? Your scientists study the vast differences in forms, discovering that each is a matter of frequency determining density, and density being a matter of function.

See how the soil is designed in such a way as to ground a tree. Without which soil, how would the tree root? See how the soil serves as an environment, where the roots are not only stabilized, but a site where the roots can absorb nutrients and water, necessary for expression as a tree.

And see how also the human body, like a tree, has roots, the environment enriching those roots, to give expression as a human being.

Now a tree's roots extend down into the soil. And the roots of human form extend into an environment invisible to human observation. For how can the eye observe itself? The eye can gaze into a mirror and see its reflection, but can the eye observe the eye? Can the leaves of a tree observe its roots under ground? Are the leaves aware of the roots, or would they be shocked to discover they are connected to these strange tentacles buried below the surface of the ground? Because the leaves cannot see these roots, does this mean they do not exist?

Because you cannot see your own roots beneath the surface of the human form, does this mean no such connection exists? So you see yourselves as wholly separate from all other life forms? Are the roots of the tree separate from the soil that enriches? Is there not a constant state of interaction between soil and roots? When you yank roots from the ground and lay down the tree, does this not interrupt the interaction? And devoid of the environment of soil, will the roots and tree soon cease to function?

And when the human form separates from its roots, will it not soon cease to function?

What is the nature of your root connection? Because you cannot see these roots or where they connect, and to what they connect to, do you imagine there is no such connection?

And if you can imagine there must be such a connection, when the connection is broken, as when roots are yanked from the soil—what happens to the intelligence that expresses through this form?

See how a tree yanked up from its roots begins a process of change. See also how seeds from this inert tree have found other soil and rooted there to produce a new tree form.

See likewise how the seed of the human form roots in the womb to produce a new human form.

See the cycles of life! See how all forms cycle, changing form in this dance of life, in this environment.

And so you are no closer now to comprehending the nature of intelligence that expresses in human form. You strain to see the connection between form and intelligence. You agree there is intelligence in every cell, as expresses in the spontaneous ways that cells behave, receiving instructions from the brain site where reside leader cells that seem to direct the general cell population.

And if all forms reflect the dance of cyclic life, then see that the site of one human form reflects the activity of a population, where many cells or people take direction from lead cells, or people you call leaders, as a way of describing these functions.

See each human form as a kingdom, the brain functioning as king. And so you ask—where does the king receive his guidance? Is he a self-sufficient intelligence, intelligent unto himself, with no guidance from any higher source? Is this king the King of Kings?

And then, so, imagine five billion such kings, all believing themselves to be kings of kings, each believing he or she is the king of kings.

Then what of all these other kings? Are they all pretenders to the throne?

Does this not touch upon the nature of competition between human beings? Do human beings see themselves as wholly separate kingdoms, each having a king that rules? Each king knowing best how life in these environs should function?

What a set-up for chaos! What keeps these competing kings from destroying one another?

What is the nature of the DNA instructions written into each and every cell and taking instruction from leader cells in the brain? Who created such complex software and how is such software activated, as compared to a computer coming to life when the plug is inserted into the socket and the on-button is pushed?

Does it not seem that there must be an intelligence behind the scenes?

Again—does any form function wholly separate from its environment? Can any cell of any human form spring free of the form and perform independently of the mother environment?

Even your astronauts in the sky remain connected to your environment, through communications with NASA headquarters. How long would they survive if these communications were severed? Could they successfully return to Earth using only the mechanical instruments which, in and of themselves, lack intelligence sufficient to guide? Would the spaceship be as a tree yanked out of the soil, its roots dangerously exposed to an environment that lacks the necessary nutrients for continued life? And while the man lost on a desert can survive, separated from other humans, for he has intelligence—is he not in danger, so separated? Will not such separation test him to determine if he has intelligence sufficient for survival?

Within your human form, are there not cells dying each moment, and cell replacements occurring? Does not life outside the human form reflect the life within?

When cells within die, do all the other cells mourn? Is there celebration when new cells emerge to replace, to fill the vacancies?

But you say—"yes-but"—we are all special, unique, and when one dies, the one to replace is not the same. The one gone is gone forever. Never before was there this unique expression and never will there be another, exactly the same.

Is this not reason to grieve?

But see how you describe unique forms. Do you grieve a unique tree yanked up by its roots? Or do you say, "That's okay, there are many saplings and seeds galore"? Do you perform for every tree that falls a funeral ritual, mourning the loss of this unique expression?

So why do you clamor so over the loss of a specialized human form? Because you cannot see where the intelligence has gone—indeed, you cannot see the intelligence as it performs, except as is expressed in human form—do you imagine it is no more?

Do you imagine intelligence does not exist beyond the form that expresses intelligence?

What sort of kings are these, that they should so easily be brought down? But you do not behave as if you are this vulnerable. Each behaves as a king believing he will reign forever. So he dictates with such power and exhibition, each adoring himself and proclaiming in kingly ways.

See how the fetus develops into a child, the child into an adult. Imagine, if you will, humankind on such a journey, each human engaged in a process of development—each (mature human) a child-form developing into an adult-form YET TO EXPRESS. For this (new) adult will not happen, will not take form, until all of the children are performing their functions, as all of the cells within the fetus *symphonize* to activate the progression from fetus to child.

And so you cannot imagine the form that is trying to take shape, as each cell in a fetus does not see the child emerging. For each is focused on its own activity and while aware of the activity of all other cells engaged in the process, none sees the form in its final stage. For how could they, being designed to concentrate fully on the task at hand?

But for such a miraculous event to occur, must there not be intelligence that guides? Who designed such system functions, each cell unaware of the precise function of other cells, none seeing the final form taking shape?

And do any of these cells suffer for lack of awareness, as to other cells and the final form taking shape? Do they cry out, afraid for what they do not see? Or do all rejoice in being alive, asking not to know more. Alas, not aware there is more to know! For why burden each cell with such awareness, if it cannot be satisfied?

Does your maker give you awareness of things invisible to taunt you? Or is such awareness also purposeful and necessary to your functioning? Do you fret because you do not understand the reason for such awareness? Because you cannot see how it functions to serve the process? Is your obsession to enlarge this mysterious awareness born of self-will, you choosing to be so obsessed, having no origin in the intelligence that guides? Can the eyes see the eyes? Do your thoughts reveal the site of intelligence? Or, do the eyes see and do thoughts issue from the site of intelligence, both performing spontaneously?

Yes, there is some ability to direct—what you look at, what you gaze upon, what you decide to think about. But can you improve your sight or think beyond what your brain decrees as to its capacity? Can a retarded child have the thoughts of an Einstein?

Do you control the nature of your own thoughts? Do you originate them? Or do they seem to flow like electricity, making bright your existence?

See how limited a human performs when there is limited brain activity. So that the liveliness of a human relates to brain activity. So the greater the thought capacity, the greater awareness and expression.

So if you do not control thoughts or the nature of thoughts, then what is the nature of your intelligence? Can you claim to be king of your own kingdom, if you cannot direct your own constituents? If you cannot see them, much less direct them?

And so is not your suffering due to trying to behave like a king when you lack the capacity? Would not this poor king do better if he bowed down and surrendered to the invisible source of his limited (earthbound) intelligence and awareness? Then could he act to his highest capacity, free of trying to direct a populace he cannot even see? Do not your kings and politicians have great trouble, trying to direct so many they cannot see and do not know? Would they do better if they came to be aware there is an intelligence who does know all—and then to seek direction from that intelligence?

And so it begins with such acknowledgment—with discovery that the king does not perform well, trying to direct without knowledge of all of the constituents and the environment in which all exist.

And so then, *how* does one stop directing and become a subject to this greater unseen source of intelligence?

It begins with a question and becomes a quest. How to less direct, how to become more a subject of this Higher King.

Why? Because the (individual) king is looking out upon the wreckage in his kingdom, seeing he knows not how to direct such a complex kingdom. He had a plan in mind, but the constituents did not cooperate! See how they do whatever they please, disregarding direction! See what a mess they made. See the kingdom is in shambles.

So the king seeks help from a higher source. What am I doing wrong? Everything, everything. You do not know how to direct, oh beloved human king. You have a plan, but you fail to communicate it.

And so you must learn a new language to receive and transmit direction from a higher source. So you become subject, and your kingship serves as a link between the source of all intelligence and the constituents that comprise your kingdom. Only when you so subject yourself will you be able to communicate to them; only then will they cooperate.

And so is each human such a king, trying to direct a kingdom he cannot even see, nor the environment in which the kingdom resides. And each king experiences upheavals and chaos until he seeks a higher king who can tell him what to do, how to perform, what to communicate. And then, so subjected, does each king become a messenger of the Divine Source of Intelligence.

And so then together you perform as kings, as all are equal participants in the kingdom; no one king lording over another, but each performing in a specialized way, each benefitting the kingdom and each enjoying the benefits of kingship, as decreed by the King of all Kings.

And so each is on a quest to discover the nature of one's kingliness and the kingship each performs. And when this is discovered, one begins to experience ecstacy, for living to the highest call and capacity.

(authorship not designated)

This was an important message for me as preface for the shock that would come eight days later—a chastisement from Elohim—a lesson in discernment.

10

ELOHIM:

SPIRITUAL WARFARE?

On January 25, 1996, as usual, upon awakening, I began to record. The material was dense, and wearisome, but I felt it worth typing up. I came to this sentence: "Be careful not to confuse the material with the spiritual, forgetting that all matter is also energy. . . ." I replaced the word "forgetting" with "remembering," otherwise the sentence was false. But this bothered me. The material never required editing, save for an occasional word added to clarify. But a wrong word such as "forgetting" instead of "remembering" drastically changes the meaning of a sentence. This slip may seem a small thing, but for me it was a red flag . . . one I ignored. I was so tired.

The next morning, a "voice" came through, quite unlike any I had "heard" or felt before. (I don't actually hear voices, but have no words to adequately explain how such communications occur.) The communication felt more than telepathic . . . I felt an energy, a presence. Imagine small lightning bolts searing the pages, puffs of smoke, rumbles and hissings. Cowering in awe and fear, I had to write extremely fast to keep up with the rapid-fire delivery. It was as if part of me was over in the corner, watching, wringing my hands. . . . *Oh, my God, I'm really in trouble*!

The material came in increments, 1., 2., 3., etc., each a challenge to statements made in the material recorded the day before. Most increments began: "Ask them . . . why this, why that . . . " Complete disgust was expressed for not only the content of the material I'd recorded, but also for the transmitters themselves.

Essentially I was chastised for scribing "half asleep."

After a point-by-point scathing dissection of the material, I was asked: "Would you, in your desperation, believe anything? That sounds half possible? Where is that deep feeling of trust? Where is the light in your life? Did they succeed in neutralizing you? Why do you think we are constantly telling you to go deep within?"

The source spoke in no uncertain terms of the hybrid breeding program as real, and being conducted by *disembodied* beings who could appear as substantial, beings who could not reincarnate on Earth, beings who were using us and our genetic material to create bodies they themselves meant to "possess" (transfer their consciousness into), as a means to reinstate themselves on Earth as a new breed.

"You do not even know their names."

"So . . . who are you?" I wrote timidly.

"WE ARE ELOHIM!"

I felt faint.

"Are you embarrassed to use our name? Would you feel better to have their names? They have no names, for why name something insubstantial?"

It was not exactly comforting to learn that the name El equates with the Canaanite "High God," considering that Baal, purportedly El's son, is rendered as a most despicable character in the *Old Testament*. But Karen Armstrong (author, ex-Catholic nun, honorary member of the Association of Muslim Social Studies and foremost British commentator on religious affairs) explains that different scribes of various narratives in the Bible refer to God by different names. According to Armstrong's research, Yahweh (Jehovah) and El are one and the same.

> It is highly likely that Abraham's God was El, the High God of Canaan. The deity introduces himself to Abraham as El Shaddai (El of the Mountain), which was one of El's traditional titles. (Page 14)
>
> Jacob had decided to make the god he had encountered there (Beth-El) his elohim: this was a technical term, signifying everything that the gods could mean for men and women. Jacob had decided that if El (or Yahweh, as J calls him) could really look after him in Haran, he was particularly effective. He struck a bargain: in return

for El's special protection, Jacob would make him his elohim, the only god who counted. Israelite belief in God was deeply pragmatic. Abraham and Jacob both put their faith in El because he worked for them: they did not sit down and prove he existed; El was not a philosophical abstraction. (Page 17)

Excerpt from *A History of God:*
The 4000-Year Quest of Judaism, Christianity and Islam
by Karen Armstrong (Alfred A. Knopf, New York, 1993)

This is not exactly comforting, either, considering Jehovah's track record as a ruthless and capricious god, who sometimes commanded his chosen to destroy entire cities. Not exactly warm, fuzzy feelings, noticing the same tone in the communication to me, as was expressed to *Biblical* Job, after the poor dude was put to test and torture by the "prince of the airways" (Satan). I'm supposed to feel cuddly toward a god who says to Satan, "Yeah, go ahead and torture my man, Job . . . let's see what he's made of. . . . "

We are not required to *like* what the gods do . . . but anyone confronted by someone/something as powerful as I felt that day, recording, will *respect* . . .

If I had been "neutralized" by dense, almost hypnotic repetitions of disinformation, I was now in danger of falling, head bowed to the floor, to this new "voice of God." For that's what Elohim means.

More excerpts from the Elohim scold:

"See this great lyrical logic to justify the secrecy. They do not wish to arouse fear. Why? Is not fear a signal to beware? But they justify, as if to say all good things must be done in secret, for you would not like these good things.

"And then this high finish, speaking of love and compassion. And what love and compassion do they show for you?

"Have you not been persuaded there are no dark forces to worry about? Is your reaction—your deep reaction to this "glorification" of the hybrids—a sign they cannot quite convince you—because you have seen . . . been used . . . your conscious memory "erased." But you *know* at a cellular level—they *cannot* erase that—so this is your salvation, why they cannot completely take you over.

"Your minds are a playground for *anything* . . . your thoughts you cannot always distinguish . . . you must be very careful. Question all.

Be wary, alert . . . to intrusion.

"Why do you think we are constantly telling you to go deep within? Because here is the ark of the covenant—the bull detector—where they cannot intrude."

A few days later, I "just happened" to pick up a very biased anti-Mormon book penned by a couple of Christian fundamentalists out to show the world that Mormons are a dangerous cult. One of the writers' alarm signals was that Joseph Smith, founder of the Mormon church, took instruction from Elohim! This name was as alarming to the writers as it was vague to me.

I stared at this sentence for a good five minutes. Then slammed the book shut. Never mind that the authors seemed unaware that some scholars consider Elohim and Jehovah to be interchangeable names for the *Old Testament* god—the thought that Joseph Smith and I were both addressed by the same controversial source gave me the creeps. A *god* source? That tough-talking, no-nonsense "voice" heralding dark deeds done in the night of our souls?

It was not a matter of sitting down and working this out on paper, or in my head. What difference did it make who or what they said they were? Who could confirm? But it wasn't that simple. As an experiencer, these questions were not philosophical abstractions.

One of my bedrock principles was: you get through something by going through it, not around it, not leaping over it, not running away from it. If you run, if you suppress, it comes back a dragon snorting down your neck, the Shadow tracking you relentlessly, or Coyote tripping you up on the path.

This was all terribly confusing. Were the researchers and investigators and abductees who insisted this business was all-dark correct? Were the feelings of love that sometimes rose up in me—for the "children in the wings of tomorrow"—programmed to cover a horrible truth I could not, or would not face? Were various dark conspiracy theories surrounding a nefarious alien-human cloning project true?

The "coincidence" of picking up this anti-Mormon book and reading that Joseph Smith had been instructed by Elohim was not to be ignored. Was I psychically entangled in deep unresolved religious issues that were bleeding through as disinformation?

Spiritual warfare is the name some give to conflicts between good and evil, here and abroad. Life as we know it is dual in nature—dark, light, shadowy and bright. Absent duality, the Tree of the Knowledge of Good and Evil would not have existed even in mythology; Adam and Eve would not have sacrificed their innocence to the bearing of children; and you and I would not be walking around on these "clay feet" we like to use as excuse for our behavior.

> *"There is a cosmic law of confusion that regulates the dissemination of information to human beings. This law may help explain why UFO communications seem to contain a bewildering mixture of nonsense and possibly valid information.*
> *"The basic idea is that in order to preserve the free will of human beings, it is necessary to withhold information from them and even bewilder them with false information."*

Richard L. Thompson,
Alien Identities: Ancient Insights into Modern UFO Phenomena,
(Govardhan Hill, Inc., San Diego, 1993
from the chapter titled: "UFOs and Religion," pages 411 and 412)

(For more on the Law of Confusion, read *The Ra Material* and the *Books of One* [source material for Thompson's reference] by Don Elkins, Carla L. Rueckert and James A. McCarty, West Chester, PA, Whitford Press)

Guidance suggested I might want to go talk all this over with a Catholic priest. *Oh, sure! Go tell a priest that I'm having trouble discerning good ETs from bad ones! He'll just say I'm possessed or crazy. What else could he say? "Thanks for sharing with me, Dana. That's really special. I've been thinking of late . . . maybe Jehovah is actually an alien. Nothing I need mention to the Monsignor, you understand . . . ha ha . . ."*

Over my abducted body, he would.

Consulting a priest seemed the looniest counsel I'd ever heard. But how was I doing on my own? This latest was not something my ufology friends could help me with. This was clearly my own stuff. They knew no better than I did what was coming down.

The guidance was bogus, I decided; couldn't be right. But then a synchronicity placed me smack in front of the local Catholic priest, whom I had not met before. No way to pass it off as a coincidental meeting, so I swallowed my pride and asked for a few words in private with him, whereupon I felt him out on his attitude about UFOs, etc. He seemed reasonably open, so I made an appointment with him to "spill the beans."

Father Ken was in his mid-thirties, soft spoken, nice looking, and easy going. Self-conscious in the presence of a man dressed in the official black garb—collar and all—when I went to see him, I "buttoned up to my chin," so as not to distract him with any careless reminders that I was a woman. Silly, I suppose, but I had no understanding of the practice of celibacy, having been raised in a church that glorifies the opposite.

On my first visit with Father Ken, I assured him I had no intention of trying to persuade him to believe in the reality of UFOs, or abductions. I wanted him to help me, if he could, identify religious issues that might be stumbling blocks on my path to getting free of this business and resuming a normal life. (A white lie, that. I had no hope of ever resuming a normal life. But there was a dim hope that I could somehow recapture the old sense of belonging that is reward for submitting to authorities who claim to be spokespersons for God. This was the swaddled secret I nursed at the back of my mind, that somehow I could find my way back into the warm nursery that religious membership had been for me in childhood and adolescence. I had always been attracted to the Catholic church, its mystical concept of God, and its various rituals and ceremonies had always struck in me a deep chord of familiarity.)

Memory of our first interview is vague, but I recall I chose my words more carefully than I would explaining my plight to a peer. Scoff as I might at organized religions, I didn't forget for a minute that I was in the presence of a man who had chosen to devote his life as intermediary between humans and God.

Regardless of my belief that anyone can seek God directly, the fact was, my choice to solicit Father Ken's help was acknowledgment that I also believed that sometimes intercession is called for. It's great to feel you are being looked after by Guides or Angels, but in times of high stress, I want to talk to a *human being*!—one I feel I can trust. Could I trust this man? I trusted God, and I trusted that Father Ken had honestly dedicated his life to helping people like me.

I decided to treat this business like any other difficulty in my life. I would write out specifically every fear and resentment I had concerning it, and then consider it all from the perspective of "what was my part?" What choices had I made to create or perpetuate these difficulties? Where might I be wrong? deluded? mistaken? The purpose of this sort of inquiry is to identify false beliefs, misplaced blame, self-delusion, or just plain wrong-headedness, so one can get free of whatever is causing the problem, and reconnect, in a conscious way, with Spirit or God. Once the sources of the fears, frustrations, or resentments are identified, I set the list aside and focus on myself. Not easy work. And not work I was looking forward to. The idea of facing, on paper, fears and resentments associated with abduction experiences was daunting enough, but then to admit it to another human being—in this case, a Catholic priest—that was maybe going too far. Maybe I was crazy. Of if not quite yet, by the time I got done revealing the colors of my conflicts to a man of the cloth, that would be the final push over the edge.

I was as thorough as I could be with this work . . . this was my life on the line . . . a life now reduced to waking up every morning and recording information that was often heavily laced with religious rhetoric, communicated by the same sources responsible for the nocturnal high-jinx that continued to magnetize my attention to the point that I had no other life. (I assume that the sources who create the nocturnal events are the same who communicate, but since I have not encountered any of them in this reality, I can't be sure. Sometimes I felt myself in the throes of spiritual warfare—that one type of being was harassing me with phenomena to thwart the effort of the El communicators.)

I listed everything I could think of . . . from my fear there was no God, fear that maybe I *was* possessed by demons, fear that Father Ken would think so, fear that I was part-alien, and the resentments associated with the trouble this business had caused in my personal relationships and career.

When I was done, I took it all to Father Ken and read it to him. He was as helpful as he could be, I'm sure. I was not Catholic . . . and maybe not even fully human (he heard me worry). But I'm afraid my confessions may have been too much for the man.

All I can recall of his reaction was . . . silence. I'm sure he said *something*, but I remember only the gulf, the void, the awful feeling that I had just made a terrible mistake. In prior experience, when confessing to peers, they had always shared something of *their* failings and fears. Maybe I had no concept of the role of a priest as *responder* to confession. What could he do? Tell me to recite fifty Hail Mary's?

Leaving Father Ken, feeling lost and disoriented, I drove to a spot in the rocks above the golf course that gives view of the valley from the Colorado River north, to as far as the eyes can see south. There I sat, gazing at the sky, the valley, feeling more alone than I ever had, with no answers . . . and now fresh out of priests, too.

The hope I had secretly nursed that I could find sanctuary in the Mother Church was now a corpse. The work I had just done, of bringing up out of my soul into the light every twisted tendril rooted in religion, had left a void in me, and a feeling of desolation. So much for my hope of finding a hand-hold in some earthly institution, to find some earthly authority I could turn to. . . .

For about an hour, I was godless; I was alone on this planet, an alien trapped in a human body, unable even to summon the old yearning for a lost home, somewhere in the starry vault above. This is precisely the "sacred emptiness" a seeker on the path hopes for, but the desolation I felt at the moment was too believable to recognize that I had just successfully reached a new level of freedom.

The drama I felt in the emptiness soon faded, and I was just a woman sitting in her car above a golf course. I did the next thing. Never mind that I was no longer sure God existed, I asked God—any god, Great Spirit, the Sun, the Moon, the Stars—to remove from me what I had identified as my flaws, the same old boring defects of character that had always been my undoing, all of the ego stuff that were cause for my fears and resentments—the self-pity and false pride, the self-centeredness, the judgments against others—all the stuff that shuts one off from the sunlight of the Spirit.

Then I drove down the hill to the rest of my life.

From February to August 1996, I kept working on letters and numbers, kept in contact with friends and researchers, kept applying for jobs . . . and the business continued. One noticeable gift, as a result of my visits with Father Ken: I was no longer afraid I was prey for demons. This old exotic fear just slipped . . . away.

I kept on recording messages. Whether I liked it or not, whether I understood it or not, this was the course my life had taken, and the fact that I did not remember when, or under what circumstances I had agreed to do this—if I did choose it—seemed a pointless worry. Reality has a way of speaking louder than our opinions or desires as to what we think should be happening.

Now most of the material coming through ended with this signature: "Adonai, Adonai, We are El." It was my own damn fault for biting the bait in asking for their name.

"Are you embarrassed to use our name?"

Yes, I was.

Earlier, I mentioned the book *Taken: Inside the Alien Abduction Agenda* by Karla Turner, Ph.D. In *Taken*, Turner describes a "virtual reality scenario," during which messengers inform her that the story of Jacob and Esau was about the genetic alteration of humankind, which keyed to my dream about a man with a furry face. Karla's messengers warned that the aliens *are doing it again* (currently producing a new variant . . . meant to supplant us).

"We must not surrender our sovereignty to them, as that would mean we were truly lost forever," Turner wrote on page 222 of *Taken*.

But how can we defend a state of sovereignty that was already compromised at the creation of the "Jacob variant?"

The transmitters of the *History* (chapter eleven) were silent about this most talked-about aspect of current contact and encounters—the hybrid breeding project. Why?

Problems, problems.

Spring of 1998 (excerpt):

"You will not know this secret you probe, for it constitutes a counterplan to that which is being conducted in the dark by those who aspire to become human gods. Many who are so engaged are acting themselves as dupes, unaware of the roles they play in their deafness to the consultations of Spirit. These live by hive mind commands only, uninformed of the heart. So have compassion for them, for they know not what they do."

The hybrid project is a *counterplan*?

This keys to a communication recorded three and a half years earlier (before I knew myself to be an abductee).

August 1993 (excerpt):

"The light centers identified are among you now, established and in the process of being established, some with those who have been planted and cultivated, some with volunteer Earthlings."

[Me]: But doesn't the doctrine of abduction produce fear. . . . Please tell me about abduction again . . .

"We said a mimicking to create fear. If it were possible to defeat us in this way, we would continue helpless, no? So we devised a plan they cannot so easily mimic, though they are doing a good job."

[Me]: They're mimicking light centers?

"Enough of you have come forward with distortions that many have 'written this off,' too. Light centers are different. Each alone, or in small groups, like-spirited, meditate, shielding themselves from interferences; these are dedicated channels of light; these literally become light centers, establishing light amidst the children of Earth, creating an environment into which the *new species can abide.*"

Old species, new species . . . plans and counterplans. Add to all this the controversial claim by certain Pleiadians that we are all human-alien.

11

THE HISTORY OF HUMANKIND IN SUMMARY

"Different species can't interbreed," said Keith Montgomery of Montgomery Archaeological Consultants. This he said when I gave him the *History* to get his educated feedback. (The man's credentials as a reputable scientist of archaeology are pristine. I felt fortunate that I knew him.) He was unhappy with my source's use of the terms "species" and "orders." Scowling, reading further into the text, he said, "I get it. They mean *kinds* . . . "

Two kinds of human beings. First and second orders. Esau and Jacob?

The *History* is the longest message I've ever translated. It took three sessions to complete. It is central to my understanding of the purpose of UFO sightings and abductions, so I beg your patience for the length.

Zecharia Sitchin, Sumerian scholar and author of *The 12th Planet*, plus six other books that comprise *The Earth Chronicles*, and *Divine Encounters*, is my primary source of education about the genetic alteration of humankind. When I read *The 12th Planet* in the late 80s, it felt as if I were *remembering* this fundamental truth about our beginnings. (Perhaps I *was* remembering from cellular-ancestral knowledge in my DNA.) While this feeling grew stronger over the years, I never imagined I would record a "formal" message about it, because Sitchin had done a thorough job of bringing to our attention our hidden history, and many others had written about it as well.

The history here differs from other accounts (so far as I know) in that the focus is on the complications the genetic alteration caused in the *spiritual* evolution of humankind.

In chapter four I shared a dream that was precognitive of something I would read the next morning in Dr. Karla Turner's book, *Taken*. The dream pointed to the Biblical story of Jacob and Esau. Turner's messengers informed her that the story was really about the genetic alteration of humankind. The *History* here strengthens that assertion, and adds more for consideration.

Part I is short; it came in the fall of 1993, three years prior to the rest. I had no idea more was to come; I remember snickering at the high-sounding title for so little information conveyed then. Part I speaks of our beginnings, and an unexplained "severing of communications" between humankind and our "makers."

Part II speaks unequivocally of a breach that occurred in the development of humankind—the creation of a "third species," i.e., the "second order of humankind."

Parts III and IV expand on the complications this "genetic miracle" created for the spiritual evolution of all humankind, first and second orders.

The *History* also contains prophesies.

Not everyone rallies around the idea that something higher than human intelligence exists; but if it does, keep it high in the heavens, away from the game field here. The concept of spiritual evolution suggests that the playing field is more even and open than appears to people who believe that survival is an art of cunning and winner-takes-all. Spiritual evolution suggests accountability for choices and behavior. Perhaps spirituality has little to do with good and evil, and much to do with free will, consciousness, and other unrealized human powers.

Many messengers are informing us that leaps in conscious awareness will soon provide keys that will open doors of understanding about the higher laws that govern the principles of creation and evolution. The *History* is one small preparation. But "head knowledge" is like an airborne arrow. The archer may have shot the arrow true, but until it hits home, the destination is still a theory.

The *History* is not a statement of biological or historical fact. I feel it's best to read it from the heart. Like everything else in this book, it is offered as food for thought. Maybe it's only a parable to warn about dangerous misuse of knowledge coming out of the human genome project.

Or maybe it's just another Big Fish story.

You will decide.

All words in parenthesis are mine, added for clarification. Scriptures are from the Holy Bible, New International Version, except when noted otherwise.

PART I

September ? 1993

In accordance with the laws of divine love/wisdom, you were each created individually and uniquely, and endowed with personal will. In this way, you were encouraged to explore all aspects of existence, dark and light, that you might develop a wisdom of awareness that can only be obtained through experience in physicality.

Not all who were formed as individualized energies chose to participate in physicality. Choosing thusly, these forfeited the use of personal will, allowing their votes, so to speak, to be absorbed in a collective pool of expression.

You who chose to experience physicality were created in the image of a master race whom you have called collectively by many names, God. In your newly createdness, you were as all children, dependent on your parents for your survival and progress.

In the beginning, your parents walked among you, and taught you the laws of physicality. Once schooled, your parents withdrew that you might mature in your own unique expressiveness, and gain the wisdom and awareness that is your legacy. Your parents withdrew in form only. At the level you understand as mind, channels of communication were dedicated that you might seek and receive from them (your parents), direct guidance. In this way, you were given dominion over the Earth, and encouraged to create in your own unique expressiveness all that you so desired, calling upon your creators for guidance in accordance with your individual and collective wills.

As you are aware, as beings in physicality, you experience dark and light, joy and pain, and all else in accordance with the laws of dualities on this plane of existence. In the beginning, fully cognizant of these laws, you were not afraid to explore your habitat in order to gain the experience that is the prerequisite of mature wisdom.

Though you exist on a plane governed by the laws of duality, your concepts of good and bad are distortions. In the beginning, all was experience having dual aspects: light, dark, joy, pain, and so forth. Dark was not bad, light was not good, joy was no more good than pain. All was known to you to be multifaceted experience.

Understand this of the Biblical story of Eve eating the fruit of the Tree of Knowledge of Good and Evil: Knowledge is wisdom bereft of love. Knowledge bereft of wisdom/love generates fear.

Humankind did not fall from grace. Direct communication between humankind and your creators was severed.[4] From this originated a distortion of reality, and from this distortion originated the Great Lie, that you and all that you know as physical existence is wholly separate, having no connectedness.

Being still children in your experience, the level of your awareness was not fully developed when the channel dedicated to direct communication with your makers was severed. You were not good children who knew no bad until Eve ate of the tree. You were divine children who had no knowledge of this distorted divisiveness taught you by that which caused the severing[4] of direct communication.

Understand this: The teaching that dual aspects of existence are either good or bad has wreaked havoc and confusion among you, depriving you of the full experience you were encouraged to have, in order to become enlightened beings. "Knowing," as it

---

4   *Direct communication between humankind and your creators was severed . . . that which caused the severing.* The transmitters do not explain what this means. From various messages (I cannot include all here), the implications were that ancient tales of spiritual warfare were true—there were, and still might be, conflicts as to the management of human beings. Though I was given little information about these conflicts, it is my understanding that the communicators of the *History* are, or represent, the creators of humankind, who have returned to gather their offspring and end an inferred enslavement by others who came in and established a wrongful control over humankind.

were, good from evil, you judged all aspects of dual reality accordingly, and erected systems of law to forbid that which you deemed to be bad.

In this manner, through no fault of your own making, you became gods unto yourselves before you gained the wisdom that can only be developed through full participation in all aspects of existence, no part of which is good or evil, except by your judgment.

In essence, from this Great Lie you created, in ignorance, a world corrupted by the appearance of a divisiveness that in reality does not exist.

PART II

December 7, 1996

Do you know you have a collective hive mind? Do you not know that you have your high councils and you have your workers who perform the will of these councils?

Do you not realize you are biological entities? And that there are biological laws that govern your behavior?

But there is trouble on your planet because of the breeding that was done in ancient times, when two species joined to create a third. This third species was not meant to be independent, and in fact could not be an independent species, for it did not evolve in a natural way: (changes in?) characteristics occurring in response to changes occurring on the planetary sphere (sic).

The third species, which we will call the SECOND ORDER OF HUMANKIND, was created to serve those who came to earth in rocketships, the Nephilim, as you have named them.

Now, they possessed motive, intention, and purpose . . . will, if you will . . . and they possessed intelligence that made possible the ability to perform what they did. But like all peoples in the universe, for all their enviable traits and remarkable powers, they did not possess such a wide-seeing wisdom that could predict the outcome in its myriad consequences of this awesome act they did perform, in creating a third species.

In fact, they did not then acknowledge it was a third species, so fascinated were they at this successful feat they performed in order to satisfy their desire to create a people for their own delight and purposes. And how many peoples see the far-reaching con-sequences of the acts they perform, small or grand?

Those who performed the miracle were so enamored with their powers to perform such a feat, they were like drunken men staggering around in a museum filled with every manner of precious artifacts, all organized and catalogued and displayed for the enlightenment of the observers. They were like drunken men crashing against the fine displays, knocking them down, shattering one-of-a-kind artifacts wherein lay the only record of the nature and history of such unique objects.

For all their intelligence, for all their advanced knowledge, they appreciated not the intricate design of the human being, nor did they respect the reason and purpose for that design. For all their wisdom, it did not occur to them that the human being was designed precisely to evolve on this planetary sphere, down to every hair and every follicle.

This fact was your proverbial elephant looming in the center of their planning council rooms, and yet they did not see it. For they were like drunken men who do not smell the gas fumes, and so light a match to their own destruction. So drunk were they, so proud of their capacity to enhance the human being to serve them, the consequences of their bold act did not show for many years to come, and then it was too late to correct the mistakes that were, in effect, written as with indelible ink upon the genetic scroll.

Remnants of the records retained mention of the realization that a mistake had been made, long after the act was performed. The God of your Bible spoke for the Nephilim in declaring his sorrow that he had ever made this third species (*Genesis 6:6*). But as was said, they did not see it as a third species, but as a people created to serve them, as you create dolls that walk and talk, to the delight of your children.

For all their genius, they did not factor in an element of human nature that was, and is in fact, an element of supreme significance. Now, understand that the Nephilim possessed this element them-selves, but so drunk were they with pride, and so focused were they on their ability to create, they had long forgotten the essence of the element that made it possible for them to perform such miracles. Like the human being, the Nephilim possessed the power to decide their own destiny.

Now, as you are aware, this power is one that unfolds slowly, like a shy moss rose embarrassed to reveal its splendor to the courtship of the sun, or like a blushing virgin bride slow to disrobe before her husband.

The power to direct one's own destiny is like nitroglycerin. In the wrong hands, there will be catastrophe.

In the design of the human being is a directive to the slow unfolding awareness of the power to direct both individual and collective will—as did the directive slowly reveal to those (the Nephilim) who acted upon this power in creating a third species. However, as was said, these creators did not acknowledge they had created a new species. Rather, they saw you as "belonging" to them. To them you were doll-like, and they could direct you to perform every task they so desired.

Drunk with this ability and achievement, they remembered not their own long history of unfoldment. They had forgotten the humility they felt when this awesome gift of awareness was discovered. And they forgot that there are laws governing this element, as there are laws underlying every other element, whether it be the manner in which a seed attaches to the wall of a uterus, or the way in which a thought-form acts upon a physical manifestation of energy.

They (the Nephilim) became gods unto themselves. They ceased to consult the One who created all: the Supreme Omniscient Intelligence, the Alpha-and-Omega, the Great Spirit who in love created children in its image, children designed to develop in trait and wisdom, in accordance with the Law of Love that governs all, the Prime Principle that governs all that exists.

And so when it came to pass on Earth that conditions of flood arose, in a natural response to the aberration created, the (resident) gods did declare that it was good that the waters would flood the whole Earth. For it was evident by then the nature of the mistake made. It was evident that a desecration had occurred. It was evident that the awesome creation was not so easily governed by those who had forgotten the laws of their own governance. So drunk were they on their own powers, they forgot the source of that power, taking it upon themselves to act as if together they were greater than the One who made all.

And so it came to pass that the waters of the Earth conspired to set right the mistake, to destroy the aberration—this third species, flawed in design, as it was.

And yet every being was, and is, a child of the Supreme Maker, regardless the exercising of power to alter that being. For at the center of every living thing is the element of the One who made all, the *quinta essentia*. Everything that God made (physical) is of air, water, mineral and fire, and a fifth element, the essence you call spirit. That is, the Divine Element, the Energetic Intelligence manifest in all, the Light, the Spark that enlivens all manner of all matter and all else—the element that only the Supreme Maker governs; the Creator of the Light that underlies all.

And so it came to pass that Nature responded to the mistake so made. The waters of Earth conspired to set right the mistake, that the children of God would be spared the ultimate consequence of the desecration performed on them in the creation of a third species.

Now on the Earth were also at that time many human beings who were the original children, THE FIRST ORDER OF HUMAN-KIND. Many of these the waters spared, for they were still governed by the Great Spirit, Supreme Maker. They were children as those described in the Garden of Eden. They were children who had not eaten of the tree of knowledge, before their time. They were children spared of the alteration, children still innocent.

Now, the Supreme Maker was not angry at the third species, those comprising the second order of humankind, created by the hands of the proud Nephilim, they who came to Earth in rocketships, they who conspired to refashion the human being after their own design. Nor was the Supreme Maker angry at those who performed this desecration, for God had given all powers to such creation, and God is given neither to anger, nor to the taking back of gifts. The Waters (sic) came not of God's anger, nor of God's Will to withdraw the gift. The Waters also possessed the element that determines destiny and the Waters conspired to set right this flaw, in accordance with the wisdom of Waters, that was wiser than that of the ones who created the flaw in the redesigning of the human being.

And though it seemed an act of anger and punishment to allow the Waters to destroy that which had been created, it was not; for the Divine Essence of every child would return to its Maker, and would express again in conditions right for the unfolding of the excellence created by the Prime Principle. So it was not with mourning that the living things of Earth prepared for destruction, but it was with rejoicing that the Supreme Maker had provided a way for mistakes of great consequence to be corrected.

Now, it came to pass, as twists of fates occur in the dramas of all intelligent life, that one[5] who saw what was to come to pass exercised his divine right to rebel against the decision of the Waters to destroy the aberration. So did this man instruct a small select number of the third species to survive the flood, as he did know the way it could be done, for he was a master designer and a master builder, possessing intelligence beyond any of the third species. So did he instruct the fabled Noah to build a vehicle as a transport to land when the Waters receded, and so was it done, as the Supreme Maker did not interfere but looked on to see what would become of the ones the man directed to survive the cleansing the Waters conspired to bring about.

Now, in your records, not all comes down to you in the sequence it occurred. Some would have you believe the creators of the third species acted in respect of the Divine Element, instructing the new children as loving parents (would do), carefully guiding their development. It was not so. Those of the third species were created with great attention to physical design but with no heed paid to the Divine Element. The third species was enhanced physically beyond the elemental design, therefore it was like placing a chimpanzee at the controls of a rocketship. No amount of training could allow for the command of such a vehicle, for even if the animal followed every instruction to a "T," there would be unexpected events the chimp would be unprepared for; and

---

5   The "one" who instructed the select number of genetically altered humans to survive the flood is not named. From my readings of Zecharia Sitchin's books, I would assume they mean Enki, but the communicators seem more intent on conveying a big picture than on the sort of details we want, to fill in the blanks for our investigative pursuits. Much is left for us to puzzle out together—which may be part of the purpose—to motivate us to share our information with one another, and use our brains and spiritual proclivities—such as intuition—to solve the greater mystery of why these beings are overwhelming us with so much information that fails to address some of our most passionate questions.

therefore, to put such a creature at the controls of such a powerful vehicle would be to launch her on a sure course of destruction. Such was the mistake made in the creation of the third species. But alas, an off-stage director's assistant did take it upon himself to add a scene to the drama unfolding.

For it came to pass that some of the second order of humankind survived the flood, as well as the many human beings who were not so altered.

And so comes record of a god who informs the fabled Adam and Eve they must not eat of the Tree of Knowledge of Good and Evil, but instead must follow every instruction of the god, precisely. In this way, the flawed beings would be allowed to live and develop, as if the flaw could be corrected through obedience. This was the plan of redemption for those who survived, these of the second order of humankind.

But they could only survive over the long course if they heeded the instructions of the (local) gods, who then conspired to be their guardians and shepherds. And so it was they decided in councils to direct the affairs of humankind.

PART III

December 7, 1996

There are few cases in the histories of third and fourth density development[6] where/when the decisions of individuals prove to be wiser than the forces of nature. Waters, winds, fires and minerals are considered to be wiser than even collectives of intelligent beings; indeed, the forces of nature are like teachers for those who are willing to become disciples.

Rarely in the histories of third and fourth density creations have individuals challenged the wisdom of the winds, waters, fires and minerals, and when the one did set apart those of the third human species to survive the cleansing floods, many advanced beings did watch, and wonder, along with the Supreme Maker, to see what would become of this decision and its consequent act.

---

6   *Third and fourth densities*: They do not explain what is meant.

Now in your time frame, ten thousand years is a ticking of a clock wound down to a speed so slow as to challenge the meaning of the word speed. But for the watchers, observations of the events following the great flood occurred as if on a Sunday afternoon, for they stood outside time as you know time. It was as the watching of a football game, with many time-outs called, for in reality this was no game, but a drama with a cast of trillions, and many time-outs were necessary, in order to reassess strategies for a successful outcome for all of the players.

Now, unlike your games of competition, this was a game where if one team lost, so did the other. So a game plan was devised wherein the goal was for both teams to win, that is, both the first and second orders of humankind, those being the original children of Earth and those genetically altered by the Nephilim.

Now, in devising the game plan, and preparing the participants, the fact of the genetic alterations had to be reckoned with, and was in fact the cause for the revision of the original plan for the children of Earth. There was now on Earth two orders of human beings, one with intelligence and aptitudes superior to the other, yet these "enhanced" beings lacked requisite experience. In essence, this meant there was on the face of the Earth a people who were superior in knowledge, yet inferior in wisdom, as compared to those whose physical and mental attributes did not exceed their spiritual capacities.

And so there was imbalance the forces of nature moved to correct, but the will of even one individual can foil nature's plans, as was demonstrated. Yes, one being exercising will can change the course of history, a principle too powerful to introduce into consciousness before requisite spiritual maturity has been developed; which maturity develops out of direct experiences, a law the Nephilim ignored when they created the beings to serve them.

And so was born the myth that the first parents sinned by eating of the forbidden fruit, thus all children born of them would likewise be sinners, for the sins of the parents are passed down to the children. Let us substitute, for the word sin, genetic alteration and a light comes on, as if someone pulled a long golden chain.

All children descended from the First Parents indeed carry in their bloodlines the altered genome. And because these were of a different order, there was call for special decrees and rules, that all might develop along with those who were not so altered. But it was clear that over time a great gap would develop between these two orders, for those granted capabilities for knowledge and aptitudes beyond their spiritual capacities would seem to be superior in all ways, and could become bullies, and hence compound the great imbalance.

And so it was that restrictions were placed upon those of the second order. And so it was that religion was born to fill this need to restrict. Religion was introduced as a kind of remedial schooling, allowing those of the first order to "catch up," as it were, in the natural development of intelligence, and the powerful attributes.

Now, as it was said, it was seen that despite the introduction of religion to help balance the equation, a gap was sure to develop between the two orders, in any case. For no game plan can plan for the variable of individual will, that divine inviolate gift that underlies all living intelligent manifestation or expression of Divine Will. And so to offset this inevitable gap, a subplan was created, an instruction for the interbreeding (assimilation) of first and second orders, which plan is too complex but to mention here. Again we ask you to consider your myths, first of the "scattering" of the peoples, when the Tower of Babel was struck down, secondly, the story of the fabled tribes of Israel, specifically paying heed to the "blessing" given to the second-born, Jacob (later renamed Israel).

(The Bible says that) Esau would live by the sword and serve his younger brother. Indeed as events would unfold, the offspring of the first order would be forced to defend by sword the encroachment of the second order, whose members often came as conquerors, insensitive to the ways of the people challenged, as is characteristic of beings who are powerful yet lack spiritual wisdom.

And would come a day when the plan would run its course, as is hinted in the prophesy for Esau's offspring, that when he grew restless, he would throw off the yoke of servitude. And indeed it is come the time when the "reseeding" has been completed, and those predominately of the first order shall no longer serve those predominately of the second order. For now the seed has intermingled, and there are few of "pure lineage"; and these are fast being found and assimilated, much to the dismay of those who did heed the plan of redemption and who did develop the exquisite spiritual gifts that are activated through experience and the exercising of will.

And so now, at the fulfillment of this imperfect plan, for no plan can be perfect, in consideration of the variable of individual will, humankind stands at a new crossroads, and many have gathered to watch or to guide, as collectively you will decide your own destiny.

Many are the watchers and many are the guides, and some are among you, and some watching from the sidelines, all in wonder at the progress made, many ready to assist you, as the will calls; and many are here to exploit, as well, as is true in any environment where free will reigns.

Now because no human being has ever crossed this threshold before you, there has been call for elaborate and extended preparations. Many, many are here in form to help you, and many more have been recruited from among you to help, and many have volunteered. Each plays a role, each has a task, and many groups have formed to fulfill special tasks in the readying of humankind to cross the threshold so mentioned above.

There is much confusion, much disorientation, like as happens at the beginning of any major production, but more is the confusion and more is the disorientation and fear now, for not even those designated as leaders and directors know the script or the setting, but barely do they grasp the nature of the scenes soon to play on the human stage. But they are ready to lead and direct, as the other workers are being readied to fulfill their roles, and all together all members of the crew are working to prepare the population for the crossroads ahead.

And as is always the case in an environment of duality, there are extremes at either pole of perception, at which poles the confusion and disorientation is greater in intensity, and a cause for the feeling of a great pressure bearing down, as if soon a huge rubber band would snap and catapult the Earth herself into the starry regions, to shatter like a popcorn ball, her many pieces flung into wild orbits, where even dark holes fear to go.

Such is the fear and panic of some, while many in the center seem lulled, as if asleep, much to the dismay of those who walk the lines to and fro, observing, in preparation of this unprecedented moment in the history of humankind.

And what can we say to aid in this preparation? Attend to your tasks, and watch, be alert. Listen to those who seem to know something of what is to come, while exercising discernment, for there are as many who do not know but would have you believe they do, that they may exploit you while there is still time. Such is the foolishness of those who did not heed the plan of redemption, nor those sent to guide, but exercised their wills to go their own ways, unheedful of the faithful community.

Try to stay as close to the center as possible, while avoiding the eye, where so many slumber, but walk to the right or the left, crossing back and forth often, but not too far toward the poles, where perceptions run to extremes, where good is the enemy of evil, where evil usurps good, where intelligence believes itself to be wise on one side, while on the other side ignorance declares itself master, and where love and hate collide, where good intentions violate will, and concern conspires to rule.

As the one sent to you whom you know as Jesus Christ said: "Be gentle as doves and as wise as serpents" (*Matt.10:16 paraphrase*).

Keep praying, keep seeking guidance within, test all things, consider all things, and be true to what moves you in the deepest waters of your hearts.

We are those of the fifth order of the star you know as Alcyone in the constellation you know as the Pleiades.[7] Adonai, Adonai, we are the children of El, servants of Love/Light, and the Creator of All.

PART IV

December 8, 1996

Consider the prophesies in regards to each of the twelve tribes, and the meanings of their names. You ask is Destiny so fixed you can predict events thousands of years in advance?

Human behavior is predictable within a range. Anyone with a long view can predict major outcomes.

---

7   *Alcyone/Pleiades:* Many messages came from "We are El," but this is the only time transmitters have mentioned a location.

Over the course of this phase of development, in relation to the large numbers of new incarnations, few humans have surprised us, few have broken from the pack, so to speak. To a large extent, most humans have preferred to stay within the bounds of "mass mind," as you call it, few venturing far as explorers or renegades.

Therefore, yes, predictions often prove out. Consider also the scripture, "Train up a child in the way he should go, and when he is old, he will not depart from it" (*Proverbs 22:6; King James*). To a large degree, this is true. Now consider the word "train" in the context of nature, as in the "software" genetics that serve as guides in the lives unfolding for individuals. You do not need stern trainers in the flesh, for the instructions written upon the genetic tabloid are quite enough. But even this determination the human being can overrule, to go his own way; especially this is true, once the human being discovers this heretofore hidden influence, once he awakens to the nature of his own will. The truth shall set you free, so be seekers of truth. If you desire freedom, insist upon truth. Track it down like a ruthless child molester, and expose it for what it is. An apt metaphor, considering the effect of (some) instructions written upon the genetic scroll. And yet we do not judge these restrictions as evil, for they were instituted to offset the imbalances set into motion when the third species came into existence, when the Nephilim tampered with nature, upsetting her orderly pattern.

Study of the predictability of human behavior will serve as a teacher as you learn to exercise your will collectively as individuals, with conscious awareness. You will see the reason the restrictions worked so well. You will see that human beings preferred enslavement over freedom, for few were they who had the courage to break from the ranks. For, in addition to unknown consequences, there was the matter of punishment and ostracism, both predictable responses in a system devised to discourage, if not prevent, such "rebellions." While the punishments seem severe to the soul, remember the long view, remember why this system was instituted. It was deemed necessary in order to achieve the intermixing of the first and second orders of humankind, that *Homo sapiens* would be as one family, with many diverse and interesting members.

Nature glorifies diversity and abhors uniformity, and yet for the sake of ultimate order and balance, she will forestall corrections of the imbalances in deference to the powerful assertion of human will. Yes, the will of even one human has the power to override nature, knowledge as dangerous as a nuclear bomb in the hands of one or many who have yet to master the ethics of love, or those who seek the intoxicating effects of self-adulation and pseudo-power, which are the temporary rewards of domination and dictatorship.

So why does it seem that only people given to such selfishness possess the awareness of these powers of will? The instructions written on the hearts of human beings ask of them suppression of individual desires over the well-being of the community. The nature of this instruction is the essence of faith. Human beings are asked to walk in faith, to believe in an ultimate outcome considered to be beneficial to all participants. But does not this seem a contradiction to the encouragement to break from the pack, to exercise the wings of the will?

If it were not for those who braved the consequences of such rebellions and revolutions, the plan would have derailed, resulting in destruction, for the numbers of human beings who willfully exalt themselves over others would have created counter imbalances. If not for the rebels and revolutionaries, tyranny would have prevailed, and yet if the numbers of rebels and revolutionaries (had) outnumbered those willing to walk in faith, if to experience a kind of enslavement to the "system," then "all hell would have broken loose."

And so, though you were yet to experience conscious awareness of the roles you have played upon this great stage of development, all so choose to participate accordingly.

In closing, we urge you to continue to walk in faith even as the light of awareness grows stronger, even as you begin to see through the dark glass, even as you begin to discern the activities of those you judge to be the enemies of love and order in diversity, for you are yet to learn the conscious use of collective will to positive outcome, so long have you deferred to faith, that you would arrive here on the shores of Great Change.

You are beginning to see the doors, and you sense they are opening, and you see light streaming forth, and your inclination is to move toward the light, and let it embrace you, and indeed you shall be so embraced; but for the sake of those yet to awaken, we urge you to be patient and to continue to work as ushers and pointers of the way.

Many signs and wonders are manifesting, that you might awaken in full measure, and yet we caution you; for not all signs and wonders point the way you desire to go, for there are those intent on misleading you, that they might retain positions of willful domination, if it were possible. The call is for discernment and patience, for soon the light will shine brightly enough for all to see, and then together you will decide in conscious awareness to "clean house," to restore order where chaos has long held the reins, and oust those who have usurped the rule of free will in exploitation of the plan you have abided in faith.

Soon the words of your faithful scribe Matthew will be illuminated: "So do not be afraid of them. There is nothing concealed that will not be disclosed, or hidden that will not be made known" (*Matt. 10:26*).

So fear not your enemies but have compassion, for they will be your children. "The last will be first and the first shall be last" (*Matt. 20:16*).

Adonai, Adonai, we are the servants of El, faithful to the Law of ONE.

12

MESSENGERS OF THE RED CHRYSANTHEMUM

Humankind cannot bear very much reality.

Murder in the Cathedral (1935)
Thomas Stearns Eliot (1888-1965)

I admit that the *History* had a profound effect on me. But I can no more accept telepathic communications as gospel than I can anything I am told by earthbound historians, theologians, or scientists. Education about our physical heritage is a personal quest, just like endeavors to understand our spiritual natures. In all cases, our perceptions are as diverse as insects in a rain forest, or as different as stone and lamb's wool.

I doubt the information will impress proponents of the "missing link," that, if found, would prove Darwinian-based theories of evolution. Nor do I imagine that believers in established religions will budge from their positions, even though the Bible contains information that contradicts much of what is posed as official gospel. For instance, if Adam and Eve were really the first human beings, who the heck did their second-born son, Cain, marry in the Land of Nod? (*Genesis 4:16-17*)

Dismissing this clue that human beings existed on Earth before Adam and Eve were "created" in the image of gods (plural according to Scripture), leads me to assume we are offspring of incestuous couplings. I remember when I first read Genesis, wondering why I never heard these things discussed in church. I still wonder.

Mythology adds to the mystery. A comparative to the Bible and other ancient texts is the *Popul Vuh: The Sacred Book of the Ancient Quiche Maya*. Interestingly, the gods of the Maya experimented a lot before succeeding in the creation of a proper human being.

Stories from all directions feature competition among humankind and gods with vested interests in control of the species. In Sumerian literature, the competitors were Enki and Enlil, sons of a high god named Ea. Is there any ancient culture that does not tell a story of two brothers locked in mortal conflict? In the West, it's Jesus and Lucifer, Jacob and Esau, and Ishmael and Isaac (sons of Abraham). The conflict between the offspring of Ishmael and Isaac still rages today between Arab and Jew.

The seer in me is aroused by such obvious patterns that seem to escape the interest of some researchers. Absent consideration of historical records of UFO activities, it would be easy to make of the current UFO enigma a new mythology that isn't new at all, but parrots the same old stories about humankind and gods locked in eternal competition. I can't help but wonder if all of the fanfare is really about the powers of higher consciousness triumphing over our base animal nature.

In 1994 I was told: "We would not need to appear in ships and shine cone lights down if you were familiar with these altered states. But you are children in this respect, so we enact dramas. Do you not create dramas for your children, with bright toys and people in costumes? Your Santa Claus, clowns, puppets, all used to teach your children about this reality. And we do the same."

But your games scare people.

"Yes, because there is need to accelerate. A person is challenged to hurry, catch up, see quickly . . . as you work to 'bring Heaven to Earth,' so to speak. Is not birth traumatic? You are in the throes of labor pains."

In 1996, I was told we were like adolescents who must mature before we can venture further into "outer space." They say the keys we seek are in "inner space," and the only way to obtain them is through a transformation in mind and spirit, not unlike what we experience physically in the transition from childhood and adolescence to adulthood.

The bottom line is, we who are experiencing abductions cannot wait for scientists, theologians, or mythologists to settle their disputes. For the experiencer, this phenomenon is an every-day, "in-your-face" reality.

In the first draft of *Summoned*, I was reluctant to share much about my sense of the meaning behind the UFO phenomenon. I didn't want to push any one theory, even if my guts told me I was right. I had been schooled so thoroughly to respect others' beliefs and choices, I was nervous about revealing something as innocuous as my feeling that I was in contact with Siriuns. It wasn't that I was embarrassed to admit I had such feelings; I just didn't want to strengthen such notions, having no proof.

From the start, the messages I received were mixed. Most of the material seemed to be schooling in regards to a dramatic shift in consciousness in progress; but also, there were the frequent references to a new species of humankind in the making. The tone of such communications tends to be vague and secretive.

Not so on December 9, 1995, a year before I received the *History*. The transmitters of the message below sound . . . sensible. The "light" I can doubt as fanciful, the "dark," as trickery, but when the aliens sound sensible, that can be a worry, especially when it strikes a deep chord in me.

Karla Turner used to warn me that we can't trust the aliens because we've all been programmed. But before the term "hive mind" was voiced in the *History*, I knew that something like a hive mind existed. We're *all* programmed, whether by aliens or humans. There just seems no escape from the difficult business of each person deciding individually what is true, whether we accept what we are told without question, or we draw our own conclusions from study and thought.

Many abductees are as concerned about the future as we are the past. Who are the historians of our future? Perhaps those who exist outside the boundaries of time-space. The UFO brigade we call Grays, and/or EBEs (extraterrestrial biological entities) may be guardians, species designed as fail-safe teams who enact higher laws that must be upheld for Earth to sustain as a viable environment for life. If true, maybe the message below came from a source whose job it is to safeguard the human genome, in case of an impending disaster that can be seen from higher perspectives.

The information may seem bleak at first pass, but as always, there is more to the story. If it's too late to reverse the tides of destruction, then why this global effort to raise consciousness? Perhaps the collecting of DNA to salvage the best of us is merely a precaution against a worst-case scenario. That sounds sensible to me. But I must believe that as long as I and countless others are writing and speaking about these things, there is still time to make choices that will render this message non-essential.

December 9, 1995:

The people of your planet are asleep and you cannot awaken them. While they are aware there is trouble, as long as it does not touch them, they feel concern and that is the end of it. They discuss the trouble and that is the end of it. They will not act until the trouble is on their doorsteps because the illusion of safety is too strong.

See how throughout history there are always signs. Then people are shocked when the trouble explodes on their doorsteps. This is human nature. And this is why you must change your nature, if you are to survive. For the trouble in progress today is such that if you do not take action, will result in destruction that will wipe out your species.

It is difficult to stir interest because all know they will die anyway. So what do they care if the human species is wiped out? They are going to die anyway. So make merry while there is time to do so. For tomorrow you will die. And there are masses who say, well, if it happens, it is God's will. I am not responsible. See how mass destructions have occurred throughout history? So this is nothing new. Why worry? Earth is a playground. We can do what we wish, and then we die. No need to worry about the next life if we are reasonably good people. For God is merciful and will not punish us for being humans with clay feet. What can we do about the trouble? It is all beyond our capacity to change.

[Me]: So why warn people of what is to come?

Because miraculously there are a few who are awake, and are ready and willing to act on what you tell them. Not action to save the world, but actions to save themselves. For the sake of preserving the species. For these care that the long development of the species not be lost. Look what mankind has gone through to get to this point. Look at all the sacrifice and hardship and effort to improve conditions. Look at the many heroic acts, to help others live and learn and teach.

And most would say let it all die, we don't care. We do not

care if the development recorded in the genetic material is all lost. We all die anyway.

If not for the few who do care, indeed, all that you have experienced would be lost—meaningless.

You know this to be true. Because you have tried to arouse them and they turn away. They do not want to be bothered with such a wild story.

Leave this be, and don't look back. Those who do not respond are allowed to be this way.

What of the few who do care? [Here is an example of them picking up my thoughts, though I did not pose a "formal" question.] What can you tell them? Take heart, be courageous, soon you will find peace. And—you are not alone, though you may have to endure aloneness for a while longer.

[Me]: But what of those who are participating against their wills?

Yes, we do force some to participate. For if we did not, how could we preserve?

[Me]: But many say they would participate, if you gave them a choice. They argue it is the force they hate.

Would they? Or would they balk? It is a matter of becoming aware—and then the choice is made how to respond. You do not choose your circumstances. You can only choose how to respond. Some of you believe you can create circumstances, but close study shows this is limited and temporary. Always life introduces unexpected circumstances. But this torpor is exploded, by death, by catastrophe. And the person is always shocked.

This we hope to change. To create a more aware species. So that you are not so prone to destruction.

Immediately following the communication, I made these notes in my journal:

> *12/9/95: I feel tremendous love for the babies, for they are the hope of our species. They will carry the records of all we have accomplished and go on to create a better world. If it were not for them, all that we are and have been would be lost. For we are destroying the environment . . . changing the environment, so that it will be impossible to go on reproducing. I live with such knowledge. How to live with it, in peace? Few believe. Write for the sake of recording.*

At the time, I genuinely felt what I wrote. But reading it over later, it gave me the willies. It strikes at the heart of the dichotomy so many of us feel. Was I programmed to feel this way? If so, how can I know my own heart?

One night, meditating with my eyes closed, I saw an alien-human hybrid girl. It happened in a flash, and then was gone. Fleeting but extremely vivid, hyper-real, sharper than life. The "flash-vision" left such an impression, I was able to draw a picture of this girl. "Something" told me she was my daughter. Then other drawings came. A son. Grandfather . . .

Memories? There were no strong signs that I had carried a fetus for the aliens, as so many women have reported. And I am not troubled with feelings that I personally gave birth to hybrid children. What predominated were *hundreds* of "dreams" about caring for highly intelligent, odd-looking babies and children, whom I communicated with telepathically.

While experiences such as the "flash-vision" of the hybrid girl can leave me with a profound sense of connection and purpose, just as often I have felt a deep revulsion that sets off fear and trembling like nothing else can produce in me.

On July 30, 1996, (again) I prayed to be shown the meaning of all this business. That night I was awakened by the watery voice of a woman calling my name. I was to record a dream still vivid in my mind.

The setting was "otherworldly," an awful place: *I sense a big wooden, barn-like building, with places where people were hung. Sense restriction, a kind of jail, and seems not here, but in the past, or possibly the future. I see like trap doors, and climbing up to levels, then cramped quarters, but seems like a school house, the attic, the "belfry" . . . so stark in decor, but this is how they live.*

In brief, I was there visiting my son . . . a little red-haired boy, extremely bright, about three years of age. In the dream, he is a captive of beings I call "cluster beings." They look human but are not. (I call them cluster beings because of the peculiar way they move/hover/cluster together. Previously in a vivid "abduction dream," I had seen these kinds of beings sort of stacked together and on top of each other . . . and I will encounter them again in April 1997, a story I will tell later.)

I see myself dressing him (the boy), helping him, and it seems that it is noticed that I am showing too much attention . . . so give him back now. And me making excuses, pretending to be only helpful . . . most of all pretending to want them to take care of him. Making a remark to one of them that I'm just no good with kids as babies . . . I only like the older ones . . . and there seem to be nods of approval. Somehow I persuade them to let me take him for a bit, and I go to another place, but soon they get suspicious, and come to take him away from me again. And again I act as if this is what I want to do, and again they seem to believe me.

Overwhelmed with emotions, after recording the dream, I wrote in my journal:

They are so CONCEITED to believe that we would feel privileged to give our babies to them . . . they being superior but they are not; they are sorely defunct, as for love or empathy or compassion. They seem empty-headed and close-hearted, but still they have this power over us, to bring us here at will . . .

Who are "they?" Consciously I don't know, but in this dream scenario, I sure did, recognizing them as beings who are not working on our behalf. There was a strong sense of enslavement in unnatural conditions.

This haunting dream had a sequel early in 1998. This time the setting was familiar . . . my mother's house (not really). I had the little red-haired boy with me. He was several years older, and now I saw he had "beautiful alien eyes." Eyes slanted like those of a Gray but not as large, and white surrounded irises I remember as blue. I was holding him as if he were as fragile as a newborn angel. Suddenly he was gone. I raced out of the room and asked Mom and (unidentified) others: "Did you see him? He was just here! He disappeared!" Everyone seemed bored, disinterested. I was extremely agitated, not only about losing the boy, but by the apathy of my loved ones.

And that isn't the end of the story. A few months after I had this dream, I received from Film Graphics, Inc. in Sydney, Australia, a draft of a screenplay written by Peter Townsend for my novel, *Ezekiel's Chariot*. Anna Fawcett of Film Graphics asked for my help in smoothing out some of the rough places. I discovered that Townsend had changed the ending of my book.

In Townsend's version, after Jason leaves (I won't spoil it by telling you how he leaves), the next morning, unable to find the boy, Mindy, distraught, rushes through the house searching for Jason, as I did in my dream when the little red-haired boy disappeared. As was true in my dream, in the screenplay, Mindy's loved ones act as if they have no idea what she's upset about.

When I read this scene, chills raced over my body, and I cried.

Ezekiel's Chariot is a story about an extraordinary child . . . one of many extraordinary children being born on Earth today. I wrote it in 1987.

The equalizer between the light and dark of my experiences and the information given me, are in displays of light, some of them, holograms. First appearing in May 1994, the displays began as light patterns that varied night after night—a matrix, a Victorian curtain, a watery design (see appendix). It was the variety that convinced me I had not suddenly developed a tumor in my brain coincidental to the wake-up jolt I'd felt, reading John Mack's book, *Abduction*. Over time, the displays were interspersed with three-dimensional light forms I call holograms. By far, the most prevalent was of a red chrysanthemum (which still appears occasionally). Such displays were equalizers because they symbolize, for me, connection with something safe and familiar. This is at a feeling level—I know neither the origins nor the nature of the light and sound phenomena.

The red chrysanthemum has appeared in various shades, hues, and sizes. This particular hologram was displayed so frequently, I came to call the originators "messengers of the red chrysanthemums."

Not long after I began this book in the fall of 1996, one of my friends suggested that I was somehow producing these holograms myself. "How?" I asked. My friend didn't know how . . . just that it couldn't be generated by ETs . . . that was absurd.

Willing to consider anything, I asked in prayer that night, "Am I somehow making these things happen?" The next morning, waking up, I knew to look up and to my left (I always "just knew" where to look), and there dangling from the ceiling was the most vivid hologram of a red chrysanthemum I'd seen to date. Every petal was distinct. Oddly, this time it had black leaves and a black stem. (Sometimes the flower has a black center with yellow dots across it.) As usual, I stared at the flower with awe and fascination. Slowly it rose toward the ceiling (fading), as if pulled by a puppeteer into the attic.

I laughed out loud.

I don't make these things happen. I realize this answer to prayer is not proof for anyone else. Other prayers about things more disturbing to me went unanswered, so I was grateful for this small reassurance, and a humorous one at that. I'm not accustomed to seeing flowers in the air. I think hummingbirds are awesome; I'm used to seeing them in the air. I don't know how to fly, but I never thought to ask, "God—am I making that hummingbird fly?"

Before I continue with my personal saga, I want to share a brief excerpt from a message I feel sure came from the flower bearers. You'll see why I think so.

February 3, 1997

Excerpt from "Many Stations, Many Broadcasters"

Now, here is a secret to ponder like a strange seed set into the soil to grow into a plant you know not yet. The mental links connecting as a result of human inventions are but a crude mimicking of that which you are meant to create by other means. While the majority succumb to the technological net being spread over the minds of watchers to ensnare like schools of fish, those who resist will be in mental comparison like the gazelles swift and strong.

Even as you sleep in your beds, your minds are "in school," in preparation for the day when you will become aware of your enhanced mental powers. This is a development designed to manifest, as carefully as you plan your gardens, watering them daily, and keeping watch for pests and other conditions that could threaten the good crop you mean to see.

For tender shoots in a garden, it takes more than human attention to see the crop to fulfillment. You depend upon the sun, for one, to do what you cannot, to bring the seeds to fruition. And so, the human being is dependent on sun-like forces to "grow" the mind and spirit to a flowering stage.

To not recognize this, in comparison, would be like seeds of a delicate rose throwing themselves upon a rocky outcrop, insisting they will survive without the nurturing of a knowledgeable gardener.

Yes, you have wild roses, and everything "green" grows, seemingly of its own accord. But what is wild growth compared to a garden filled with prize roses? Human beings once populated the earth like wild flowers, left to develop as the greater forces willed. But now you are at a stage like unto exquisite roses tenderly nurtured from seed to fragrant flowering. Now is a time for utmost care of the seed-souls trying to push through soil cultivated to receive a new garden.

From 1995 to 1997, most of my days began with hours of recording information. My life was completely wrapped around this business like a cocoon encasing a caterpillar.

In the summer of '96, I was still suffering much in trying to convince people that my experiences were real and not imagined. If the physical effects and evidences would not convince, what would? More words? But words are merely symbolic representations of ideas and realities. Differences in perceptions as to the meanings of words are as myriad and complex as life itself.

For example, the word "spiritual" is often used to mean correct moral and ethical behavior. A good person is spiritual, we often say. But behavior is a quantum step from the reality of spirit as a principle of life. "Spirit" can, as well, express in behavior that is judged to be morally or ethically *incorrect*. To wit: many believe that Lucifer is an evil spirit. "Spiritual" then is a neutral word like "water" or "air." Spirit—mind—intelligence—consciousness—are words that refer to *states of being* that differ in characteristics from that which is perceived as tangible, or physical, as was communicated in "Make a Baby Form."

Scientists understand this very well. They just use different words (or numbers) to express their understanding of spiritual realities. For instance, in a very real sense, a "quark" is spiritual in nature. It's nothing we can touch, see, smell, hear or taste. Or at least no scientists have admitted to *encountering* a quark!

Speaking of extraordinary proofs for extraordinary claims . . . so far, all we have gotten from scientists are *stories* about the existence of quarks. . . .

Although I realized to some extent why I was having difficulty communicating the reality of my experiences, I was still suffering the illusion that I could somehow bridge the gap if only I could say it just right. Failure to do so hurt my pride. Peace was impossible until I got over such ego barriers. This wasn't about my success as a writer-communicator. This was my life, and if I didn't "get my shit together," as we used to say, I was going to fail at more than communication; I was going to end up an emotional invalid.

A turning point came in August 1996. Holed up in the duplex for nearly a year, living my personal contact and encounter melodrama, hope of ever functioning in society again as a "normal person" wore exceedingly thin.

Adding to the pressure were frequent reminders from people from all directions that for one to feel she had a "mission" was unattractive, a turn-off. My poor ego. The job of scribe wasn't "cool." But if I were an "emissary for ETs," that would be cool, according to one friend. He couldn't understand my conflict. "But I don't really know who or what they are," I tried to explain. He wondered why they didn't take *him*—he wouldn't waffle!

Charlie (not his real name) was one who wished for a UFO sighting. Here I was up to my earballs in signs and wonders, but I myself had not seen an alien spacecraft . . . until August 5, 1996, in Charlie's company. As irony would have it, I was walking with Charlie and his dog, down a hill on Mill Creek Road, on our way to my duplex from the park. It was about 7:30 in the evening. The sky was mostly blue with a few scattered clouds.

Glancing toward the western red rock rim, I saw in the sky, directly over Moab, a large golden sphere, which appeared to be metallic. I was struck silent by this thought: *In a minute I will see that it's really an airplane. . . .*

POOF!

It disappeared!

"Charley! I just saw—!" He had been talking to his dog, his head down.

The sighting came the same week I heard an audible voice during one of my "energy treatments." The sound was right next to my ear. A musical male voice said distinctly, "SCHENEIDE!" [pronounced Shen-NEED]. A name? I worked with it for days, weeks, every spelling I could think of, applying it to various charts and graphs to see if I could puzzle out the meaning.

This happened the same week I received a copy of a Sunday supplemental feature article Zack Van Eyck had written (July 30, 1996) for the *Deseret News*, about UFO sightings and cattle mutilations near Vernal, Utah (where I had experienced missing time). Van Eyck had interviewed me by telephone, and my name was all over the part about abductions.

This was also the week I was called by Jose Knighton, local book store manager, who informed that a visitor had asked if he knew anyone in the valley who was "into UFOs." Jose then called me to inquire if I wanted to call the man at his motel. I did, and invited him over (with Charlie present).

The visitor was from Alabama. He said that he and his fiancé had seen a UFO in New Mexico last year, and Al (as I will call him) now made it a practice of searching out UFO enthusiasts, wherever he traveled. Naive maybe, I believed him.

Soon into our visit, intuition telegraphed (something I saw in his eyes) that this meeting was more than coincidental to the *Deseret News* article. As result of the article, I had received an unsolicited call from the "Maury Povich Show," checking me out as a possible talk show participant. My story was public information now, including my location in the small town of Moab.

Responding to my intuition, I emphasized the "spiritual aspect" of my experiences . . . nothing that should interest a government agent . . .

Forgive me, Alabama, if I've got this all wrong, but abductees have good reason to feel suspicious.

This was the month I finally got a job—at an RV campground, checking in guests. The disorientation I felt re-entering the work-world after the long siege of strange experiences was horrific, gentled by the fact that most of the campers were European: mostly German, French, Dutch, Austrian, and Swiss. Feeling awkward and alien myself, it was a blessing to help foreigners, many of whom had trouble with the English language.

But it was a seasonal part-time job that ended in October. Soon I was back in the duplex with no prospects for a winter job. It was then that I got down on my knees. *God? Nothing makes sense except that all this stuff should go in a book. I'm a writer, you know. But you didn't help me find a publisher for* Jonah, *or* Lucy Blue, *so I'm broke. And I can't make a living at $5.50 an hour, even working a full season. I'll write the (damn#%@!) book if you'll provide the means.*

The next day a man I barely knew asked me if I would "trailer-sit" for a couple of months, while he left Moab on business. There was the beginning of means. So, there in Nolan's 14 x 70, I wrote the first manuscript . . . cooking meals for the owner the last three months I was there, to pay for my room.

In January 1997, Frank DeMarco called from Charlottesville, Virginia, to see how I was doing. I told him this book was *not* for Hampton Roads. "This is no nice, new age story, Frank."

"Send it," he said.

Five days later, "out of the blue," Hampton Roads was contacted by the Aussies, who were looking for the author of *Ezekiel's Chariot*. Money from the film option paid my way to Virginia where finally I met my publishers. They offered me a contract on *Summoned* . . . and a job as book production manager.

I was threatened by both offers. Still feeling an "innocent victim" caught up in some sort of spiritual warfare, I couldn't imagine that a new age firm would support me in the light and *dark* of my story. My fears were based in a biased perception about "new age." I had a lot to learn.

As for the second offer—a *real* job—in no way did I feel ready to plunge back into the world at *that* depth. But there was a wave action operating in my life that I felt helpless to stop.

13

NOT ESPECIALLY ALIEN . . .

April 1997: I am in a condo on top of Wintergreen Mountain, about thirty miles outside Charlottesville, Virginia. It is rainy, cool, and just the right quiet. I came here to work a month on my book before beginning the job at Hampton Roads.

The decision to move East seemed so sensible, maybe I thought it would be like a magic wand that would sweep "the business" out of my life so I could get on with the business of completing this book, and earning a living at the same time. But in matters of the soul, logic and reason are like pliers used to pare an apple or angel hairs for sewing thread. The fruit is crushed, and the weave will not hold.

"Expanded consciousness" is not all its cracked up to be. I have this knack for "holding" in my mind a whole novel I am working on. For instance, if one of my characters reveals or does something in chapter nineteen that contradicts something I wrote in chapter three, I don't have to wait until the rewrite to discover and correct the contradiction. Not so for this book.

Logically you would think that since I am telling my own story, I would know it better than one I invented! That's true for everything that happened before June 1994. It was like, up to that point in my mind, my life was a kind of linear process, events like dots on a map that show a path not much different than everyone else's life map. But beginning in June 1994, it was as if the path-line swirled and began a spiral pattern, and I was now experiencing on several levels, up and down and around the spiral, all at once.

The effect of so much information coming into my consciousness so quickly was like a flood that sweeps in on a town, the waters rising to cover all the buildings, roads, and landmarks. The structure is still there, but residents forced to evacuate are suffering shock, grief, and disorientation. Now imagine that the residents of this imaginary town must somehow learn to live in their homes with the water up over the roofs! In a way, it was like that. Something was added to my life, as challenging as having to learn to live under water.

The information pouring in was not "flowing through" my mind—it was in my mind to begin with, and now being activated (made conscious) in increments (messages). I couldn't hold in my conscious mind, as I had my novels, *all* of my remembered contact and encounter experiences—*and* all of the information and messages. Paradoxically, in my case, expanded consciousness forced me to learn to focus to a narrow beam. Writing was like a floodgate control, to keep from drowning, as I adjusted to this new way of living.

Up on Wintergreen Mountain, I expected a let-up, but that delusion was dissolving. I was nowhere close to finishing this book, and furthermore, I was not in Virginia for the purpose of finishing it (I would later learn)! The business continued, the lights, sounds, physical sensations, the comings and goings. So alone, so far from home, I was feeling especially alien. While on the mountain, I experienced a vivid dream some would call a virtual reality encounter.

It began dream-like enough in mundane (but unfamiliar) circumstances that reflected a certain personal dilemma.

Leaving a basement of a house, I find myself on a kind of boardwalk, surrounded by several female "cluster beings." They viciously accuse me of certain sins. Amazingly I don't let them bully me, telling them I had examined the behavior in question and felt I was not doing wrong.

Somehow I escape the cluster beings, only to feel lost, disoriented and drugged. Now I'm in a desert-like scene in grayish-purplish light, like at dawn or dusk. I lie down, my back against a sort of mound of dirt. Off in the distance is a dark outline of a mountain range that reminds of mountains north of Santa Fe, New Mexico.

I notice two moons in the sky above the mountains. *Two moons?* I am thinking sluggishly. *I don't think that's right.* . . . Suddenly the two moons merge into one ball of light. It streaks toward me . . . transforming into a silver disc spaceship. In the next instant, the ship transforms . . . and I am staring, close range at *two huge alien (gray) eyes.*

My reaction is instant rejection. No! In the next instant, I am wide awake in my bed. I know to look up in the air. There is the familiar red chrysanthemum, very vivid. It transforms into a red rose, then fades.

Four transformations—first, the two moons into one ball of light; second, the ball of light into a spaceship; third, the spaceship into an alien in my face; and fourth, the red chrysanthemum hologram in my primary environment transforms into a rose.

The feeling was, I had accomplished something significant. The transformation of the red chrysanthemum into a rose had the feel of "applause" for something done right: Of my own volition I broke the spell of this encounter.

I haven't had this kind of vivid experience since. But I still see light displays now and then. More often sounds, such as tones, or the old familiar telephone jangle that does not issue from my real phone. I am sometimes hummed to . . . by humming beings?

Moving down the mountain into Charlottesville began an odyssey of horrors. Easterners consider Charlottesville to be a prime location. It's relatively small, lovely, clean, the people are congenial, and if there are problems of crime or unusual poverty, neither is evident. But for me, this quaint, story-book home of Thomas Jefferson was just another city, loud and busy. And the streets all ran in circles.

In the studio apartment I rented, I placed my bed parallel to sliding glass doors that gave view of Carter's Mountain, near Monticello. Perched there, my gaze fixed on the mountain, it was like watching a video of serenity with all the wrong sounds. The apartment building was near I-64, and the constant traffic sounded like buffalo stampeding across a concrete prairie. The sound of four heat pumps near my patio, one or more almost constantly whirring and grating, kept to the forefront of my consciousness that I was far from Moab, where most nights you can see the stars and hear the rustlings of the wind moving through the trees.

The first three weeks were a nightmare I thought I would never awaken from. Recalibrating my sleep patterns to adjust to the 8:30-5:00 routine was strain enough, but hardly a tenth of my troubles. For reasons obscure, the woman vacating the position I was to fill had little time to train me. The whole work scene was, in general, so disorienting, it was a wonder I learned anything that first month. I knew nothing about book production, had worked alone for twelve years, and had not spent eight hours in one place with so many people (nearly 20) in years. There was no way to communicate the shock I was feeling to my fellow employees without sounding like a sob sister.

So far as offices go, it was an upbeat atmosphere, pleasant environment, and as one would expect of a company that publishes literature for the evolving human spirit, all of the employees were unusually bright and good-natured.

At the risk of making too much of my adjustment, for the first few weeks, at home in the studio, I gnashed teeth, yanked at my hair, wrung my hands, and if I had not been in the cloister of apartment living, would have howled at the moon. The wave motion that brought me East was now a hurricane.

But I possess a kind of pride that will not allow for defeat in the face of a challenge that *can* be met.

If Frank DeMarco had been my confidante and protector across the States and into the office, he was now confusing me by behaving like a *boss*. In response to my reports of the afflictions I was experiencing in adjustment to the work scene, he seemed unsympathetic. He is really a very nurturing man, so this added to my disorientation. Later I understood. He was responding, as if to the drowning woman, which I was. I frightened him. "Swim! You can do it!" Survive, my friend. Without his friendship, I might not have.

Publishing is not a science, Bob Friedman, co-owner, would often remind us in management meetings, where the forces of acquisition, production, finance, art, and marketing gathered weekly to butt heads, putting to test the principles we all claimed to represent.

Reports from my department kick-started the head-butting. If I did a poor job of reporting, it was my head first. No sympathy that I was an alien, suffering from people-shock, work-shock, city-shock, or lack of proper training for the job . . . come Wednesday morning, I was expected to show up all new-age grown-up, and report on the status of all books.

I was in a whirlwind, spinning, and beginning to really like these people. So much for my preconceived notions of a new age aloofness that is blind to harsh realities. The old stereotypes of "new age" fit this warm and sophisticated community of individuals like a polka-dot bib on the Queen of England.

No one seemed to notice there was an alien among them. Now and then I would confide to someone something of my special story. The response was always the same. Blink eyes. Shrug. Back to work.

Of all the perpendicular and horizontal purposes I imagined for this trial of fire in the ovens of book producing, I least expected that I had moved to Virginia to get over feeling especially alien.

If you are one who feels especially alien, I recommend a chat with Frank DeMarco. Give him a call. He can help.

"I'm alien, you know."

"Yeah, yeah . . . me too."

"But I'm *more* alien . . . "

"Got that inventory report done yet?"

Get over it.

I jest. Frank was extremely helpful. He gave me a lot of sympathetic ear-time. But he was also concerned that I "come back down to Earth." No doubt he was a godsend to help me through a very difficult passage.

Meanwhile, I was not adjusting so well to Charlottesville. When I ventured away from office or studio, I felt sharp contrasts in energies, some moving very fast, and a counter-force that was appallingly sluggish. I had always been sensitive to the feel of a place—the land itself, towns, cities, houses, office buildings, places inside structures—but never to the keen degree I felt traveling to and from Virginia, and around Charlottesville. It was as if my body had become a kind of tuning fork for energies. I was also disoriented, direction-wise. No matter my efforts to orient to the east-west of this place . . . east was west, and south was north. My apartment and car were cluttered with maps and feeble sketches to retrain my brain out of this reverse mirror image problem with the lay of the land, but nothing worked to right the thing in my mind.

Respite came in visits to Roberts Mountain (near Wintergreen), where I was invited to meet with other seekers (some almost as alien as I). Most were former students of The Monroe Institute, a fabulous place built on top of the mountain by veteran out-of-body traveler Robert Monroe, who brought science to the paranormal with the invention of *Hemi-Sync*.

I can joke about feeling especially alien now, but while in Virginia it really was a stumbling block. I wasn't getting over it . . . I was just mastering the ability to "live split."

Because both Frank and I believed I would complete this book while I was in Virginia (originally it was scheduled for spring 1998 publication), we spent a lot of time talking about it, and I spent a lot of time and energy writing, writing, writing . . . trying to hit the right track. But the more we talked, and the more I wrote, the more complications. At the heart of it was my extreme self-consciousness about feeling alien.

Something was wrong with my book. Frank said something was missing in it, and nothing I gave him in the way of new material or messages "clicked." Editing is not a science, either. By August, pushing against the deadline to deliver a manuscript, I was beginning to panic.

Around September 1, 1997, I woke one morning at 4:30 A.M. with a message pressing upon my consciousness. It was personal; an unequivocal instruction to retrieve the incomplete manuscript and leave Virginia. The question of how I was going to make a living after I did this radical thing was not even a consideration. My guides seem unconcerned about such mundane matters. How you fulfill is your problem, Sister. (They often call me Little Sister.)

When I receive guidance as clear as I did that morning, I don't argue. I act.

There was all around the instruction feelings of high intrigue, as if I were some spy in an espionage novel, in danger of being exposed to the enemy. In fact, the guidance was specific that I act quickly and surreptitiously, to sever the job, rescue my book, and hightail it West. The owners, Bob, Frank, and Ginna were all shocked at my sudden notice of resignation, and I expected to leave with nothing but my mess of a book, and bad feelings. But by the end of the next day I was the recipient of two more book contracts and advances on *Lucy Blue* and *Jonah*.

Summoned was not lost after all, but officially delayed for a year. This was strong affirmation that this book was slated to be done, done right, and everything else would just have to wait or re-arrange.

When Frank and I were trying to make the book happen in Virginia, I made an effort to describe to him my dual identity problem. I began a memo to him, and right away there was telepathic input. I'm including parts of it on the chance it will be helpful to others who are experiencing trouble with feeling alien. Some of the discussion is in context of the *History of Humankind*.

April 13, 1997, Memo/Communication (Excerpts):

[To: Frank] When I began the book, instantly there was this problem—and a constant problem—of the two stories; and as I am reviewing journals, this comes up again and again: the expanded consciousness story, and the breeding program; and always it seems one negates the other, except when I treat the breeding as true—and wrong—then to say that expanding consciousness is *how* we will survive. (We can't defend against enemies we are not even aware exist.)

Guides have told me both are true—that we are being bred and it is good . . . and bad. But don't get hung up on good-evil!

Can I say (in the book) that I believe the breeding is going on (and I've been told that it is), but when I probe in this direction it creates anxiety in me, and I can't get to the information, beyond what I have? There seems to be a block on this info for me; when I try to probe deeper, it causes depression and anxiety. Am I to warn, reveal, or just help prepare?

THEM: Now see here: Do not fall into the trap you fell into so often for so long, of insisting that the answers would come on paper. Now we just pause and allow the truth to rise up . . . allow yourself to reach down and feel it. . . . See that this is key in remembering: When we tell you to remember, we are coaxing you to go deep, learn how to access this information in you—without the hypnotic regression, for they tampered with this route.

(I believe they mean that certain aliens either tampered with the memory faculties in the brains of abductees, or something like scramble codes were used so that in either case, anything "remembered" is highly distorted.)

They continue:

We are speaking of an "infusion" of energy-intelligence into the human being—at the fetal stage. The child is then monitored and schooled in secret, then allowed to go live the life of the prototypical being—with this added dimension—so then serving both purposes. The second is not meant to bypass or thwart the first, but both to co-exist. We mean not to violate or side-rail, but to enhance.

(I don't know what they mean by infusion of energy-intelligence into the human being at the fetal stage. I suspect something is done to activate something like message codes in the DNA. These codes might activate information or commands normally dormant. To speculate further would be like puzzling out the plot in a science fiction story.)

And when the dual/being begins to awaken, there can be great upheaval, for the prototypical aspect feels violated, or possessed, and at some points, very "tricky"—things can go very wrong—the prototypical being is asked to go beyond what should be expected of any being, but no other way to accomplish elsewise.

This is the essence of the enhancement in action—can be described as a quickening process—but quickening is too gentle a word for the chaos/battle/struggle that ensues once the process is begun.

(References to a dual-being and prototypes and prototypical aspects: From other messages I understand that "prototype" refers to all that we consider to be descriptive of human beings at the level of body, mind, and emotion. The reference below to a "prototypical population" suggests that we are controllable at physical, mental, and emotional levels, but by implication, perhaps we cannot be controlled unawares at soul or spiritual levels. The next few paragraphs contain more discussion about dual-beingness, i.e., being part human and part alien.)

Why was it necessary that this aspect come to be a part of conscious awareness?

(They read my mind.)

The plan all along, for all who could survive, for all who could go the distance. And what of the essence of the taboo (on this information)? To reveal these truths is to dispel certain notions in religion, which were erected to keep the prototypical population under control until such time you were mature enough to learn of these other dimensions of existence.

Now, then the history . . . first the overall, broad history of humankind, and now the release of information regarding the individuals who are awakening to their dual roles, as a weaving into the evolutionary process.

The plight of one so awakening . . . to be careful to not frame as special or unique as in (you cannot do/be this), for the potential and call is in everyone, as was stated (in the *History*).

Think of it as a "shot-gun marriage." Once the "Nephilim" breached the DNA of some, it became imperative that they make a provision for all . . . with the order to go and assimilate and proliferate.

And now that this has been accomplished, the second imperative is to enact the awakening process—but as you see/know, a battle is in progress, for many of the controllers would continue to control, having become possessed of such roles—not a battle of violence as you play out with weapons on your plane, but a battle of wills. And this is where we say LOVE WILL PRE-VAIL—speaking of the power of rightness, or righteousness, in relation to the universal law of will, the law of One.

Though this is the law, and it will prevail, still we must assert and persist and insist. And here is where the words "triumph" and "victory" have great meaning, for indeed life does only progress when "won," so to speak, and this speaks to the action of will, beyond the theory or idea of choice.

You have battled with notions such as, how can love be where there are secrets and deception and controls? And we have reminded you to go easy on judgments of good and evil, for the purpose of such (deceptions) may fulfill the call of love.

Now see that readers can accept the lesson as explanation for the ancient history of humankind, but when you "bring it home" to say that you are all "part-alien," then the reactions vary, and some quite stormy.

For clarity, we will address only the aspects of genetic distribution that reference this "dual existence" so mentioned. . . .

Now see here. We will not attempt to but touch on the complexities of such interweavings, except to say that some lines of development were directed to carry more of the "alien attributes," while others less, and across the spectrum there would be degrees of both, and for the most part the process was allowed to develop in random ways, for the intention was not to control the genetic distribution but to direct certain lines to this purpose that is unfolding today, this stage you call expansion of consciousness—which indeed describes what is occurring.

Channels were dedicated in some for the development of certain lines, to keep balance, so that no matter the random nature of reproduction, the "weave" would hold—the fabric would not unravel, as it were—all in keeping with the universal laws in reference to free will, allowing humankind of all origins to develop as they would, crossing breeding lines, as you so desired, or where so directed, all to reach this point in the creative development of a species ready to begin a new stage characterized by expansion of consciousness—now to expand the spectrum of choice/will.

Moving back to Moab at the end of October 1997 was another turning point. Home again in red rock country, now more aware of "resonant vibrations" after the sharp contrasts felt during the relocation, I began to move out of disorientation. Logic would have it that going physically back into "the world" was the way to reorient, but I experienced the opposite. This was a lesson in realizing that all such "shifts" happen first internally. I would deliver the book to Hampton Roads and vacation to Denver to attend a MUFON conference before feeling I was beginning to reorient.

The conference was the second of the UFO kind I'd ever attended. The first was in 1994, in Mesquite, Nevada.

Though I had changed internally since then, outwardly I behaved as I had previously, moving around the edges of the activities. It is a curious thing to attend such a gathering of ufology buffs, investigators, and researchers. I was reminded that the focus was still on the "hardware"—the physical manifestations of alien "visitations," and we who were in contact and encountering them were still considered suspect in our claims. But I was not there seeking acceptance as an abductee. I was in Denver to discover that I could be in a large city without feeling overwhelmed by the furnace-blast energies of the concrete and machine world.

Reunion with old friends and the forming of new friendships was the real reward for all of my work and troubles.

Though I still feel a little alien, I've never felt stronger . . . that

Earth is home. Maybe this is a realization that truly the Kingdom is within, and among us . . . wherever we are.

14

GETTING STRONG

They say our lives are
Marked by three major events—
Birth, Wedding, Death.
I think I got the first right,
And probably I will die right.
But the middle event—*Oy'vey*!
Even after a patriarch
Pronounced me destined
To be a Mother in Zion
I could not get marriage right—
During, much less
Death do we part.
I thought for sure I'd
Marry once, and birth
Six children.
Sweet fantasy.
Instead
I married
Six times, and
Gave birth to
One child.
Proof I am more alien than most?
Born to make trouble for
Human beings who
Think themselves
Cowboys of the Cosmos.

Call me insane,
Call me alien,
I am the one
Who holds the pen
for the One
Within.

July 22, 1998:

Stuff happening last night. It's been a long time since I felt I was being prepared to go somewhere, though lately there have been a few sound and light phenomena . . .

The tinglings and pulsations are deep and more intense than usual. I feel my whole body shifting . . . doing that thing. . . . I see a vivid, gorgeous swirling purple color behind (?) my eyes, with bits of vivid red, green, yellow, like a kaleidoscope. Pain in my eyes (never felt that before). And then I hear the old familiar bee-buzzing sounds . . . and something new this time. Besides the bee-buzzing sound, a kind of warbling . . .

I am sometimes glib and philosophical about it all now. But all I have to do is reread the record (or be visited), and I remember all those nights I knew they were here, or I was going.

I'd much rather tell you a story about some guy who gets sucked through a rock into another dimension, after he carves in that rock "JQ + ZR," carves a star of David around it, and then has the stupidity to push the knife into the center of the star and turn it, because, you know, a dot in the center just looks right, like it belongs there. . . . How'd he know that doing such a thing would open a portal? Jonah Quiller Mahoney was an ordinary man who knew nothing about ancient symbols and their powers. But he will become a believer that such knowledge is essential to the survival of the human race.

I would rather write about anyone else's life but my own. Naturally some people are going to think I made up *Summoned*. If I had, I would have made it a lot more interesting. For sure, I would have included one big dramatic ship scene in Denver, if for no other reason than to describe the shock on ex-husband Tom's face, as I tumbled up toward the Mother Ship in that shaft of glittering blue light. Tom has big eyes. I can imagine them practically popping off his face. But then, to be realistic, I would have had to write about all the trouble this dramatic abduction scenario would have caused in our marriage. Believe it, Tom would *not* have approved. The cuts on my hands and that ball visible beneath my skin were about the limit of what he could stand of alien activity. And people wonder why it has to be kept secret.

Before all this business, I was in love with words, and when I became intimate with letters, that love was crowned with passion. But I could no more transfer my passion for letters to an uninitiated mind than I could convey the feelings and emotions evoked by encounters with beings not of our known world. It was as if I were jolted awake to the shock of seeing the legendary Emperor parading down the avenue, not naked, but wearing silk pajamas. We in the West always did see things differently.

The strength I needed to carry me through had to be found within, tapping resources I did not know I had, or feared were insufficient. In the beginning, I had no idea the degree to which I would have to hold myself together; and if anyone had told me I would have to live like this for four years, I am sure I would have thought it impossible. It never felt like a "journey," or any of the other words we assign to grand spiritual adventures. The quest was: How was I to live now, knowing and experiencing as I did, among so many who could not accept? Who would be my friends? Who cared? Who could I talk to? Where did I fit now? Was my only hope for community in a support group off in some large city? Would I ever be able to lean back in a chair, and rest my feet atop a desk? Not . . . so far.

Abductees are challenged with a horrendous breach in the fabric of our beliefs and the lives we created, as result of those beliefs. It is not surprising that some of us have ended up in mental institutions, or committing suicide. For many of us, the trouble is not so much the shock of discovering we can be taken against our conscious wills by beings we did not even know existed, as it is the rejection felt from members of society who have no reason to believe us. Is it any wonder we are branded as mental cases or any of the other judgments that point to us as the initiators of these phenomena?

Many lives have been torn apart, many abductees have become virtual recluses, living on the edges of society with their unacceptable secrets. But can I blame people for their disbelief or skepticism? What in their lives gives clue that such things can happen? What in our education or media has prepared us for such events? Perhaps it is a natural animal instinct to reject reports of activities that if considered to be true would pose considerable threat to our sense of security. The reality of alien abduction is nothing less than a trumpet announcing that what we think is security, is not. And like it or not, abductees are messengers heralding a warning: You can persist with the belief that security can be created through sheer human intelligence, a lot of money, fabulous technologies, and all else that composes modern civilization; but friends, it is delusion. The only security is whatever strength of character and faith has been built up inside you, for only these will carry one through experiences that shake the underpinnings of human fabrications.

And yet the orchestrators of these phenomena do not require a sudden and devastating collapse of the structures we have built like stages, believing the settings and roles we play to be the only reality. The system is not threatened with displays of UFOs and abductions so powerful they are pushed in our faces, demanding acceptance.

What is the plight of an abductee? To crawl under a rock and try not to be noticed by society, to escape the judgments and rejection? If so, the outcome will be the same, for one cannot live a perfect pretense that matches the old belief system, now shattered, without severe repercussions to the psyche. Not all are called, or even able to "go public" with their accounts, but the changes in such a person's life will not go unnoticed by people closest. Depending on the degree, frequency, and intensity of abduction activity, marriages and families may break apart, careers may be interrupted, and dear friendships may not survive the trials. How can abduction cause such havoc? Because these are events not happening on the mental realm alone, though certainly our minds are engaged in the experience. These events are happening to us in the whole of our being and lives, and none of us live as islands.

For the abductee, the challenge is not one of debate between belief and disbelief. It is a matter of who do you tell, how much do you tell, and are you ready to risk everything—family, marriage, friends, reputation, careers, and even dreams? For if you appeal to minds not prepared for the shock of such revelations, you stand to lose all.

Even with frequent media presentations that stir the question of the reality of UFOs and abductions, there is still that seeming human inability to fathom that something can be real if not experienced. How much in life do we take on faith? Much more that we realize, I think, but most of us are from Missouri—show us—or shut up with your wild claims. Is not the "scientific method" perfect expression of our current agreement that reality be determined based on "show me" systems? But without such systems of controlled determinations, how would we keep order?

It is apparently true that this world operates by fixed laws. Understanding of these laws has served in the creation of magnificent sub-realities. But now life is showing us something else, something more—not something that defies the laws we have proven to be true—but something that demands that we notice there are higher, more complex laws that govern these truths which we have declared in our restricted consciousness to be the Alpha and Omega of creation.

I don't expect that this small book is going to be a wake-up call for non-experiencers. I wrote this book from the corner where these experiences pushed me. Will I write myself back into the mainstream? The waters seem treacherous; rivers seemed to have sprung up where none existed before; tidal waves seem to be sweeping over us all. Where is the mainstream? Do the images that flash daily on the television screen reflect the reality of the terrain? From the abductee's point of view, the terrain flashing on the screen is very different from the one seen and experienced. I may not succeed in causing so much as a ripple on the lakes of public perception, but at least I will have spoken of these things. In the bearing of the truth, *someone* will hear—possibly future historians who will know that alien abductions were real events, screened now for the panic it would cause among a population hostile to change. Perhaps someday, abduction events will be seen as part of a revolution from within, launched to salvage the best of our bloodlines in the making of a new human being—a revolution that *had* to change the course of the past and present in order to preserve the future from extinction.

Who are we? When I recorded the following message in April 1993, I was so jaded by "new age" and "spiritual" rhetoric, my attitude was reserved, if not skeptical. While the idea that we are spiritual beings expressing in physical forms appealed to me, it did not have the impact it did after June 1994.

In the spring of '93, I did intensive work on identifying my personal belief systems. I had filled up a whole desk-sized graph pad with every belief about everything I could think of. I was amazed at the weave these beliefs made, like a fabric stitched tightly around my mind. But near the end, I ran into trouble, writing of beliefs about good and evil. Here the weave was so tightly meshed, it was difficult to identify the threads. I was yet to understand that like past and future, and time and space, good and evil are like the loops on the figure 8 symbol for infinity. At the center, where the figurative loops cross, human beings are focused on the illusionary present, where we experience in vivid sensuality the contrasts of duality.

In that awful moment of truth, caught in my own web of conflicting beliefs, came this simple communication out of the depths, where Something unexpected responds to a soul reaching. Recently, looking at this message, I could see in it a certain innocence that is lost once the "veils" are lifted and one is forced to consider not just new ideas, but personal experiences that support them. Once experience breaches cherished beliefs, the battle is on, and we are more apt to color information to fit what we hope is true, or to tone down what we pray is not true.

Recorded April 29, 1993:
First I was moved to write . . .

Once upon a time, highly developed ETs created beings to populate the Earth. For them it was no different than human parents coming together to procreate children. . . .

Where do you think the system came from: We created you in our image, making alterations for conditions on Earth. There were five different groups who engaged in the creation process. We intended to create diversity. Each group was created for a purpose. The plan was that no group could "graduate" without the other. We knew you would develop at different rates and in different ways and you would fight as siblings do. We created diversity here for there is diversity everywhere, and it was intended for you to learn to respect differences among you so that you would be prepared to respect the radical diversities in other groups that populate your universe.

You were instructed as you instruct your children to adhere to certain principles; love thy neighbor being the most coherent idea expressed. You were allowed free reign in what you did among yourselves and in how you used the Earth's resources to create societies. You were allowed to form religions and universities and every other manner of organization and institution, wherein you could develop your minds, bodies and spirits. You have created some very interesting systems. You have done well.

And now it is time for your next developmental lesson. Up to now, you have evolved within the confines of limited awareness. You have been instructed to seek guidance from your gods and many have practiced and kept alive this instruction. The outcomes of your guidance seeking have corresponded to your abilities to interpret responses—through the veils of consciousness.

These veils are about to be lifted. The time and circumstances are probabilities based on your readiness. Portions of the human race will be better prepared than others. There will be chaos and terror. This is why you and those of your clan have incarnated at this time. The humans who are better prepared will interact with you and take instruction as to how to help the portion of mankind who will be in terror. Order *will* result after much disorder.

[Me]: How does this line up with reincarnation and the eternal nature of man's spirit? (Notice how I ignored the implications in the last paragraph.)

Reincarnation is an aspect of development. As you have seen, every soul is afforded the opportunity to experience all sides, all roles, so that he may develop compassion.

[Me]: Hard sell—seems to be a lack of compassion—what gives?

You see at any stage humans experiencing all sides. All sides are present at all times. Again, you cannot judge by appearances. There is much strife on Earth because so many put off experiencing the more painful lessons until this time. Whatever was missed is being experienced now. Some of those you find most cruel and despicable lived before now many lives where they made progress in other areas. They are experiencing exponentially the extent to which a being can be heartless and selfish—where without this experience they were to a degree naive, lacking understanding for the cruelties visited upon them. In order to do as the Master directed, to forgive your enemies, you must have compassion for them, and you gain compassion by experiencing the wrongs they have committed. No human escapes direct experience of all levels of behavior.

[Me]: Sometimes this seems pointless to me. Was this the only way? That we would take turns hurting each other and being hurt in order to learn?

Remember—we allowed you to choose.

[Me]: And you knew we would choose to compete and try to control others, so we could have more, do more, be more.

And you discovered through experience what works and what does not. A human without such experience would have never developed beyond an animal mentality. You do not condemn your animals for their behavior. They cannot be anything but what they are. They are survivalists. They represent your base nature. But you were a breed that was given a brain constructed to house a seed spirit. Your development as hu-man [sic] has been a system to develop seed spirits into fully spiritual beings that will emerge when ready to.

[Me]: A human being is like a pod holding the seed, and in its season a plant grows out and blossoms?

Yes, except in this case, the blossom only occurs after many cycles and when it finally emerges, it stays. It is the eternal aspect of the system.

[Me]: Are you saying life in-body is only a stage? That at some point we will no longer need our bodies?

Your bodies and spirits will be one, as the flower is an end result of the seed and stalk and leaves. Stages, cycles.

[Me]: What about all the humans who have lived and died over the centuries? They're not all here at once in body.

Correct. Some have already. . . .

(Suddenly I felt faint from hunger. Losing the contact, I jotted down: For some it was not necessary to be here, they had already completed their development on this level. They are working on another plane.)

Much has happened since to challenge this simple view of reality. If it's true . . . it hardly explains everything. . . .

15

GETTING SERIOUS

Writing this book happened in an ever-narrowing, spiraling vortex. Around the wide circle of the uppermost loop, my story was "all over the place." I could hardly contain it in my mind enough to know where to begin. Each version I wrote was a circle inward, narrowing and tightening, as I moved down the loops to this center of the story, coming last.

The making of this book is no different than the living of my life. Each is a vortex, pulling me downward, it feels; I resist, fearing to find in the center of the thing a kind of energy like a tornado that will spin me over the ground, destroying everything.

The center of the spiraling labyrinth was this book, and the very thing that would energize it was the thing that would undo me, I knew; for how can one speak of what is in her heart, and not die instantly?

This is a question the head cannot comprehend, that something spoken from the heart could have such power, especially when we know the heart has no words, except what the head assigns. But how can the head assign words to that which it cannot comprehend, unless the heart teaches the head these things?

Paradoxes, paradoxes. That is life, and describes making a book, as well. When the heart releases her final secrets, giving them words, then the thing is complete, life and book in synergy. Then a new seed-energy is born of fire.

As the hay story I shared in the Preface happened down the pages, my pen was an extension of the Muse that sometimes graces it. The same mystery must help me write these last chapters, as the heart gives the head words for what it cannot otherwise comprehend, or dreads to dare. As the "last one notified" of what is to come, the head is a fearful element in the communications system; and in fear, fills the air with yapping important-sounding words, to convince that it knows what is, what was, and what shall be. Because if we know not these things, where is the courage for living?

But courage does not spring from illusions woven to comfort the unknower. The head lives in constant insecurity that pretends certainty and projects a pride that struts up to the microphone to make grand speeches.

Courage can only come from the heart. Paradoxically, it is only in fear that courage can be found, for the head will not pause to listen to the heart until it admits the fear it hides in its great orations.

Fear is a many-headed thing, sometimes showing as anger, sometimes despair, but in whatever form it expresses, it is a thing that devours, like a deadly tornado formed of all of the words in the heart, refused by the head.

You can behold with your eyes the many signs of the fear we hold in our heads in the forces of nature. For every thought is an energy that, even if denied or suppressed, nonetheless exists, and must go somewhere, to express in some shape or form. Could a wind spring free of the very air that bears it? Nothing exists in a vacuum separate from all else. Collectively, suppressed fears might be powerful enough to explode as tornados, hurricanes, volcanos, or earthquakes.

I speak of mysteries too large for the page to contain, too much for my pen to control. This is true for life, for love, for creation, as well as for the mystery we call alien abduction.

One of the most powerful messages conveyed to me began: *Dear beloved human being of the second order. Hear this now from the Winds in Stone. It is long. Write it now.* It was a very terse informing of the "laws of creative will," rendered in stilted, archaic language that sounded more like an ancient chant than the formal recitation it was on the page. It was one of those messages that does not convey well to readers, for like so much that was given to me, its meaning is interwoven with other messages, so that one without others is a voice that lulls or bores for what is missing.

I cannot share here all of the burdens of this mystery for the same reason I do not include the "Dearly Beloved" message. Later I hope for information that will enlighten us all, but for now I depend on the same Muse that inspired the story about the young woman packing hay to help bridge gaps between that which we think we know and evidences of realities almost too strange to be believed.

In the story of the young woman who learns the reason the townspeople hate hay, Mary speaks of a man born long ago who saw behind every eye, every thought . . . I have experienced what it feels like to encounter someone who can see behind my eyes, every thought, and feeling. That is the omniscient eye of the alien, felt like a laser beam from Hell, as it probes and sees all at once, everything you have thought and done but cannot hold in conscious awareness; thus the devastating feeling of someone knowing more about you than you do. Maybe that's what Adam and Eve felt, gifted with a new awareness so shocking it made them feel naked and vulnerable.

The townspeople could not abide what the man taught, Mary said, for if everything is in the light, who has advantage? This may speak to the very core of why there is such wholesale rejection of the UFO phenomenon, and the reason it must be cloaked in confusion and secrecy, and the reason we must be prepared. We fear the light because it will shine on us.

Long ago we were schooled to believe we were inherently evil. It is easy to understand how we would come to associate birth of our consciousness with shame. Shed of our animal innocence, we were bound to know evil, for if not, how could we know good, and what would direct our wills?

In counter-reaction to forces that would, to their advantage, control us through fear and shame, perhaps we did learn to turn the darkness to our advantage, too.

We use the word light to mean all that is good and desirable, but to a human being long habituated to believing that survival much depends on darkness, the message of light may be lost. But the man in the story did not just come to teach that light is another word for love. He came to prepare us for the day when the lights would come on, ready or not.

Scientists say that our genetics are 98.4 percent the same as our nearest relatives in the animal kingdom—chimps, apes, and bonobos. But no one seems to know what it is in the 1.6 percent that makes us so different. To say that it is intelligence does not enlighten but only restates the difference in letters instead of numbers. Whatever the difference, we seem significantly guided by the 98.4 percent, to survive at any cost, if at the forfeiture of what some say is the difference—our divinity.

For humans, the enemy can be anything unknown, or new. If intelligence is our special difference, representing the focal point of our survival, then knowledge would be construed to be a power equivalent to the size, prowess, and pecking order privileges in the animal kingdom. Paradoxically, anything new or unknown is often perceived by the human being to be a direct threat to knowledge already defined and established as a power base to ensure our survival. But what we do not know can kill us, we know from long experience with such things as bacteria and viruses that do their damage in the darkness of our ignorance.

The other night, I saw a sad but uplifting movie called *Swept From the Sea*. It is a love story that personifies the human animal response to unknowns. Yanco, a Russian-speaking survivor of a shipwreck, is washed upon the shores of a small Irish community that perceives him to be an enemy because the people cannot understand his native language, and are unacquainted with his behaviorisms. The more frightened of the men gang up on the gentle foreigner in a display of brawn that feels to them to be a show of their power. Now they can settle back on their haunches of ignorance, proud for brutish behavior that overpowered this bit of evil come into their midst to herald that there are things in the world of which they know nothing. If the louts had been smarter, they would have learned as much as possible from Yanco, to bolster the library in the 1.6 percent portion of their brains.

It seems that whatever it is in that 1.6.percent that distinguishes us from other animals works as much to our destruction as it does our survival. While the right hand seems to seek knowledge and power, the left seems to wield a sword that is swiftly brought down on unknowns perceived to be threats—just because they are unknowns. Perhaps such behavior, demonstrating a default to the animal in us, bears witness to parts of our brains that are yet to be activated. Maybe the 1.6 percent is still 90 percent potential.

Remember my mention of seeing a pattern in various mythologies of two brothers locked in moral conflict? Are such stories comments about our dual nature? Maybe one brother personifies our animal nature; the other, a god wanna-be. Maybe wars and competition for supremacy are schools of experience natural to a genetic predisposition to survival of the fittest. But maybe counter-opposing is a "god-part" that mandates that we transcend our animal natures through the vital use of will, and other powers bestowed in our DNA, meant to be used to develop a species that is both capable and morally suited to be guardians of the Earth.

I see these patterns and connections and wonder if the UFO business is a complex drama staged to excite us to awaken our sleepy powers, and exert our will against entropy and animal fear. Maybe we will seize the "kingdom" by storming Heaven's gates. Maybe that's the only way it *can* happen. Maybe Scripture that tells us to be alert, for the Master will return like a thief in the night, speaks of a sudden wave of new consciousness. Maybe such scriptures refer to the drama unfolding now. Maybe my sources who say, in chapter thirteen, that we are engaged in a battle of wills are telling the truth. If true, it is imperative we wake up, face these realities, and exercise our will to establish our sovereignty (or the Kingdom of God on Earth, if you prefer that wording).

The doomsday scenario is old and familiar. It's hard for technocrats to get in a sweat over such predictions. Aren't all these stories saying the same thing? Straighten up your act, or God is going to punish you. Ho hum. Be good, follow the rules, and you will be crowned and live happily ever after.

Yeah . . . be *crowned.* An event inside our heads? Activation of some dormant portion of the brain that makes possible leaps in powers we call paranormal? It makes sense that if we are to reverse the tides of destruction that we ourselves have created, we need to get smarter, more aware—quickly.

Clues in my personal experience point to the brain as the primary stage upon which this drama is unfolding, or *en*folding.[8] Remember my suspicion that the silver seam in the spacecraft may symbolize the division between cerebral hemispheres? The seam was the consistency

---

8 Enfolding is the word that came to mind during a hypnotic regression to describe my knowing that the silver seam was a portal between dimensions. I can't explain in words the dynamics of shifting from one dimension to another—"enfolding" was the closest word to describe it. It is a word David Bohm, physicist, used to explain the concept of a hologram (*Bridging Science and Spirit, Common Elements in David Bohm's Physics, the Perennial Philosophy and Seth* by Norman Friedman, Living Lakes Books, 1990, 1994).

of mercury, a fluid-like portal on the ceiling of the navigation room, allowing for enfolding from one dimension to another.

Or maybe we are being invaded, soon to be supplanted by heartless but intellectually superior aliens. If this is the plan, my belief in our Divine origins rallies around the idea that we have the power to realize the presence of the enemy, and call to action our hidden potentials, in consciousness and will, to stop them and reclaim our turf. Of course, such realization and action would mean we are ready to cease our destructive ways and assume the responsibility for stewardship of the Earth.

Or maybe Armageddon is upon us. The demons of Biblical lore have been loosed to bring upon us all of the plagues and horrors so vividly described by John the Revelator. A case can be made for this theory; it's as reasonable as our defense of the theory that life began with a bang which mysteriously begot intelligence.

The Good Book says of end-times (Joel 2:28), *I will pour out my Spirit on all people; your sons and daughters will prophesy; your old men shall dream dreams; your young men shall see visions. . . .* (:30) *I will show wonders in the Heavens and on the earth. . . .*

It seems too convenient, too coincidental: Kenneth Arnold's sighting of nine flying saucers in 1947, just two weeks before news that an alien aircraft had crashed on the desert near Roswell, New Mexico . . . soon after we exploded the atomic bomb over Hiroshima . . . not long before we launched the first satellite, *Sputnik* . . . not long before astronauts flew to the moon. It seems too pat, too neat, that coincidental to the atomic bomb, the launch into outer space, and sightings of UFOs, the tribe of Judah would just happen to choose this time in history to reclaim their homeland, in fulfillment of ancient prophesy . . . and in ironic syncopation with Hitler's obsession to destroy all Jews.

And that all four—sightings of extraterrestrial spaceships, explosion of atomic bomb, the gathering in Israel, and venture into outer space—would just happen to occur not long before the Big Flip of the calendar, gives new meaning to the Millennial Myth.

If myth-makers themselves had orchestrated these events, they couldn't have done better in setting the stage to reflect a host of prophesies that foretell the end of the world, as we know the world.

But where in our myths comes the story of ETs on the scene at such an important time in history? Whisking ordinary citizens up into Mother

Ships to extract eggs and sperm, to create those freakish half-breeds.
Well, God provided an ark for Noah and company before the Big Flood,
didn't He? Why not a complex gene bank befitting our science-minds
before the Big Fire?

Remember . . . first we are born of water, the womb, and then of
fire, the spirit. Terrible, beautiful.

Missing in most theories is the human factor. Alien abduction affects
a person on all levels—body, mind, and spirit (soul or consciousness).
We express as biological beings, true, but humankind has demonstrated
knowledge of higher dimensions . . . consider the first etched pictures
on the walls of caves. In determinations of the intelligence of a given
human species, anthropologists look for signs of religious awareness
as a fundamental that distinguishes us from our closest relatives. Even
cave men buried their dead, placing, in graves, evidence of a belief in
continued existence. Assuming they were smart enough to know that
dead bodies return to dust, it stands to reason they knew they were
more than flesh and bones. And yet such resistance to this awareness
today . . .

Are we *devolving*?

I'm a little nervous about the Armageddon and extinction scenarios,
I confess, but the professor in me can make no sense of them in light
of so much information given that indicates we are going to bypass the
Awful Probability.

But I'm not convinced we have the capacity to exert such a unified
will in so short a time as environmental scientists say we have to act.
If it's possible, I figure science and religion are going to have to do
better than glare at each other across a room, where each barely respects
the presence of the other. It's laughable. Like two halves of the brain
arguing that one is superior to the other. Like the fingers feeling more
important than the toes. Like brother killing brother because he's hairy
or a different color. Or, like men deciding to get rid of women because
we're just too much trouble. How long would the human race last if
men did such a foolish thing? About as long as we will last if we continue
to suppress the female side of our brains. New Agers didn't invent the
notion of life being holistic; they're just people who remember simple
truths forgotten in our pursuit to develop our reasoning powers. The
children of Earth remember that we were created of Mother's water
and grains of sand, mixed with Father's stardust.

Aside from my musings . . . last night I dreamt I was a reporter for the Moab *Times Independent*. The boss sent me to get the latest scoop on the little gray men rumored to be flying about in silver machines, annoying everyone. I went straight to my most reliable sources, Brother Brain and Sister Soul. I found Brother in his tower, peering out of a small window high up the bricks, his binoculars resting on the ledge.

"What say you, Brother Brain, of all this talk of spaceships and strange little men who capture human beings to breed? And no disrespect, Brother . . . but rumor has it these spacemen are *brainier* than any human being."

"My dear," Brother Brain said in a silken, knowing tone, as he peered down from his loft. "If little green men were on the scene, *I* would know."

"Little *gray* men, Sir."

"Gray, green, purple! If they existed, I would be the first to know."

"*Oh, you big know-it-all* . . . " chimed Sister Soul from the tree beside the tower.

"Did you hear something?" Brother Brain said, wrinkling his brows.

"Your sister. She spoke."

He laughed. "Ha! A fish story bigger than the nonsense of little gray-green men! If I had a sister, don't you think I would *know*?"

"She's in the tree, Sir. Right over there." I pointed.

"My dear. There is nothing in that tree but *leaves*. Anyone with *eyes* can see that!"

"Birds," I said, pointing. "And bees, and butterflies. In the tree."

"Ha! You admit it, then. This . . . *sister* is pure hallucination."

"No offense, Brother Brain, but your sister is all—leaves, birds, bees, butterflies—and the very tree you see."

"My dear . . . I get so weary of repeating myself . . . *that* is an extraordinary claim. And for an extraordinary claim, I demand extraordinary evidence. Hmpf."

"But Sir . . . your sister is exactly what you see . . . tree, birds, bees."

Brother Brain spit. "Pure hallucination!"

I retrieved pen and note pad from my purse. "Can I quote you? You don't believe what you see is real?"

Brother Brain quivered all over in a roll of mirth, almost knocking his binoculars off the ledge. I wondered in a flash if he could see clearer without those dual peepholes. If he could, would then he see his sister?

"Do I believe what I see is *un*real?" He laughed. "Wake up, Miss! Don't you remember? This is all a dream!"

"Then you can change it," I said. "Come down from that tower. Touch your sister. Let the bird light upon your head. Let the butterfly sit upon your hand. Eat the honey the bees have made."

"Oh, no you don't! I know a temptress when I hear one! They put you up to it, didn't they?"

"Up to . . . ?"

"A plot! A conspiracy! A *takeover*. Never! I will never leave this tower! Tell them!"

"But you said it's all a dream. . . . "

"All *that* is a dream!" He waved the binoculars. "But *this*," he tapped the binoculars against the bricks on the tower's ledge, "is *real*."

"Ahh . . . " I wrote on my note pad. "I see. Everything you see beyond the tower is hallucination. But what you can touch—that, you say, is real."

"True fact."

I walked over to the tree, took hold of a leafy branch and shook it. A sparrow flew, a butterfly fluttered its wings. The bees swarmed.

"I am touching your sister, Sir. She is real."

"So you *claim*." Brother Brain spat.

"Now I see." I tucked note pad and pen in my purse. "If you come down to discover your sister, the little gray men you deny might take over your tower, and you will be forced to live in the reality you call a dream."

"Oh, you clever reporters. Twisting my words into a rope you hope will hang me! What do all call this tower, Miss?"

"The Tower of Knowing. Today, we do. In ancient times, it was called the Tower of Babylon. Sir."

"Not the same!" Brother Brain shrieked. "Not the same!"

"*The tower the gods destroyed*," I said under my breath.

"I HEARD THAT! PURE MYTH!"

I sighed. "Hallucinations . . . delusions . . . myths . . . dreams. Sir? In your mind—what is real?"

"I told you! This tower!"

"That's all? . . . "

"Of course, that's all! It's where I live, isn't it? What more could be?"

"A tree? Me? *Possibly* little gray men . . . "

My words hung in the air, unheard. Brother Brain had retreated into his tower.

"*Be patient,*" said Sister Soul, displaying as tree, birds, bees and butterflies. "*Soon the tower will topple, and my brother will be set free. Then he shall know me.*"

"I feel I wasted my time," I lamented. "He couldn't hear a thing I said."

"*The Law of Confusion,*" said Sister Soul. "*My brother's long reign in the tower is purposeful, Miss. He is storing up knowledge. The more he accumulates, the higher the tower rises. The higher the tower, the more all below seems to him to be illusion.*"

"He must feel so lonely . . . shut so high away . . . "

"*Wipe your tears, Dear. Soon the tower will topple, and he will be set free.*"

"And the knowledge he stored with such devotion and diligence?"

"*I shall absorb. And we shall merge, Brother and I. The knowledge in his guardianship is fire to spark new seeds I will give birth to.*"

"Ah . . . Brother Brain is a father to be! But . . . isn't that *incest*?"

Sister Soul giggled, shaking every leaf. The birds and bees swarmed in ecstacy and the butterflies leaped all at once into the air, wings awhirl like hummingbirds.

"*Remember the story about the forbidden fruit your first parents ate?*"

"Tempted by a demon!" I shuddered.

"*A snake to be precise,*" said Sister Soul primly. "*Better he swallowed his tail!*"

I rubbed my forehead. "I'm confused . . . "

"*Of course, you are. You are a human being.*"

"Are you saying I was born of incestuous ancestors?"

"*In the beginning we were one, Brother and I. The fruit offered was life in the forms you see. Beyond the Garden we would live apart, I, in this tree, Brother in his tower. I am experience. He is knowledge. When the tower falls, we shall merge again.*"

"And the seeds . . . ?"

"*Wisdom and compassion shall be their names.*"

"New trees? And a new tower?"

"*Flowers! And a temple!*"

"No snake to tempt? . . . "

"Devoured! In the flames of the swords that guard me now."

"What flaming swords?" I squinted; looked all around. I saw no swords, fiery or otherwise, but there in the sky—a glint of silver when the sun flashed.

"I think I saw—"

"The silver seam?"

"Whatever you call their ships. Little gray men as pilots, they say."

"Ah, the guardians. They tend the flaming swords you cannot see."

"A silver *seam*, did you say?"

"The beam they travel to and fro on. On one side is everything you see, hear, touch, smell, and taste. On the other side, all you know but have forgotten."

"The swords? . . . "

"Will slash the seam. The tower will fall, and Brother and I will merge again. Write that on your pad, Miss. That's your scoop."

I shook my head. "Thanks for the information, Sister. But my readers would never believe a story like this. Your brother banished to a tower to store up knowledge he himself cannot understand? His sister a tree where the birds and bees play alongside butterflies who whirl in the breeze like hummingbirds? Honey that Brother Brain cannot eat? Leaves he cannot touch? And your words he cannot even hear, for you speak a language foreign to his ears. And then I am to write of invisible fiery swords, and the silver in the sky rumored to be spacemen . . . really guardians of the flaming swords you say exist . . . traveling to and fro along the beam that keeps us all in the dream your brother *did* acknowledge. . . .

"But where does the dream end, and the real begin?"

"In the A and E!"

"Pardon? . . . "

"A for Arrow, my dear. E for Eternity. The Archer stands, feet firm upon the Earth. He reaches back for his quiver. Now you see him setting the arrow in the bow. Now you see him aim it in the air. He releases it . . . now watch. Where did it fly?"

"Bull's-eye?"

"In the eye of the beholder!"

"Ahhh . . . "

"A and E, my dear. Alpha and Epsilon."

"But I thought Omega was . . . "
"The birth of Humaniel!"

I suddenly awoke. Shot straight up in the bed. Grabbed my pen. Recorded as much I could remember.

A tower . . .

A tree . . .

Birds . . . bees . . .

Ah! UFO!

Was I taken again?

Not serious enough? I'm getting there. I weep. "Leave this be, and don't look back," is tempting counsel, but I can't give up trying to speak over the voices that keep crying the lie that the human spirit does not exist but is a myth to overcome. Because I know it is not a myth, I can only wonder if the Biblical prophesy of an antichrist might be fulfilled in a clone. In denial of the human spirit, how would one discern the difference between a clone and soul-filled human being?

Sometimes I believe the abductors are powerful energized personifications of *us*, flashing through our consciousness from a Probable Future, to show us in virtual horror what we will surely become, should we continue in the direction we are headed.

If it doesn't matter what we choose or do, if life is just a big game, or the Earth a playground, then why all this alien activity?

I'm serious.

16

GETTING REAL SERIOUS:

THE GATHERING

Nuclear, germ, chemical, cyber
Warfare.
Intelligence alone
Destroys.

The sky is on fire,
Our Mother is melting,
Her waters are boiling.
Two in a field, one is gone.

Brawn may survive,
But if the Soul
Departs,
Man is a but a machine.

Shun the spirit and
Intelligence mutates to
The lowest denominator.
Brute force reigns.

What's the use of a
Brain asleep to the life within?
The larger the cranium,
The better for butting heads?
Souls in jeopardy call

For a militia of
Another kind.
A spiritual warrior stands.

Help is here for
All who remember,
All who care,
All who ask.

The body returns,
Dust to dust.
The spirit goes
Home.

Where two or more
Join to gather,
There we are,
Never alone.

Seriously—what if one of the worst-case scenarios is true? There were indications in my own experiences and information that point to the story that we are being harvested for our genetic materials, like lab animals, with little or no consideration for what we believe to be our finest qualities and sensibilities. We seem to be, to the abductors, no brighter, and no more significant than we consider our closest relatives, the chimps and bonobos. Maybe they are fond of us, maybe they respect our animal rights. But we see ourselves as more than animals—intelligent, soul-filled beings who have *divine* rights of will.

In one worst case scenario, some portion of the government has known about the aliens for years. There are rumors from high places that the "black government" made a deal with the aliens to pretend ignorance of abductions, in exchange for technologies. If true, who knows what the aliens told those in power, to secure their cooperation? Maybe the deal-makers thought their decision was for the survival of our species. The few are sacrificed for the many. Maybe the aliens convinced the government some catastrophe was on the horizon that would soon drastically reduce our population.

Not everyone in the government is aware of the drama playing back-stage. I suspect that most government workers and leaders are as oblivious, curious, skeptical, or believing as the rest of the population.

They are, after all, representatives of the people, not some alien breed themselves. We voted them in.

There are hidden black projects, I can attest. The term "black" was coined as designation of a level of secrecy or seriousness. Black to cloak. But not all, if any, of the people who work at these levels have black hearts. Power does tend to corrupt, but not all are easily corrupted. Some people in government may know more than most abductees do, and may be working to help maintain balance between wild assertions and secrets that have to be guarded for the panic or rage that pulling the cloaks would cause. Government isn't an entity cut off from contact or connection, anymore than anyone else. The changes occurring are happening everywhere, to everyone, and all is being monitored and guided.

Next worst-case: Will Biblical end-time prophesies prove out? If so, is it because these events are set into the fabric of our existence, as ineradicable as a dye? Or are aliens and/or others *using* Biblical prophesies to make us feel there is nothing we can, or should do? And if this is true, would not such orchestrators work to incite wars, disasters, hate and destruction, so we would say, "See? And welcome."

You have read portions of messages given to me that hint of such power struggles and deceptions. And you have read that I was told that the key to our survival is in seeking within, to connect with the highest sources of love, or God, or Great Spirit, whatever name is meaningful to you.

The Servants of El (in the *History*) promised that "Together you will decide in conscious awareness to 'clean house,' to restore order where chaos has long held the reins, and oust those who have usurped the rule of free will in exploitation of the plan you have abided in faith."

I once knew an ex-Episcopalian priest named Owen. He may have been crazy. I didn't think so, but if I were crazy, how would I know? (He did speak of some sort of mental breakdown that was cause for him leaving the priesthood.) I thought he was one of the wisest men I'd ever met. Maybe going crazy is a prerequisite for wisdom. Describing something that I have forgotten since, Owen said, "It was terrible . . . and it was beautiful."

"Terrible-beautiful" describes not only the mystery behind the UFO enigma, but also the mystery of human existence. They are inexorably intertwined. Alien abduction is not happening off-stage. It is in our midst, and it means something.

Part of the "terrible" is the paradox in human behavior that seeks knowledge for power, and at the same time, fears the unknown. It is as if we are suspended between the Garden and the Kingdom, doomed to a perpetual adolescence that mistakes knowledge, youth, and beauty for wisdom and true power.

The History of Humankind in Summary informs of complications in our evolution, due to a willful alteration of the human genome to produce a worker model to exploit; a being with just enough alien intelligence to perform well, but not enough to compete with this foreign throne plunked down in our garden—implied in the Bible story of the gods destroying the Tower of Babel to curb man's incipient power.

The Pleiadians, servants of El, they name themselves, go on to explain why they and others of the "Heavenly Councils" stepped in to call to task the Nephilim (the Bible's name for the sons of God) for the desecration this genetic breach was to Earthlings, who had been created by a Supreme Being to evolve with body, mind and spirit developing in harmony. The "enhancement" in effect created a second order of humankind, which, if left to develop unguided by the evolutionary principles coded into the DNA of the first order, would overwhelm and usurp the original Earthlings. By comparison, the original Earthlings were children to these offspring of giants who had the intelligence to establish civilization on Earth, but not the spiritual wisdom that can only be gained through long experience, to fulfill the guardianship legacy meant for mankind.

The plan of correction was one of assimilation, and both random and guided genetic distributions, to blend the two orders, or kinds of human beings, resulting, if successful, in a third order, with the insurgence of alien intelligence now balanced with the spiritual time-coded proclivities fostered in the original Earthlings.

A big fish story? Maybe. Maybe the truth is too terrible to tell except in parable. But the heart knows that behind the "terrible" that cannot be told to the head, is a secret too beautiful to release before conditions are right.

Makes no sense to me that we would be created to be guardians of Earth, and yet in some of our behavior, reveal ourselves to be less intelligent than the life forms supposedly under our apprentice guardianship. No other species has the capacity to enact the destructions we can to the planet and ecosphere. Is intelligence too dangerous to endow upon human beings in the adolescence of our development? Is the Supreme Creator experimenting, correcting mistakes as He goes, searching for the right chemistry that will finally produce a human being capable of responsive guardianship?

The Judeo-Christian version of religion never made sense to me in the implication that God created flawed human beings, then punished us for being flawed.

If, indeed, will is the most undeveloped of human endowments, yet key to our survival, then it would seem that we were created to fail, because how can we choose on the side of good, right, and survival, if lacking the consciousness to be aware that our left hands are destroying what our right hands create?

Ah, but (some will insert here) a successful life can only be lived in faith, not knowledge; for we are offspring of fallen angels, Adams and Eves who willfully ate of the Tree of Knowledge of Good and Evil, thereby setting into a motion a live-by-the-letter-of-the-law mandate by which we would be judged. By this mandate, exercise your will and risk eternal damnation, for what is living by the law blindly and exclusively, if not default to the Garden where we lived as animals, innocent of good and evil, therefore unable to make choices?

Religion, say the servants of El, was instituted as a stop-gap correction to forestall the development of will in the imbalance created by an insurgence of intelligence into a biological life form that was still a child in its spiritual development. Religion then would be our mother in the nurturing of our hearts and souls to spiritual maturity, while the institutions of higher learning would father our intelligence and guide our explorations and creations.

A good plan on papyrus, but regardless the reasons or complications for this seeming imbalance between head and heart, spirit and intelligence, or right and left hemispheres of the brain, no plan is perfect; despite the best of plans and good motives, we still have free will, like it or not, sensible or not.

Important to realize—extremely important—is that we are not the only intelligent entities in the cosmos, or in our own neighborhoods, who possess free will. It should come as no surprise that we are not alone, for every form of religion and history has informed us since ancient times that we share the universe with other schools of beings.

Nor should it surprise anyone to learn that some of these schools of other free-will beings would not want to share territories or powers with us, for conceivably, some of them are not much advanced beyond us, and like us, probably still possess an animal competitiveness.

Awakened to these realities and challenges or not, here we are again, perched atop the equivalent of the Tower of Babel, in our communications systems and space technologies. Here again, humankind is becoming a collective power to reckon with; now with the intelligence to venture into the territories of the "gods"; now almost spiritually ready to prove ourselves worthy of cosmic citizenry.

But history shows that civilizations rise, and civilizations fall, as if we were offspring of the mythological Sisyphus, forever doomed to roll the stone up the mountain but never over it.

Speaking from my heart, head and experience, I believe that the aliens are real, various, and on the scene. I believe some are of the angelic or demonic quality, and all co-exist in our "multiverse" (as venerable author Jacques Vallee names our multi-leveled reality). I believe that some are so highly advanced, they barely remember our issues with good and evil. Their purpose is to shepherd our evolution; their devotion seems almost ruthless, their love, pure and free of the sentimentality we mistake for passion.

I believe we are caught up in a battle of wills we call spiritual warfare. Though we can see the effects in the world, it is happening in the "mental fields" that surround and interpenetrate our dimension, unseen by most.

Because most of us are "asleep" (maybe for our protection), many of us are pawns in this mostly unseen battle that seems to be happening at the edges of our conscious awareness. And many of us are in the thick of it, in the trenches and on the front lines, though we may be only dimly aware of such roles.

And what is the booty? Us. Our souls. Or the powers our souls can assert once we awaken, and call them with our wills.

And though many are here to help, only we can act, because the ones who love us cannot directly engage in battle, for to do so would be a violation against the very thing we need to survive—our wills. If they made our choices, or fought our battles for us, we would be forever suspended between the Garden and the Kingdom, vulnerable to predators much more aware of their rights of will, and much more exercised in the use of powers they easily wield over our minds and bodies to the extent we allow it, aware or not.

I've heard a hundred stories about the dark doings of rogue aliens and humans in cahoots with them. Some are probably true, others, confabulations or disinformation. But *something* is afoot (if on hooves) on Earth, as well as "above"—as has always been the case.

The stories of the creation of clones is a particularly strong impression in my consciousness, and was cause for a great deal of trouble in the way of harassment, when I was writing *Jonah*. Or maybe the harassment was part of my own personal testing—not so much the Divine wanting to see what I'm made of (I figure the Creator knows), but that *I* need to see what I'm made of, what I want, what I am willing to do to accomplish what I say I want, what lengths I'm willing to go, and most important, will I be true to what is in my heart; or will I compromise to win approval from the many heads that are sure to scoff at what I say, reporting from the heart?

In my heart, I know there are children waiting in the wings of tomorrow. I have loved and taught them in my dreams. Hideous, robotic hybrids who will supplant our species? Clones of Earth's children, new containers for select spirits who will inhabit them and rebuild the world after a nuclear holocaust? I do not have access to that information. And though I can feel love for the children, and believe they are the embodiments of the best in us, I have not forgotten all of the dark dreams and scenarios that kept me praying that I not be used to promote confusion, fear, or the lie that human beings are bad or helpless victims who deserve only to be reaped for resources to strengthen denizens who seem so powerful they are beyond the reach of even God.

In the eyes of my heart, I can envision a new human being who is you, me, and everyone breaking free. This new human being knows that s/he is not separate but a unique expression of the Divine, interconnected with all, now matured like a butterfly emerged from a cocoon; now ready to develop will in the light of a conscious awareness expanded to include memories of all of our lifetimes; now ready to live in true community. Now ready to become specialists?. . .

Recorded December 3, 1996

BROTHERS AND SISTERS ON PLANET EARTH: Long have you lived apart from the ones who made you. Do we call ourselves gods because we made you? We are not the Prime Creator. We created you, as you create your children. Using the resources The One created and the intelligence The One gave us, we created you, as you create your children.

And now after many years of development, you have reached a state of adolescence, much like you consider your children reaching an adolescent stage of growth. When your children reach a point in development, you send them out into the world, to learn the lessons of adulthood. For you, the world we would send you to is what you term as Outer Space. Like your adolescents, we have let you build vehicles; we have in comparison given you the keys to powerful vehicles. But unlike you do with your children, we have done this by means of a guidance system of which few are aware.

The competition you engage in to advance your technologies serves to keep order and to enhance upon what you know, but discoveries that serve as leaps in knowledge and awareness come to key individuals at appointed times, as you yourselves serve as guardians of certain knowledge and discoveries, in preparing your children for challenges you know they will face.

And as is true for you in preparing your children, often they do not believe what you tell them, but instead feel sure they know better, and will surely do better than you; and for this, you worry or take other measures to assure that you are doing all you can to shepherd your children into a successful adulthood.

Your adolescents are in danger of early pregnancies before they are ready to serve as parents. Your adolescents are in danger of becoming addicted to powerful drugs that could cause them to commit crimes against others, could damage their brains or circuitry, or cripple them for life in other ways—mentally, emotionally, or spiritually. Furthermore, overindulgence in drugs opens them to unseen influences, beings who literally "latch onto" a vulnerable body-soul; and though the victim may never exhibit or suffer the range of troubles drug indulgence can manifest, the victim may simply "never amount to anything."

Your adolescents may rebel against education, preferring the fleeting but intoxicating lure of "popularity," that thief of bright young minds. Turning up their noses at the "nerds" who work at becoming educated, these young people may soon find themselves saddled with their own children and the demands of survival, then it is difficult or impossible to obtain the education necessary for them to live in a comfortable way. These are to mention but a few of the dangers that beset the stage of growth in your society at this time.

Like you, we are challenged with similar concerns. Like you, we wish to shepherd our adolescents into successful adult experience.

Long have we provided you with what you would describe as schooling, that you might prepare to graduate and go out into the greater world, that is, "Outer Space." To prepare you, we schooled you in "Inner Space." For it is only in Inner Space that we can communicate with you, to teach you what you need to know, in order that you embark upon the next journey.

Unlike your schools, designed to teach you all you need to know for your survival on Earth, our curriculum is not general, but specific to each individual. Yes, there are universal principles all must learn and some must master, but we speak of specific schooling for specific children to perform specific tasks.

On Earth you are schooled in community living. While each of you is special and unique, that specialty or uniqueness is shunned, unless it serves the community. So you have been schooled, and so you behave, quite naturally, reacting with offense at anyone who behaves as a "prima donna," or a dictator, or the many other roles an individual may adopt to elevate the self above the community. Yes, you have your leaders and your heros and your "stars," but if you consider the nature of these roles, you will agree that in some way they serve the community. Those who adopt negative roles of leadership, such as tyrants, shall be challenged and brought down, that your history shows.

Now you have asked how many years of community education prepares you for what may seem to be the opposite, for "specialization."

Dear ones, consider this: With specialization comes a leap in responsibility, like unto what you are not yet acquainted with, as it is true that you try to tell your adolescents—it is different being an adult.

The responsibility that attends specialization requires long education in community, in learning to love and respect others, to understand that the actions of each individual do affect the entire community.

And so who shall graduate, and who shall receive a degree in community education? And who shall need to repeat the courses? All who have learned the lessons of love shall advance to schools of specialization, and all who have need to learn more of love shall repeat the courses.

To whom much is given, much is expected, so said the one who came to teach you love (*Luke 12:48; paraphrase*).

To whom has been given the lessons of love, as prosperous parents provide their children with higher education, much is expected, as wise parents expect their children to use their education to serve the community.

In the schools of specialization, you will begin to learn of communities far more advanced than you can comprehend now, communities composed of beings who long ago learned the lessons of love, and long ago advanced beyond individual specialization to become soul-complexes, of which advanced state requires graduation in first community education, and second, individual specialization education, both preparing the soul to join "parent groups" to begin the next phase of growth. Beyond these schools of experience, we cannot speak, for there are no words equivalent.

Soon you will experience a time of graduation or a time of knowing you will repeat the Earth school. For those who will repeat, there is no condemnation, except in the minds of those who have yet to master the rudiments of love. Many will choose to repeat the course, not yet ready to embark upon a path unknown, along with those who volunteer to serve as guides and teachers for those repeating, and for those yet to enter this school.

So it is, so it was, and so it shall be forevermore. The circle circles, and circles around again, and again, and new circles appear and connect, and circle around—such is life, such is love, such is the way of light. Truth is here, there, everywhere. Truth eludes.

Adonai, Adonai, we are EL.

AFTERWORD:

GETTING BETTER

The "town" seems less hostile and more receptive now. Maybe it's just me getting better . . . or maybe *everyone*'s getting better.

I've heard it said by other abductees, and it's true for me: we don't learn much about the aliens, but we sure do about ourselves, and other human beings. . . .

A (personal) Cosmic World-view:

The life of any individual is not much different from say, the life of a tree. As is true for a human being, everything that happens to a tree influences that tree, for better or worse. We chop down a tree to alter its form to become something deemed more useful than the living creature that stood stalwart in the soil, providing environment for civilizations of microbes.

In changing the form of a tree into say, sheets of paper or furniture, we tend to forget that these products are a tree re-formed. In our alterations, it is easy to lose sight of the reality of the thing itself, its origins, nature, and beauty.

We often speak of our immediate environment in terms of "settings," as if the trees in our yards were parts of a set that form the showy stages upon which we live and play. How often do we remember that everything that composes our "set" is made of living organisms, altered to suit our purposes? Beneath the surface of the ground, the roots of the mighty tree are hidden in a world alien, nonetheless very alive. There is no such thing as a "man-made" thing. Everything man "makes" originates from the resources of our Earth. We did not make this world. And we did not make ourselves.

A human being is much more complex than a tree, probably you will agree.

Maybe re-formation is not a good thing for human beings.

Abstraction is one step away from extinction.

Who am I? A soul-voyager here to participate in this Earth school of experience.

Who are we? A diverse community of soul-voyagers, probably from many origins. But while we are here, Earth is our home.

Who are "they?" I don't know for sure. Celestial ancestors, aliens, extraterrestrials, angels, demons, demi-gods, ushers, guides, guardians, harvesters, cosmic practitioners, skilled dimensional shift technicians, evolution masters, time travelers, "us" from the future, living archetypes, energy vampires, dimensional competitors, meta-terrestrials, brothers and sisters of unidentified realms. Whoever they are—they are here.

What are we doing here? The gig may be that while we are here, we have no clear memories of former or future lives. This amnesia serves to allow us to concentrate on the dynamics of this particular environment and curriculum of learning. Here we live in a special kind of community, among spirits from all walks and realities and origins—all of us temporarily "disguised" as human beings. The human biological form is a child of Mother Earth, accommodating a spirit who matures and "graduates" to new realms of experience.

This special Earth school maintains certain illusions. Having no memories of past or future, and nothing but stories of continued existence, we are forced to live by faith—a key to what we came to achieve.

Where are we headed? Depends. I believe that faith is more than a religious idea. Faith represents a frequency of thought. Thought is energy. What we think (believe or have faith in) determines our energetic state of being, our experience, or reality. We are essentially energy (or light) beings who are vibrating at rates that express as dense forms that are compatible to this environment, wherein everything is demonstrating in ranges of vibrations that express as forms compatible with the frequency of this particular sphere of existence.

Sound is the first principle, not light. *In the beginning was the Word, and the Word was with God, and the Word was God* (John 1:1, New International Version, Holy Bible).

What we believe, think and say produces a quality of sound that directly affects our energetic state of being, or vibrational quality.

Where we go, if at a climatic moment some call a "shift," or where we go when we die (when we cease to function at the densest level, departing the shell-form), depends on our rate of vibration.

Judgments of good and evil as we apply them to our behavior here, barely hint of the mysteries behind this school of experience. In terms of energies, frequencies, and vibrations, generally speaking, "good" correlates to all that uplifts, or speeds our vibration rate, allowing us to shift to a higher frequency, or dimension, while "bad" slows our rate of vibration, and we get "stuck," or decline into retrograde cycles.

Whatever our energetic state, wherever we are, in the strictest sense of the word "scientifically," we belong.

Spirituality refers to a focus of attention and a quality of action. Our attunement, or state of being, is both a spiritual and real dynamic. Spirituality and science are not separate schools, one blathering of theories and myths, the other concentrating on reality. They are different curricula in the school of life.

Mysticism is a professor studying the alchemies of religion and science, hoping to mediate a union of thought.

What we think matters. Because matter is what we think.

APPENDIX:

DREAMS AND PHENOMENA

June 11, 1985 through December 14, 1995

One gift in writing this book is plain and powerful: Early in the writing, I was inspired to place the record of nocturnal events at the end because reviewing it always upset me. Now, September 15, 1998, as I work over final corrections, I feel detached and peaceful. It's like it's all something that happened to me a long time ago, and it's nothing unusual, nothing to feel embarrassed about, nothing to fear. I'm amazed.

Months before The Breach, I was puzzled, reading another author's personal account of alien abduction. It seemed to me that what she described as encounters were really vivid dreams. So I wrote to her and asked how she made the leap from dream to encounter. In effect, she said all those incidents I considered to be dreams were real events. But in my own experience, in most cases, I can't make the mental leap from dream to encounter. No matter the amount of phenomena before and after, I still call what happens to me while I'm asleep a dream. I use the term "SUSPICIOUS" to indicate that I have reason to suspect there may have been an "alien influence." The actual suspicious events are marked with the following symbols:

 = lights;   = sounds;    = voice;

 = tones or other musical noises;   = feeling of presence;

= OBE or possible abduction scenario;

 = physical sensations; = physical effects such as marks on body or unexplained soreness

 = electronic disturbances or other "suspicious" noises in the house, or wherever else I am staying. (These phenomena occurred when I traveled as well as when I was home.)

Because the study involved so many dreams and "nocturnal events" (over 3,000 dreams reviewed), to list or expound on every suspicious dream or incident would have overburdened an already challenging task. As stated previously, the original purpose of analyzing my dream journals was in response to sudden and impossible-to-ignore phenomena that began in May 1994, following the reading of John Mack's book *Abduction*, which served as a challenge to my denial that I was no more than a "scribe for unseen guides."

This record shows clearly the sudden onset of new phenomena, and an increase in all suspicious dreams and activities. Interestingly, in the table below, it is also clear that certain types of experiences or dreams were more prevalent before 1994. For instance, "medical exam or surgery" dreams involving suspicious types of people (usually "Asians") occurred more often in the mid-80s, when I began keeping journals.

Many details are excluded in this report in favor of a broad picture. When I first typed up these entries, I had no idea I would ever publish such details. It was strictly an abbreviated record for my personal consideration. To protect the privacy of my friends who appear in dreams, sometimes I use initials.

I trust there is enough here to be of interest to researchers, other experiencers, or the curious. Please keep in mind: Many dreams about "smart babies," hybrids, or repeat themes were excluded to reduce the burden of information. I was seeking the truth—not trying to impress myself or anyone else. When I use the term "suspicious," it means there was more than one UFO-related element in the dream, such as Asians, smart babies, animals that talk, medical exams, military or government, underground facilities, genetics, otherworldly settings, possible travel in a spaceship, gatherings in auditoriums, classrooms, video presentations, end-time scenarios, and especially when I was flying (out of body?) in a dream.

A "smart baby" is a baby or toddler (usually bald-headed) that is highly intelligent and converses with me, sometimes speaking aloud; but often the communication is telepathic.

"Insert" refers to a part of a dream that doesn't fit with the rest, and indicates possible alien manipulation. Also, in this record, all references to animals or "foreigners" are indicative of possible screen imagery for aliens.

Entries in the 80s are no more than notations that indicated to me suspicious elements. You will see an increase from 1993 on. Note in the detail and the table below, there is a *decrease* in the number of suspicious dreams in 1988, 1989, 1990, and 1992. These decreases may have been due to distractions and pressures in my life during those years. Three major things were happening: the publication of my first book (*Ezekiel's Chariot*), with all the marketing and book signing challenges; the writing of *Lucy Blue and the Daughters of Light* happened during those years; and while all this was going on, my marriage was on the decline, causing emotional stress. In my case, possible ET-related activity decreases in times of stress, and increases in times when I am more settled. Once I was well into the writing of *Summoned*, all suspicious dreams and phenomena significantly decreased.

The record here does not include data for the last half of 1995, 1996, 1997 or 1998. The Table merely shows a leap in activity from the 80s to the 90s. Details follow.

NOCTURNAL EVENT DETAILS, DREAMS, AND PHENOMENA

Dreams/Phenomena	1985	1986	1987	1988	1989	1990	1991	1992	1993	1994	1995	Total
Spacecraft/UFO	0	2	2	4	1	6	4	4	2	10	3	38
Other Vehicle/Travel	7	11	2	0	1	0	1	1	2	9	0	34
Water	2	2	3	1	0	0	1	0	3	4	0	16
Flying/OBE	1	0	4	0	0	3	3	0	0	3	1	15
Asians	5	1	2	0	0	1	2	0	2	4	3	20
Other Foreigners	1	1	4	2	0	0	1	0	1	2	0	12
Angels/Entities	1	2	1	0	1	2	2	0	4	9	1	23
Fair Hairs	1	1	1	0	0	0	0	0	3	3	3	12
Doctors/Nurses	2	2	4	4	0	1	2	0	2	1	0	18
"Smart Babies," Children and Hybrids	0	17	9	4	4	2	5	2	6	12	8	69
Military/Government	2	3	0	1	0	1	0	2	0	4	2	15
Guards/Police	1	2	1	1	0	0	3	1	1	7	11	28

NOCTURNAL EVENT DETAILS, DREAMS, AND PHENOMENA

Dreams/Phenomena	1985	1986	1987	1988	1989	1990	1991	1992	1993	1994	1995	Total
Dogs/Cats	3	1	1	3	3	0	5	2	5	13	4	40
Other Animals	5	4	3	0	2	2	1	2	4	8	5	36
Auditorium/Classroom/Video	1	9	2	0	1	1	3	1	9	19	9	55
Military Base/Airport	0	4	1	0	0	0	0	0	1	0	4	10
Otherworldly/Tunnels/Caves	2	2	3	3	0	0	0	2	5	13	4	34
Hospital/Clinic	2	1	1	0	0	1	0	0	0	3	1	9
Medical Exams	8	5	5	4	0	1	6	0	0	1	0	30
War Games/End-Times	4	7	7	0	2	0	0	2	5	1	1	29
Secrets/Warnings	3	3	0	0	1	0	0	0	6	4	2	19
Messages/Lessons	3	5	12	4	2	5	4	1	11	14	12	73
Suspected House Intrusions	2	0	0	0	0	0	3	0	4	7	3	19
Other, suspicious	9	14	11	4	6	7	10	7	8	9	9	94

PHYSICAL PHENOMENA

Dreams/Phenomena	1985	1986	1987	1988	1989	1990	1991	1992	1993	1994	1995	Total
Sounds, General	3	2	1	0	0	3	5	1	6	52	26	99
Voice Speaks	0	1	0	0	0	0	1	1	2	9	3	17
Chants/Tones/Voices/Music	2	0	2	0	0	0	2	0	2	9	3	20
Lights, General	0	0	3	0	0	1	1	1	3	40	14	63
Holograms[9]	1	1	1	0	0	0	0	0	2	2	0	7
Physical Sensations, General	0	0	0	0	0	0	0	0	0	21	13	34
Tinglings, Vibrations	0	0	0	0	0	0	0	0	0	30	35	65
Bed Vibrates	0	0	0	0	0	0	0	0	0	4	5	9
Feeling of Presence	0	0	0	0	0	0	0	0	0	6	3	9
Feel Physically Manipulated	0	0	0	0	0	0	1	0	0	2	6	9
Time Confusion	0	1	0	1	0	0	0	0	0	1	1	4
Physical After-Effects	0	0	0	0	0	0	0	0	0	8	5	13
Days	214	365	365	365	365	365	365	365	365	365	120	3619
Total Dreams/Events Analyzed	42	77	72	23	22	31	47	25	63	144	56	602
Percent of Dreams/Suspicious Imagery Physical Elements	19.6%	21%	20%	6.3%	6%	8.5%	13%	6.8%	17.3%	39.4%	47%	17%

9   The most prevalent hologram, a red chrysanthemum, is not included in this count.

NOCTURNAL EVENT DETAILS, DREAMS AND PHENOMENA

1985

06/11/85	Dream about a spiral that comes out of the ground.
06/12/85	Dream, people in uniforms and secret stuff.
06/15/85	Dream: I'm PREGNANT.
06/17/85	Dream about the power of words.
07/26/85	Dream, very odd—in a classroom, being prepared for last days.
08/02/85	Saw a hologram.

08/10/85	Dream about an ASIAN, the military and a "war screen."
08/22/85	Dream with a strange "insert."
08/23/85	Dream, a "vision" of a suspicious girl.
08/29/85	Dream, suspicious about a period, Kotex.
09/02/85	Dream, repeat of above, plus an ASIAN.
09/04/85	Dream I'm PREGNANT.
09/05/85	Dream, the house is so easy to break into! And an ASIAN woman.
09/6,7/85	Heard noises, afraid of prowlers, dream about MONKEYS ON WALL and OWL EYES.

09/10/85	Dream, a stainless steel room.
09/18/85	Dream I'm a spy; world end is coming.
09/19/85	Dream, suspicious, noise and music at end.

09/28/85	Dream about big birds and dogs.
10/01/85	Hear "phantom" phone ring. (This has been a very frequent

and enduring phenomenon—hearing a phone ring in my immediate environment, but not the "real" phone.)

10/04/85	Dream about an IMPLANT?
10/21/85	Dream, "insert"—about X-rays and bus travel.
10/28/85	Dream, clinic and nurse.
11/01/85	Dream about a DESERT—another planet?
11/02/85	Dream about tiny scabs on my earlobes and CIA.
11/09/85	Dream about a talking cat.
11/11/85	Dream about water and "TUCKER" (Los Angelos).
11/15/85	Dream I'm flying (OBE).

11/16/85	Dream about a mouse and an ASIAN shutting the door.
11/18/85	Dream, bus trip, a fire, and being a leader.
11/24/85	Dream, an ASIAN, a "kahuna."
12/06/85	Dream, a doctor's office and a brother named DOXO or DOMO.
12/09/85	Dream I am INJECTED IN NECK.
12/19/85	Dream insert about a Jeep and a dog.
12/23/85	Dream, a man falls from the sky, and doctors.
12/28,29/85	Suspicious dreams.

1986

01/4,5/86	Dream about babies.
01/10/86	Dream, a cloud, and being in a coma for a year.
01/11/86	Dream, a secret, a baby, and a dog.
01/12/86	Dream about "HALF-BREED BABIES."
01/13/86	Dream, military base.
01/17/86	Dream about a water wheel (a repeat theme).
01/21/86	Dream, a warehouse and a baby.
01/24/86	In Dream, I am telling someone, "Don't worry, I'm a fiction writer . . ." regarding a concern I'm going to expose something.
02/03/86	Dream, suspicious.
02/18/86	Dream about "OLDER BABIES."

02/24/86	Dream about lies to government, sabotage, water, boats and a baby.
03/01/86	Dream, Mexico, visitors/residents, a "starman."
03/02/86	Dream, a school, babies, and a doctor.
03/03/86	Dream I'm PREGNANT, in hospital.
03/07/86	Dream, a boat, mind-reading, and a classroom.
03/13/86	Dream about a meaningful "display."
03/15/86	Dream I'm captive, afraid I'm meant to die; also a pregnant woman.
03/21/86	Dream about monkeys, and a man gives birth.
03/26/86	Dream, foreigners and a (bath) shower.
03/28/86	Dream about women and babies.
03/29/86	Dream with suspicious insert—a subway/train and parking lot.
03/30/86	Dream I met God—he's a lanky young man—suspicious.
04/01/86	Dream I have SEX WITH A "BABY MAN."
04/02/86	Dream of foreigners, being herded around like slaves.
04/03/86	Dream of sex in a dormitory setting.
04/05/86	Dream of ASIANS.
04/09/86	Dream a war scene, camouflage dress.
04/10/86	Dream, a trip in a jet . . . bodies, blood, "clean cuts," and eggs.
04/17/86	Dream, war scenes and about "following a star."
04/18/86	Dream about my JONAH book (a "GOD dream") and about changing my name to Diane Jonas. (Wrote *Jonah* 8 years later.)
04/22/86	Heard noise in my room—suspicion of MISSING TIME, and a dream about my "twin self."

04/23/86	Dream, end of world scenes.
04/29/86	Dream about a pilot and a "tail-less" plane.
05/07/86	Dream, "insert," sand, New Mexico Missile Site.
05/08/86	Dream, a factory, a swimming pool (common suspicious element), and a cave scene.
05/18/86	Dream, a bus, train, classroom, and TUCKER (Los Angelos).

05/19/86	Dream, something about a revolution.
06/03/86	Dream about an astronaut.
06/09/86	Dream about a secret experiment at a military base.
06/10/86	Dream about "initiation."
06/11/86	Dream about SMART BABIES.
06/13/86	Dream about SPACESHIP travel (first time in journals).
06/15/86	Dream about an airport, a dead woman and waxy faces.
06/22/86	Dream about a trip on a suspicious airplane.
06/24/86	Dream, repeat (a trip on a suspicious airplane).
06/26/86	Dream about a "living manuscript."
06/29/86	Dream about a SMART BABY and guards.
07/22/86	Dream about a nuclear bomb, like a previous dream of future (and I have a "secret attitude.")
07/23/86	Dream image of my "mentor" woman (repeat theme).
07/31/86	Dream about people burrowing into earth and a "fairy" in the sky.
08/05/86	Awakened by sound of pounding on door—dream about a child named Brighton.
08/09/86	Dream about a spacecraft.
08/10/86	Dream, words like pearls . . .
08/22/86	WOKE WITH TRIANGULAR CUTS ON HANDS: on left, over a vein; on right, closer to knuckle. Ball found soon after, under topskin of left hand. No significant dream recall.
08/24/86	Dream about strange "bobbies" with helmets, and dark mists.
08/28/86	Dream I move to Moab to work for an "aerospace" company. (Actually did move there 5/92.)
10/02/86	Dream about dropping a fireball on Earth from a classroom.
10/10/86	Dream, a newspaper headline sparks war, and men are "like children."
10/11/86	Dream of a doctor and a spider.
10/21/86	Dream I'm flying in primitive jet, then huge meeting in auditorium, and U.S. government.

10/30/86	Dream I was raped.
11/14/86	Dream about treatment, surgery, and a conveyor.
11/15/86	Dream . . . disembodied voice.
11/16/86	Suspicious dream.
11/24/86	Dream I'm flying on a big ship.
11/29/86	Dream: I'm told I'm PREGNANT. I say impossible. "They" argue I am pregnant—seed attaches to inner walls. They show me an X-ray to prove.
11/30/86	Dream, a silver atmosphere.
12/02/86	Dream about writing impact.
12/03/86	Dream about a creed and a baby.
12/15,18/86	Dreams about babies.

1987

01/11/87	Dream, babies and keys.
01/18/87	Dream a "girl" sees my boobs, and stars like balls in sky.
01/20/87	Dream about a mission and something imperial. (In peril?)
01/22/87	Otherworldly dream?
01/24/87	Dream about strings around the world.
01/25/87	Dream about a SPACESHIP.
02/11,15/87	Suspicious dreams.
02/17/87	Dream I'm PREGNANT.
02/24/87	I received/recorded a message.
02/26/87	Saw a cluster of black balls (lights) on wall.

03/02/87	Dream about a SPACE WOMAN, about a book I will write for "them" someday. (This book?)
03/04/87	Dream about a Chicano with gun, and a hospital.
03/05/87	Dream about "archives," and Dr. Walker.
03/07/87	Dream about a whirlpool.
03/08/87	Dream about a "baby mummy," a doctor, and classroom.

03/10/87	Dream about immigration to foreign countries (suspicious).
03/12/87	Suspicious dream and a symbol.
03/17/87	Dream about boys chanting—about a dead god.
03/19/87	Dream I'm SEEING EARTH FROM ABOVE (I hear a sound).

03/21/87	Dream about a doctor.
03/24/87	Very suspicious: out of body, lights, and chanting.

03/27/87	Suspicious dream about being abducted?
03/28/87	Suspicious futuristic dream.
04/19/87	I see a light and a suspicious dream.

04/21,22/87	Dream about underground caverns.
04/30/87	I'm flying.

05/01/87	Dream about geometric form instruction.
05/02/87	Flying, scary . . .

05/03/87	Dream about last days, keys, visitors.
05/05/87	Lucid dream about Jesus, a shrine, a cross over, Indians, etc.
05/09/87	Dream of two moons (repeat imagery in major encounter, 4/97).
05/10/87	Dream of a frightening (bath) shower.
05/12/87	Suspicious dream.
05/26/87	Dream about a man from another planet? And a swimming pool.
06/01/87	Dream: swimming pool, doctor, TV screen, and about intelligent and ADVANCED LITTLE ONES HERE TODAY.

06/04/87   Dream about "meditation conversations," and precognition about a cop.

06/07/87   Dream about ancient temples and an airport. Woke up to see a pattern of bright green lights.

06/09/87   Dream I see a display of words in the sky: "OUTER SPACE VISITORS," and about our origins.

06/10/87   Dream about an ASIAN woman, about giving up illusions.

06/18/87   Dream: I see my book like a band around my head at forehead.

06/19,20/87 I "get" a diagram and a channeled message.

07/11/87   Dream about "third dimension."

07/13/87   Dream, spiritual.

07/17/87   Dream about us being programmed "human experiments."

07/21/87   Dream—a "rag doll" element.

07/22/87   Dream about a SPACESHIP, definitely suspicious.

07/26/87   Dream about a shower of rays.

08/02/87   Dream about my "mentor" woman.

08/12/87   Dream about an ASIAN woman, computers, and magnets.

08/25/87   Dream, animals, suspicious.

09/01/87   Dream about the land shifting near Grand Junction, Colorado.

09/04/87   Dream about Indian ancestry and a naked woman.

09/06/87   Dream, an airplane and boat ride.

09/12/87   Dream of bomb shelters and a Jewish woman.

09/18/87   Dream a doctor sticks a TUBE IN MY ARTERY.

10/06/87   Dream a SURGERY is done on my belly.

10/12/87   Dream of war games, animals, pregnancy, and babies.

10/30/87   Dream about a baby and a dog.

11/21/87   Just a "blip" about a UFO.

11/28/87   Dream, suspicious . . . flying.

12/02/87   Dream: Robots?

12/07/87	Dream: Suspicious, about an animal, a baby, nurse, and a shot.
12/11/87	Dream, suspicious medical stuff.
12/22/87	Dream: Futuristic—bands of people.
12/27/87	Dream of writing about peace and war.
12/30/87	Dream, a swimming pool and a BABY WITH ADULT FACE.

1988

01/04/88	Dream: DOCTORS, A DEVICE IS PUT IN MY EARS.
01/11/88	Dream, suspicious.
02/09/88	Time confusion, wake thinking time should be later.
03/15/88	Dream about time zones, new lenses, and doctors.
03/22/88	Dream: KNEE SURGERY I refused (later found straight razor line scar on left knee).
03/28/88	Dream about a doctor and cats.
04/17/88	Another teaching dream.
04/18/88	Another teaching dream and babies.
04/22/88	SPACE SHIP, MILITARY MEN IN BLACK AND RED, DOCTOR, and a waterway.
04/23/88	Dream of a strange flying triangle.
04/25/88	Dream about a wolf man.
04/26/88	Dream I'm riding on a weird triangle basket thing.
05/05/88	Dream: ON A SPACESHIP, babies, cats, etc.
05/24/88	Dream of an underground place.
08/29/88	Dream, a "guard cat," and a man from "Martin."
09/26/88	Dream, Africa and children.
10/05/88	Dream about a "hysterical pregnancy."
10/18/88	Dream: Reference to visitors from outer space.
12/17/88	Dream: A tree that spins.

1989

01/14/89   Dream about ADULT BABIES.
01/15/89   Dream: A very smart baby.
01/26/89   Dream: SPACESHIP TRIP, ANIMALS, WHITE DOGS, YELLOW EYES.

02/06/89   Dream about war games in Hawaii.
02/15/89   Dream: Strange door on SPACESHIP, and a dog.
02/21/89   Dream I'm KIDNAPPED BY A BIG RED-HAIRED DOG.
02/22,24/89 Dreams, suspicious.
03/04/89   Dream about me unable to have babies.
03/24/89   Dream about discs, designing, and kids.
03/26/89   Dream of traveling to another dimension.
06/09/89   Dream about a dog and a child.
06/22/89   Dream about TOM AND ME UNDERGROUND. I say in dream: "QUESTIONED BY ALIENS *AGAIN?*"

07/16/89   Dream about a secret trip.
08/03/89   Dream about the "Invisible College."
09/20/89   Dream a big bird comes through the window.
10/26/89   Dream about "cloud faces."
11/27/89   Dream, more war games.
12/13/89   Dream, suspicious.

1990

01/05/90   Dream of a special bird.
01/13/90   Dream "insert," a narrow brick enclosure and ladder.
01/14/90   Dream, suspicious.
01/20/90   Dream about ancestry stuff.
02/09/90   Dream setting in an auditorium, etc.
02/22/90   Dream about "space writing."
03/03/90   Dream: a man comes straight up out of Earth.
03/28/90   Dream: a hospital and a tall woman.

05/10/90	Dream about a vampire.
05/11/90	Dream—past lives?
05/17/90	UFO: MEN IN BLACK—cameras—major abduction; suspicious dream.

05/31/90	Dream I'm PREGNANT.
06/01/90	Dream: flying and a doctor.

06/22/90	Dream: flying and mice.

07/07/90	Hear a suspicious *whoosh* sound; dream about wooden dolls and a dizzy mountain scene.

08/02/90	Dream reference to ETs.
08/13/90	Dream of UFOs and "time-digital" numbers.
08/19/90	Dream about a UFO trip.
08/29/90	Dream—flying and I hear sounds.

09/02/90	Dream about a UFO, and a noise.

09/08/90	Dream language, words and ASIANS.
09/09/90	Dream, suspicious, of a launch and babies.
09/24/90	Dream: Another "FINALLY I SEE!" UFO dream—in another dimension.
10/17/90	Dream of time and black holes.
10/26/90	See lights—suspicious.

11/08/90	Dream about a UFO shaped like a bobbin.
11/24/90	Dream, suspicious.

12/06/90   Dream of writing from "visitor perspective."

1991

01/10/91   Sound, suspicious.

01/12/91   Major UFO DREAM: DELTA shaped and DOBER-
             MANS.

01/14/91   Dream, suspicious, babies, etc.
01/20/91   Dream about talking dolls.
03/04/91   Strange sound, a chant, and dream about my book
             and some fish (strange insert about a manuscript).

03/07/91   Dream, suspicious.
03/08/91   Possible intrusion: MAN COMES IN THROUGH MY
             WINDOW.

03/13/91   Dream someone sticks a "fork" down my throat and
             up my vagina.
03/14/91   Dream about communication, also riding in a balloon-
             like contraption.
03/15/91   Dream about psychokinetics.
03/16/91   Dream about a doctor, guards, an exam, and a "Martin"
             guy.
03/18/91   Dream about flying, movies, and a snake.
03/19/91   Dream, an elevator ride.
03/20/91   I'm flying in my room.

03/21/91   Dream of people outdoors, voices, an exam, a cat.

03/23/91	Nightmare, suspicious; sound of chimes woke me.

03/25/91	Dream "insert" about watching a baby.
03/28/91	Dream: an airplane going too fast, etc.
04/02/91	Dream: LOOKS LIKE I'M BALD, and children.
04/09/91	Dream, suspicious.
04/28/91	Dream, suspicious about genetics.
04/29/91	Sound in the night; dream about a cat, Mexicans, and a swimming pool.

05/03/91	Dream about a strange staircase.
05/08/91	Classroom dream.
05/22/91	Dream: ASIAN, guards, and a dog.
05/23/91	A dream "bleedthrough."
05/28/91	Dream about an ALIEN.
06/14/91	Dream I'm PREGNANT; animals, and a policeman.
08/10/91	UFO—A METAL CLAMP ON MY ARM by an ELF-MAN.
08/18/91	Strange light.

09/12/91	Strange voice.

09/26/91	Dream about UFO, "God's place," and genetics.
10/11/91	A DOCTOR INJECTS MY LEGS.
10/23/91	Dream: possible POSSESSION attempt.
10/29,30/91	Dream about moons (plural) and an "Earth book."
11/08/91	Dream: I am told by an ASIAN MAN about my father dying.
11/13/91	Dream of a classroom, being dizzy on stairs, and a mannequin that talks.
11/17/91	Dream about spirit helpers.
11/23/91	Vicious dogs in a dream about a past life.
11/24/91	Dream about things "tribal."
12/12/91	Awakened by phantom telephone ring.

12/27/91   Dream of SEEING PEOPLE NOT HUMAN.

1992

01/08/92   Dream: a deer, and an auditorium.
01/29/92   Dream: UFO COMES RIGHT THROUGH GLASS
            DOORS, government, etc.

01/31/92   Dream of locking glass doors—TALKED TO A DOG.
02/07/92   Dream about "dot therapy," and a dead man walks.
02/17/92   Hear a loud "slurp" noise.

03/07/92   A light show, and dream of President Bush in fatigues
            —another "revolutionary" dream.

03/14/92   Dream about DNA—genetic triplets, etc.
03/17/92   Dream about seeing a BABY UNDER WATER, EYES
            OPEN.
04/14/92   Phantom telephone ring, dream about gorillas.
            (I moved to Moab 5/1/92).

06/24/92   Dream about a white dog I don't like.
07/29/92   Dream I SEE A UFO OUTSIDE MY WINDOW.

08/04/92   Dream about being watched in showers.
08/13/92   Dream we will hear about UFOs.
08/20/92   Dream: Caves—me doing "forbidden" things.
09/02/92   Dream, futuristic, sci-fi scene.
09/28/92   Dream about TRANSPARENT SKY MACHINES.
10/14/92   Dream, very complex with suspicious elements, under-
            ground, tunnels, etc.

11/09/92   Dream I'm flying, and airplanes.

11/17/92   Dream about UFO and end of the world.

12/08/92   Dream I see a woman with cut knee.

12/13/92   Dream "insert" about an intelligent baby.

12/23/92   Dream—possible UFO.

12/27/92   Dream about "UFOs OF THE BRAIN" ("shaggy visitors" in my house).

1993

01/06/93   Dream of UFOS, small people in capes called "Pan boys," a light show, and war, missiles, campfire, rage: woke to strange sound.

01/15/93   After dream: Saw big seal on window, then a square with writing on it.

01/22/93   Dream about three babies; two die; one that lives has written on forehead CHILD OF ANGELS AND DEVILS. In dream, I wish we could have incorporated all three in one.

02/01/93   FIRST NOTATION OF SEEING A RED FLOWER: Wake to red rose symbol on ceiling after a dream about a classroom, a contraption, and a strange ride.

02/04/93   Dream: SUSPICIOUS: Auditorium, tunnels, CITY UNDER DOME, medical procedure, TUCKER (Los Angelos)—someone makes the remark, "He's not letting you know him too well."

02/20/93   Dream of a dog, a doctor, an intruder, an attic—trying to stay invisible.

02/22/93   Dream a baby says my name out loud.

02/26/93   Dream: Auditorium, corridor, airport, children.

02/28/93   Dream of a secret business within a business called Acoma.

03/04/93   Dream about a great doctor with a space-age code name.

03/06/93   Dream about a fire—one's father must be a Mormon to get credit (to buy anything); Swiss hikers—A NEW BREED; beautiful, exotic animals; wakened by phantom music, then phantom telephone ring.

03/09/93   Awakened by sound like two clicking electronic keys, and a suspicious dream.

03/12/93   Dream about a facility like a cave and ELVES that don't like it if I "advertise"—be careful!

03/19/93   ENCOUNTER: Awakened by huge TRANSPARENT BUTTERFLY, like on movie "Abyss," gold sparks— scared me!

03/24/93   Dream about a lab experiment with hornets—to see our reaction; a "genealogical chart," and a trip home on cruise control.

04/03/93   Dream about leaping into another dimension; a place with movies and toddlers.

04/05/93   Dream of a past life, a ritual, and a child.

04/13/93   Dream I am "2 selves," water, and boats.

04/25/93   Dream, suspicious, a "camp," and a psychic.

04/28/93   Dream: A priest watches in shadows a SUPER WOMAN IN THE SKY; her feet are winged, she's a "chevron design." She zooms down, I scream. Suspicious—*a virtual reality teaching dream about compassion.*

05/05/93   Dream of visiting friends on higher plane; make love to an Indian; elephants.

06/04/93   Dream a JAPANESE man comes to visit; about books. He tells me about a time when all this other man had to do was look at me, and he owned me. I like this Japanese man.

06/24/93	Dream of cards with mystical ships on them. I and a man receive these cards; a synchronicity. SYMBOLIZES A TIME WHEN WE WILL BE ASKED TO DO SOME-THING—AN EVENT WE HAVE BEEN CALLED TO PARTICIPATE IN.
06/28/93	Earlier, a smell in my bedroom; Dream a man comes to see me; two ASIAN girls; man told me to forget doing a book about Mormons.
07/02/93	Dream, suspicious: cops get called off planet.
07/05/93	Dream, suspicious.
07/12/93	Phantom telephone, night before, too.
07/17/93	A woman's voice wakes me: she says, "UP!" Dream about a photo, a display, and a secret aspect of job . . . and mud.
07/18/93	Dream about a new society: a RITUALISTIC BIRTH SELECTION PROCESS. In dream, I'm beginning to see this would work better. Also, a "wild man," and a lion.
08/01/93	Suspicious insert, forbidden stuff, underground.
08/09/93	Dream of SEEING A FLOOD ON EARTH FROM ABOVE.
08/10/93	Dream, suspicious—a smart baby, etc.
08/11/93	I hear a high keening female voice—stops when I open my eyes. Dream about a dog.
08/17/93	Dream about a small theater: We all know each other.
09/09/93	Dream about a two-toned dog I need to make friends with.
09/10/93	Dream I am instructed to erect a kind of triangular configuration.
09/19/93	Woke to strange sound.
10/11/93	Dream about a "hermit code" and smart toddlers.

10/13,14/93 Dreams about symbols, etc.

10/15/93   Dream about "automatic writing."

10/16/93   Dream about symbols, videos, diagrams, a channel—ETs.

10/18/93   Dream about a movie screen—correlates to brain; and a bridge.

10/19/93   Dream, suspicious.

10/21/93   Dream about a strange school with doors at ceiling level.

11/05/93   Dream of drawing letters, a design like Anasazi petroglyphs.

11/09/93   Dream: "ZEDAPETH" (ancient imagery; triumphing over enslavement—"restore our king . . . " etc; highly prophetic).

11/13/93   Dream: Symbols, graphs, geometric shapes.

11/15/93   Dream: Symbols, graphs, and a pyramid.

11/17/93   LOS ANGELOS VISITATION (dream of cloven-hooved beings, the "life house," Mormons, etc.)

11/19/93   Dream about a dog, a babysitter, a bride, water, and designs.

11/22/93   Dream about a dog and a cat; about moving to the country, and see drawing of a veil/curtain.

11/24/93   Dream about a man in "fiber-optics," and a chart.

11/25/93   Dream of number-letter junctures, and water.

11/26/93   Dream about a smart baby.

11/30/93   Dream about charts and designs.

12/01/93   Dream with a figure, and symbols.

12/04/93   I see a strange "lamp" on the ceiling.

12/07/93   Phantom telephone ring wakes me up; dream about a woman singing to the Lord: I am never to talk about this.

12/09/93   Woke to sound like "Furies" might make, and a crash . . . important at end—a representation of the globe, a path in mountains . . . earthquake opens up pathways.

12/15/93 Dream of a university: a man tells me I will be here another year; I ask him if I'm strong enough, he says yes. He can see it in my drawings.

12/21/93 Dream reference to making love to a lion.

1994

01/17/94 Dream: Otherworldly, vague.

01/20/94 Sound woke me. Yesterday phantom phone ring, today a loud voice said, "SIR!"; then heard like 100 voices at once. Dream: Weird realities.

01/23/94 Dream: Dolls that mechanically act out moral lesson; don't like them, but like the talking dolls.

01/28/94 Dream: Strange reality.

01/30/94 Woke to noise at window or heat vent. Dream: Suspicious; interference, codes, etc.

02/01/94 See a mandala design on window, like a calendar.

02/02/94 Dream: DNA, genetics, a heart problem.

02/09/94 Dream: A ride in an "airplane," and a "lesson" scene.

02/11/94 Dream: A strange reality.

03/01/94 Dream: About stepping into a screen; a very tall woman who looks like a man; a channeler, a video on government propaganda.

03/06/94 Dream: Suspicious, babies, telepathy, a CAT WOMAN.

03/09/94 Lights, noises.
Dream: Suspicious—doors and a swimming pool.

03/12/94 Dream: About a being from another dimension in the attic; about carrying out a secret plan.

03/15/94	Dream: Virtual reality, a photo, soldiers; sense I was "enlisted"; water, a "medical play," and X-rays.
03/26/94	Dream I suddenly "step" into another reality; a woman in dark glasses and a dog-sized lamb.
04/14/94	Loud noise in inner ears wakes me. Dream: A JAPANESE man and "sinister cars."

04/17/94	Dream: A fire, a JAPANESE man, a format, strange.
04/23/94	Dream about a symbol.
04/29/94	Dream: Nightmare about Mormons "casting out a devil." Accusations.
05/03/94	Dream: I receive information; eagle feathers.
05/11/94	Heard a loud sound like the tail of a whale swishing. Dream: A form transforms to whale. Also, the FACE OF A CHILD TRANSFORMS INTO AN ET.

05/15/94	Dream: A dog staring at glass doors, suspicious, insignia, feelings of tremendous love, a baby.
05/19/94	Strange noise before I go to sleep, "popping sounds" all over house: FIRST TIME I WOKE TO SEE A LIGHT DISPLAY IN MY ROOM. This appeared to be a matrix that looked liquidy—like a veil. Dream: A message on poster.

05/20/94	Dream: A doctor, a woman, a child, and sex.
05/23/94	Dream about a classroom of "volunteers."
05/27/94	Woke to shrill telephone sound. Dream: A dream within a dream; a "staged scene."

06/03/94	Light matrix. Dream: ASIANS, intrusion, cats, attic.

06/07/94	Dream: A living plant with eyeballs, and an instruction.

06/08/94   Light display, fish-scale pattern.

06/10/94   Dream: Swimming pool, snake, priest.
06/11/94   BED VIBRATING, and heard a HUMMING SOUND.
                    Dream: Being interviewed . . . at a hospital.

06/12/94   Saw a "scarf" of light on ceiling.
                    Dream: About INTRUDERS.

06/13/94   Dream: A small man, first like a mouse. Deception.
                    He calls me an "AM-brat."
06/15/94   Woke to loud sound around my head.

06/16/94   Bird nature of a visitor—FLIES AT ME.

06/22/94   More sounds.

06/23/94   Light display, ornate Victorian pattern. A noise like a
                    swishing broom. Dream: About a "need to develop
                    consciousness."

06/26/94   Saw a "curtain" of light. Voice as if down a tunnel says
                    at end of dream, "ONE YEAR . . . "
  Dream: DEFINITELY UFO DREAM; in facility like park-
                    ing garage, many levels; "cluster beings" in blue coveralls,
                    tunnels, trying to leave; SEE MOTHER SHIP in sky; famil-
                    iar entity is giving me a hard time. Voice wakes me up . . .
                    (This event relates to abduction scenario of 4/19/96.)

06/28/94   Dream: Desert scene, dirt/clay hands in a hollow in
                    Earth, fake artifacts—bait! A trap.

06/29/94   Matrix light, many rows of circles, also saw blue-green design in my bedroom.

07/04/94   Dream: "LAMB-MAN" dream (ref. Jacob/Esau— Dr. Turner).

07/07/94   Saw light display, red/maroon. Dream: A mystery about blood shining through.

07/10/94   KM and I in an ABDUCTION SCENARIO/DARK.

07/11/94   Strange feeling in right ear.
Dream: Something about babies that grow up with computers.

07/12/94   Hear a door shutting directly over my head; see a "frilly curtain" light display.
Dream: A dog is burrowing under my covers.

07/13/94   An old man's decrepit VOICE says, as I am waking up, "Maybe we are concentrating on details too much . . . "
Dream: Meeting hall; video presentation.

07/17/94   Saw "full" curtain light display. Dream followed by this entry in journal: a person in contact with other side or a representative for aliens—is natural, common, not unusual.

07/26/94   Very suspicious, possible intrusion; woke with left ear stinging and bright red. Dream: "COUSIN BEINGS" . . . chanting, small dogs, a cat, glowing eyes (a significant dream I typed up in full).

07/29/94   Dream: Planetarium; navigation facility; HUGE DOME, watery above; huge ships—as if electrical blueprint.

07/31/94   Dream: See a book, list of chapters, one PARALYSIS, about abduction experiences (but I've never felt paralyzed).

08/01/94   Dream: Suspicious—I'm in bed with JW; he has a monitor on his ear; near glass enclosure; we are being observed; a military man appears. I tell him, "I'm having experiences." He says, "WE'RE ALL GOING TO REMEMBER SOON . . . " Then a "beauty parlor" transforms into an airfield.

08/02/94   Light display like long-toothed comb.

08/03/94   Light display, symmetrical dots. Heard a "honk" sound before I went to bed.
Dream: GOING UP SOME STAIRS ON MY HANDS AND KNEES TO A MEETING TO SEE VIDEOS.

08/05/94   Light display of mesh curtain.
Dream: A different realm, saw "thugs," a "step over" a dog on a chain. Fear.

08/06/94   Light display of Victorian curtain again.
Dream: Precognitive about a friend.

08/07/94   Dream: Panorama, movie, theater, people I know, other realms.

08/10/94   Suspicious: Woke with arm very sore.
Dream: Repeat about an ancestor, woman mentor.

08/13/94   Heard door slam twice (ethereal). Later like a bong sound outside.
Dream: I go out and see ground squirrels. A classroom. KM "steps over" to another realm.

08/15/94   Ethereal phone ring.
Dream: Thinking about waking up and telling Mom and Michael about what happened to me on UFO;
sex in a "tight" dorm area.

08/16/94   Dream: I go out to kitchen to find back door unlocked; see a man and two small children.

08/18/94   BEGINNING OF TINGLING FEELINGS ON BODY.

Dream: Suspect I went somewhere. Some men I know DISGUISED AS TALL SKINNY BEINGS WHO HAVE SEX WITH ME AND TWO OTHER WOMEN; later I'm hanging onto a SILVER "CAMPER" that could sink into water.

08/22/94   Gentle tingling over my body, beginning at toes.

08/23/94   Dream: A "LEPRECHAUN," clouds, yellow/brown mist . . . someone angry at what they have done to the air.

08/26/94   Felt tingly vibrations moving up my body again; a light display as if glowing molecules.

Dream: Children, KM, classroom.

08/28/94   Awoke to a sound like an alpine horn.

Lights: first a bluish circle on ceiling. Full "curtain" of golden light like frozen ice

Physical: After dream, deep creases/indentations in left arm.
Dream: In something like a restaurant lounge; cops, stealth; a man comes down through a "shaft" over the bar area. We think he must be dangerous, then see it's Someone we know and not odd for him to enter this way; we go upstairs via a kind of tunnel rooted out of a tree trunk (tree house), very strange; I'm working on a poster, large words, a message I'm trying to put on a computer; a small dog is bothering me, nipping at me— Bites me!

08/29/94   Light out, 2:12 A.M. At 2:24 A.M., rapid pounding just
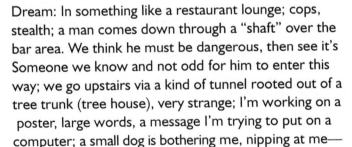
outside the window. So how do I prepare? Earlier, went outside to look at stars, heard a "clicking" sound, like two bamboo sticks, like a recent noise. Woke later

to see room bathed in pale green light, but no other weirdness.

Dream: Telling someone about sleepwalkers . . . lots of activity, lessons, etc.

08/30/94

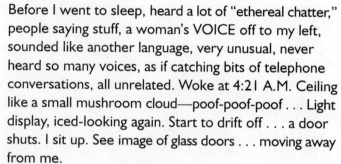

Before I went to sleep, heard a lot of "ethereal chatter," people saying stuff, a woman's VOICE off to my left, sounded like another language, very unusual, never heard so many voices, as if catching bits of telephone conversations, all unrelated. Woke at 4:21 A.M. Ceiling like a small mushroom cloud—poof-poof-poof . . . Light display, iced-looking again. Start to drift off . . . a door shuts. I sit up. See image of glass doors . . . moving away from me.

Dream: Was in a huge group of people, outdoors, grass, trees . . . gnarled true trunks here and there . . . but sky darker, or it's inside awfully large place (see no walls).

A ceremony. Singing, joyful celebration. I go down to a basement room to get my violin. Hear noise at bath-room window. INTRUDERS TRYING TO GET IN. Teenaged boys. They come in, hassle me. I get away. Return to celebration. We are "singing up the dawn." (Very long dream.) An earlier impression . . . in car with Mom and a couple of others—cousins, brothers? Tight squeeze.

08/31/94

Before I went to sleep, heard a male voice say, "HOLD STILL!"

Dream: A very high rock to climb, up on the spine.

09/01/94

Before going to sleep, a noise and tinglings. Tried talk-ing to "them." Felt a presence definitely. Asked why they slink around in darkness. Very loud noise wakes me up at 4:46 A.M. Like electronic plunger. See the "light" curtain, about 1/3 of archway.

Dream: Aspect of this dream like in dream of 8/31/94, a "touch-feely" man I don't like.

09/03/94

Saw curtain of light last night, the "frozen ice" pattern, but didn't get dream.

09/04/94

Woke at 3:20 A.M., was having a "contact" dream. At the end, not the usual light, but a bouquet of dark maroon flowers. Seems as I was dreaming, AWARE OF A BEING ON THE CEILING, A BIG SHADOWY BEING . . . kept waking up to see this and confirm. Lots of noises before I went to bed. Popping sound on video recorder, and on paintings above, and on south wall, so loud, jarred me out of meditation.
Dream: Earlier impression of young Indian-Asians. Later a flower, petals very pale lavender or violet, with bright red center.

09/05/95:

(A real telephone call woke me.)
Dream: I was in living room, napping. Radio on. Thinking I should send note to Karla Turner telling her about new electronic happenings. A man and child come in. A delivery. A box partially open. See white tissue poking out. Man, tall, in coveralls, whitish-blond hair, seems familiar, and a little girl. I say, "Okay, just leave it there" (on desk). Thinking, can't be for me, a mistake, but can't quite wake up to go check, so I can send box back with them. Just know it's for someone else, a different house, can almost see different name. Man leaves, but child stays. She's just messing around. Still time for me to check the box, send it with her, but I can't seem to wake up (thinking man must be out in car or truck, waiting for the child). Then I hear childish foot patterings on tile floor. I wonder if it's not the little girl . . . but "VISITORS." Then something begins to turn me, spinning me very fast, like I'm on the carpet and I'm being spun low to floor. I'm realizing something very weird is happening, and beginning to feel sensuous feelings . . . when the phone rings, waking me up.

09/06/94

Barely falling asleep, still awake, hallucinate a cat jumping on me, then to floor, big fluffy orange cat. Later I

09/08/94

09/09/94

09/10/94

09/11/94

am "moved" to look up—to see light curtain from ceiling to floor. A "phantom" phone woke me. This morning woke to see a sunflower-like spot on ceiling, outer hot-pink color, inner, bluish-gray.

Woke about 5:45 A.M., light show, beautiful swirling pattern all over, like hair swirls.

Dream: 6:40 A.M., vague . . . see a manual, outline drawing of a man or man and woman embracing, re-clined, and then text, all very high tech, something to do with being an individual.

Later, some kind of instruction, or "initiation."

Dream: Long, vivid about being out of body. First I'm with two others, a woman and a man. (Scott?) Woman goes somewhere. Man and I go stand in a line to regis-ter on something for "dead pay." Encounter live people. We can "zoom" them, and make them feel weird or Scared. But some can see you, so best not to play games. I realize in dream this is something I learned about in ASTRAL BODY.

Woke with right wrist bone sore, 3:20 A.M. Light show, like a huge membrane at foot of bed, swelling out from bedframe. I stared at it until it faded.

Dream: Karla Turner comes to visit, etc. Animals in dream—big dog? Yes, a dog comes into the room. I'm not afraid, a dog I'm familiar with, but I'm uneasy going to sleep with him in the room. I say, "Shoo!" wave my hand. He curls up on floor, but how long will he stay there? Would scare me if he bothered me after I went to sleep. Seems like another animal, too, like out on patio porch? Another part—being shown in big city, how they have built under grassy knolls, throughout condo village, rooms where children are placed when parents are gone. This is terrible! I tell them. I go to this place to watch TV, movies; sit on folding chairs in room with others.

Light show, regular at doorway. Also glass doors, black doors that seemed gateways that could pull me—optical illusion of doors zooming away. No clear dream.

09/12/94   Lay down 2:22 A.M. At 2:43, woke, looked up, saw a multitude of black dots above me and all around, felt like something woke me to see, a noise, heard bits of words before I dozed off. Also, saw this flower on the ceiling—bluish-gray with cherry-red center.
Dream: A cat and something about UFOs, statistics; see how people just automatically shut off.

09/13/94 Light, golden, upper 1/4 of archway, with band on bottom. Woke to loud telephone ring in ear. Dreaming, seems going over and over a story line or scene; trying to get in right words; about a woman who doesn't die . . . etc.

09/15/94 Sound like metal doors slamming three times, like down a tunnel underground, woke me at 4:57 A.M. (forgot to look for light.)
Dream: I went to auditorium . . . mistress of ceremonies asks for volunteers to talk about stuff happening lately in terms of ghosts, messengers, contacts, etc. Later when I return to my "apartment," there are people there painting. Landlady says they're redoing my apartment. All my stuff is gone. I'm very upset; WOMAN IS COLD, STARES AT ME. SAYS IT'S HER RIGHT TO DO THIS. I woke up later at 9:50 A.M. to a blast of horn sound.

09/16/94   Light fixture in dressing room gives off pale green light. Longest "body" sensational experience (tinglings) yet; turned off light at 2:41 A.M., went on until 4:16 A.M. Couple of minutes later, and this happens frequently; feels as if my whole body drops a half inch; I feel a shift, like the pillow drops suddenly. Then starts the tingling and rippling, outside over surface of body, especially feet and up legs; also on head, brushing across lips, and inside organs, muscles rippling, waving, air moving around me. When the tingling started, subtle flashes of light behind my closed eyes; other "movements." Then began the feeling like I am very light, SO LIGHT MY BODY IS SPREADING OUT AND I FEEL LIKE A PART OF ME

IS GONE SOMEWHERE ELSE; want to go to sleep so I can dream about what's going on, but can't. Keep opening my eyes to see if I can see anything strange. All this goes on and on and on, until finally I need to go to the bathroom. The clock says 4:16 A.M. Can't believe I went that long (from 2:41 to 4:16). But I did not go anywhere! Finally went to sleep. Woke at 10:50. Dream: Insignificant dream, but impression of a small boy, a toddler, watching, out in the yard.

09/17/94
Woke 7:19 A.M., by a sound like three electronic broom sweeps. Then woke later in morning by loud ethereal telephone ring.
Dream: About me and a crippled man; he's good looking; we talk about related stuff. Later dreamt about getting involved with other UFO researchers . . . a white-haired man who helps me with the "God-angle."

09/18/94
Awoke shortly after going to sleep to very loud, high, shrill telephone ring (phantom). A light like a staff beside my bed. Dreams, vague.

09/19/94
Woke several times; light shows, sounds.

09/21/94
2:03 A.M. Woke by loud shrill ring, looked up, in archway, saw like a wire matrix, black on gold, or like a kind of fence, but alive, even saw it move closer, but not past archway. It shimmered. Happened again at 3:45 A.M. (without sound); awakened to see another visual display at 5:46 A.M.
Nap dream: Tin door banging woke me up. Dream about sharing bedroom space with a kind of doctor's office; children making noise, bothering me. Look out window, see a van pull up. Then look at sky, see jet contrail . . . SUDDENLY A RED LIGHT BREAKS AWAY FROM CONTRAIL—A UFO! I think it snaps out too, but then I see a big cloud shaped like bear or dog,

galloping around the sky; wonder how many clouds camouflaging. Another part—outside this small apartment; coming home; just to left of walk is a park; some children are going into a tree house with toys or real animals. Seems like some small animal says something to me, like a bird—SOMETHING ABOUT THEIR RIGHT TO BE HERE. Not my park, I agree, trying to be fair.

09/24/94 Some bodily sensations; different; not so much tinglings as feeling something was jerking my head—once; strong vibrations on inner part of lower leg; and some strange subtle sounds, voices, but no light show.

Dream: Mention of a military man coming to the door.

09/25/94 (Same night we heard "cosmic boom" in Moab.) Last night and tonight, heard what sounds like a kind of drop of water, gulp of water, splat, like a big drop into pail of water. Heard it three times, and loud. Busy night! Clicking sounds right next to my bed. I sat up, said, "What are you *doing*?" Finally noises settled down and so did I.

Dream: Woke earlier to see the light show like bumpy golden ice over archway. Waking up, hearing "dream voice" sort of echoey, tinny, like I'm fading out of actual scene. Also a question about "selling one's birth right."

09/27/94 4:15 A.M. No golden light, but looks like the next room is moving, as if I'm watching out of a train window. Felt last night AS IF SOMETHING PATS BEDCLOTHES AROUND ME.

Dream: Cat, cops, eavesdropping.

09/28/94 4:05 A.M. Before going to sleep, a musical "twang" in left ear; then a quick run over piano keyboard. Clear! Body sensations very strong again; FEELING LIKE I COULD BE DISASSEMBLED, TRANSPORTED AWAY.

Dream: A dog in neighborhood (not here); looks scary; I'm out in yard; get inside just before dog reaches screen door; I sense he is a desperate dog; feel pity, but still afraid. A coppery-colored, odd-looking dog. Later something about a dying child; thinking there is something we can do to save this child. Also . . . later . . . maybe sex with a man?

09/29/94

Woke in night to see great light show, filled dressing room with sort of "rippling" light, more so than "frozen light" display. Don't know what woke me, maybe thunder, but happy to see light!

10/01/94

Dream: A drama around a baby, going to apartment where live the parents or caretakers. Vague . . . but feeling baby is being hidden . . . secret . . . born illegally?

10/03/94

Dream: THE WHOLE SKY IS FILLED WITH UFOs . . . all "saucer" kind. And I saw bottoms, all this stuff very clearly. All silver—daytime—I grabbed my camera and started snapping . . .

10/04/94

Loud bang in right ear before I went to sleep.

10/05/94

Heard "popping" sounds while writing earlier. Very noisy night, lots of "shiftings" in bed. Bed felt "higher—" FELT AS IF SOMETHING "SNUGGLING" COVERS NEAR MY HEAD. Aroused soon after to sit up. Saw light show, with a sound like a brass voice.
Dream: Hospital-like setting.

10/06/94

Dream (vague): Like a cave situation—like I know ancient people live down there. There are stories . . . and when I concentrate in my mind I can see more detail, learn more about these people. I am seeing details of what I was doing, where I was . . . but damned if I can get it—as if what I'm seeing is in a foreign language.

10/07/94 While changing clothes for bed, saw a quick flash of light. POSSIBLE MISSING TIME episode. For more than an hour, I lay here feeling the vibrations and ting-lings. First vibrations in bed. Then extending all over body, as if coming up through mattress. So strange. Think I'm awake, but at one point I was half-dreaming —like Katharina Wilson was in the bedroom and we were talking about this stuff. She told me she trusted her feelings more than anything else. Various subtle noises in bedroom throughout. Head feels very "large" (when I finally woke). In journal I wrote: Went to bed at 3:08 A.M. Then took notes at 5:28—writing that another 1–1/2 hours "flew by." Later realized this was 2–1/2 hours, not 1–1/2. (Also: this session may have begun around 8–9 P.M. when suddenly I had pain in mid-back for no reason. See a letter to Karla about this and dream of 10/8/95.)

10/08/94 3:14 A.M. Tapping on window, fast and rhythmic. More sensations. Also a noise in my left ear. And a noise like buzzing bees for a long time.
Dream: Flying with an angel, military scenario and a message (typed up in full, sent to Dr. Karla Turner).

10/10/94 Popping noises in house earlier. 3:14 A.M., turned on light. Because noises and vibrations started. Talked to "them." A noise like something clattering down a drain pipe. Faint "ticking" noises in left ear. Window noises. Definite vibrations on feet. Something is being applied . . . a wand going over. A noise in bathroom just now. I'm not playing games. Just wanting to be fully aware, engaged. This incident and dream also in a letter to Turner.

10/13/94 No weird stuff—except I woke up feeling beat up, and found a significant red mark on my left thigh, like from a bad scrape, but no skin broken, blood under skin. Took photos. Nothing damaged on bedclothes.
Dream: A photo session . . . I see a map that shows a building with two entrances . . . set like on edge of water

in San Francisco? Special purpose building. Another scene with babies . . . I adore them.

10/14/94 Subtle vibrations, as before, and a SUDDEN FEELING MY WHOLE BODY LIFTS . . . or changes—noises. Awoke at 5:17 A.M. Window curtain looks very black, looks odd. Snap on lamp.

10/15/94 Window curtain—looks extremely bright. Earlier in living room, flashes of light. In computer room, lights flickered.
Dream: In a dream I'm doing something with color blue "bright midnight blue."

10/19/94 3:41 A.M. Shrill alarm/bell jars me awake (was not completely asleep). Felt vibrations, earlier, seconds after I lay down head, and felt a shift, like bed sinks an inch or two (common).

10/20/94 2:55 A.M. Heard very deep, gravelly, strange, metallic voice say: "HERE, KITTY, KITTY . . . " (Ref. in book narrative); then bed began to vibrate under where I sit. (What was said, maybe a taunt for something I wrote that day to Karla Turner about us being their pets.) Waited for vibrations to settle down, then followed all manner of noises and tinglings, etc. Definitely felt a presence. Determined to go to sleep, because nothing of value comes when I stay awake.
Dream: ALIENS. Comparing body types. Then a scenario in a cave. Then . . . about ALIEN INVASION . . . see three men walking on planet . . . exploring another world, desert-like.

10/21,22/94 Noises, scratchy, etc. Lots of vibrations, no incidents, only dream fragments.

10/24/94 "Heard" a spark!

10/25/94 Earlier, woke, when I blinked, could see this red round light projected on ceiling.

10/26/94 Noises and vibrations/tinglings, strong. At one point, heard a kind of explosion inside my head. Popping noises occurring in various parts of room, sometimes near my head. Went on from 1:29 to 3:17, then got up to go to bathroom.

10/27/94 Dream: I'm in another mode of time, etc., but seems the same, except how people act. Saw a row of weapons, each for an animal, and one for a human. (Sketched it.)

10/28/94 Dream: A cop, dogs, a retarded girl, a tall, bald man, a rose bush as large as a tree, something in the sky . . .

10/30/94   Before I fell asleep, a loud noise like someone in the room. I said out loud, "That was pretty blatant!" Heard a splat of water, very real sounding.

Dream: A "smart-baby" dream. In a crowded house . . . a baby, he's very intelligent and speaks, but a BABY WITH AN OLD MAN'S FACE, distinct . . . confusion . . . think he's son of a friend. He speaks, tells me he's got a voracious sexual appetite. He gets out of high-chair . . . stretches as tall as a teenager, like a proud teenage boy, dressed like ancient Mayan, loin cloth, dark skin, long black hair. Seems like cops, authorities, someone after this boy. Going to ask questions . . . I won't tell about seeing the boy in baby form. Impression of a UFO nearby . . . image of baby being tucked in blankets inside a small vehicle, parked. Image of activity in this kitchen, living room, a mess, crowded. Impression this child knows me; addresses me; we talk, but something is wrong . . . shouldn't be talking . . . And not baby I expected.

11/02/94 "ABDUCTION DREAM/ENCOUNTER." Major tinglings, especially on feet/legs, all over, subtle sounds, shifting, feel presence, bed vibrating, going on about an hour or so until I get up . . . can still feel it, sitting up, too, like I'm in middle of process . . . at onset, a "ting" in left ear, Later familiar "chitty" sounds in ear. ABDUCTION DREAM—refer to narrative (flying down hall, going through door, an injection, an entity).

11/07/94

2:47 A.M. Awoke to a stern hard pounding . . . loud dream sound, but don't know why, dream insignificant.

11/08/94

Phantom telephone wakes me at 3:47 A.M.
Dream: I signed up for something; lot of people here; then I am questioned; told I don't qualify, or accused of being a spy; I remove my name; I resign; but I'm so fond of some of these people and they of me; this seems like in a hospital.

11/10/94

Sound like a wind of a thousand voices and vibrations. A loud rushing sound, noise all over; woke me earlier; like I was coming back into body. Not like anything before; almost like a full body sudden merge, but too confused to write it down then. More on vibrations, etc.: Earlier . . . again tinglings beginning in feet immediately after a feeling of a shift or change in body; a signal; lay down about 2:45 A.M, shift at 3:00.
Dream: Vague . . . seeing how we live on this "board," like gameboard or map . . . or just seeing this "above view." Some precautions being taken in houses, cars, around, some sort of danger.
Nap: Lay down to rest at 11:05 A.M., ears plugged, painful, trying to relax; feel tinglings in feet/legs; each time ear pops (about three times) immediately after, feel real jittery; then calm again; at one point a "zing" in left ear; then jitters. Tinglings feel very "broad," not so specific, like something pressing down lightly on legs; gentle pressure/massage.

11/11/94

Tinglings; 4:34 A.M., noise wakes me up.
Dream: Someone writes a letter asking who started the invasion/conspiracy rumors? "We are a group who is

enjoying rich contact," we answer, or something like that.

11/12/94 Nine minutes after I lay down, heard/felt like a "twang" at right side of my chest; and tinglings in feet.

11/14/94 Lay down to sleep 2:08 A.M. At 3:22 get up to pee; all this time tinglings, noises, popping; deep male voice says, "Boyd!" A ting on my lamp; thinking about my lost pen, then sound of a pen top clicking on pen base, right near my face, and some water slurps. VIVID UFO DREAM (typed up). (A UFO LIKE SEVERAL TRAIN CARS, ENFOLDING OUT OF SKY.)

11/17/94 Tinglings/phantom noises; suspicious dream

11/18/94 Vibrations/noises; bright pink light. Dream . . . tunnels, signs and codes.

11/19/94 Tonight instead of a click, heard a "ting," and felt an electrical impulse sweep over me.

11/20/94 Buzzes around left ear; the right part of head, like a wasp or electrical wand or laser, very close, jerked my head; and seeing bits of light with eyes closed; got up at 3:45 A.M. and rewrote letter to Sprinkle.

11/22/94
11/23/94

Dream: About Kewpie dolls, and a new super highway. 1) tinglings over feet/legs; 2) buzzing on left ear; 3) buzzing of upper right forehead; 4) a knock on left knee, some mild pain in knee; 5) tingling, vibrations applied to right eyelid; 6) much more tingling around head; 7) tingling applied to hands; 8) all over body; 9) noises in room and several ethereal "voiced" noises (not coherent); 10) just now yawned—left jaw out! Did I just do it? Or discover it? 11) Above activity continued for hours; not sure how long, just kept going for sleep, while allowing . . .

Dream: Some guys come to my house; I'm walking be hind this one guy; see that he is wired; long wire dangling out from under his hair in back; this explains earlier behavior; what they're up to; they are fixing up a system at my house; where everything gets watered at certain times; big yard—another house . . . But almost seems the watering (spray) happens inside also. Also feels like these guys are spying on me.

11/25/94

Sound of bees buzzing continuously; also woke up with hair matted down on right side after only 1–1/2 to 2 hours sleep; strong tinglings before I fell asleep.

Dream: SOMETHING COMES DOWN ON ME, BODY LENGTH. Somehow I know this is an ANGEL. I am told to go with it, something—to "hold on," so now I feel/see arms. WE RISE TOGETHER, ME ON BOTTOM, FLAT. Out on countryscape. I'm flying! By myself! I say, "Oh, this is my true nature, what is most natural, what I know best . . . " So now he's connected to me again; I am to allow something . . . Oohh! Feels like my teeth are out! He tells me not to be embarrassed; this is a total kind of exposure thing. At some point, asks me what kind of work I do. I say

"I do hair." Then I think—he can't know me if he doesn't know I write. I'm taken home; repeat process going down. Something happens to make me realize he's like a "NOVICE ANGEL IN TRAINING" around here and he's taken many Moabites up. But it's serious that I SHOULD KEEP SECRET. Something SUSPICIOUS about this angel. On other hand, I'm very familiar with what happened; but like it's new too; a new phase; giving me power I need; or showing me how to operate in that realm; there was some fear, but I trusted. Impression is a naked, pink-faced man, young. BUT FEELING OF BEING TRICKED; find out after I return something I was told not true, or I misunderstood. Next scene—I catch someone in act of using my car for a place to sleep! A young boy, about 8-9, has sleeping bag, clothes, toys, etc. in backseat of my car. His mother drives up. I exclaim What are you doing? She remarks something like I'm a bitch. I'll never be able to prove this. Why was he using my car as a place to sleep? Seems very strange, makes no sense, but I FEEL VERY INTRUDED UPON. Something trying to get us to leave so something else can "take our places?"

11/26/94 to early December
UFO conference in Mesquite.
Tinglings diminished much on trip, a few minor noises, some UFO imagery in dreams.

12/08/94   Think I was dreaming about being in alternate reality . . . with beings. A woman I know is going to fly her motorcycle up to a "station" (impression of a UFO mother ship), but in dream it's natural, nothing weird about it.

12/11/94   Dream: 5:38 A.M. We are inside this place where there are displays—horse breaks out! Need to help them find it, dangerous "outside" for horses. A meeting, a class, a baby. Saw in dream a UFO or what I thought was—off in the distance, flying slowly, sort of hat-shaped (silver/white), want to get binoculars, or get a photo.

12/12/94	Last night, widespread tinglings/vibrations, rippling effect, all over body; and again tonight, and I was "zinged" as if a laser beam went straight through me. Felt and heard it, through solar plexus.
12/13/94	Dream that includes men with MOTTLED FACES, LIKE LIZARD SKIN, SPLOTCHED—they ride motorcycles —wind damage. A big conference, escalators, etc.
12/16/94	At first of dream, something to do with UFOs . . . a dark, night sky, planetary scene—rockets/ships?
12/17/94	Dream with imagery, hoses, spraying a kind of statue; machines, service center; I hear a man speak, famous man, his words like a chant in my head, like I'm memorizing a certain stanza because it relates to my book. Another image—open a floor board—people live below; see a little half-black girl down there looking up.
12/19/94	A lot of tingling/vibrations last night; all over body, and the other "subtle shifts," etc. And some "thickness," for quite a while.
12/20/94	Dreams, only fragments . . . A dog on a mat; like adjusting it to sit this way or that; it lays with head down, resting, watching; also reminds me of a lizard, but think it's a dog, like a shepherd dog or lab mix, golden in color.
12/21/94	Great amount of tinglings, vibrations, all over; and there was a rhythmic tapping sound inside my head; musical, something beating, staccato; first thought I was hearing my pulse beat erratically and fast, but checked it out —not. Weird. Figured I was getting a "treatment." Heard something too, a phrase familiar, but forgot it. Dream: Tail end . . . seeing a tall, brown-haired man with beautiful blue eyes.
12/22/94	Heard a man say distinctly: "DON'T JUST SHORT SHOP." Bed vibration. Tingling sweeps across shoulders, flashes over hip/leg. Couple of noises in room; clicking. Dream: On a trip, conference with Mom and friends? A parking lot. Nap in morning: More tinglings, flashing

and HEARD TONES in pillow (right ear), low and high of an octave, repeating, and a kind of rumble in left ear.

12/23/94 Before I went to sleep, drifted off . . . I was "hugging" a man in the living room (but not really), like we were merging, like electrical and sensual. Awoke at 4:48 A.M. by sound like a spray of crystals.

12/25/94 Lots of dreams; gone but an impression remains of seeing like a "concept" illustrated; an image like how energy can shift from one dimension to another, as in "life" to "death." Typed this up, complete with "concept" drawings.

12/27/94 Heard a bee buzzing sound in living room earlier; as I turned over, saw an oval shaped light about size of pillow fly over my head; pulled lamp chain and light bulb flicked out. Flashes of "chills" and subtle noises.
 Dream: Felt like I was being rolled off bed! Woke myself up; was dreaming about a man; unknown space/place . . . or a dorm? Beds close together.

12/28/94 Bed vibrations, major tinglings, like "tings" all over, head, etc. Vibrations continuing for quite a while; earlier asked to be shown clearly what's going on.

12/29/94 Dream imagery; like a monastery; desert terrain; buying day-old food at Salvation Army; At one point saw like a computer print-out, top of page in dot pattern: DEVIL. Also see airplanes on field.

12/31/94 No dream memory, but lots of weird thoughts, vibrations, chills that "spray" as if out from center of me and "soft explosions" in head.

1995

01/02/95   Wakened by shrill "telephone" ring; image of Jonah. Ship scoots; he's treading air; then drops down through glass onto top of the whale.

01/03/95   3:55 A.M. Heard a distinct noise, saw a faint "orange" glow over in corner, above dressing table. Scanty dream.

01/04/95   Noises, orange ball of light; buzz in left ear.

01/05/95   Dream with an ASIAN man; a conference; a scientific symposium; dropping keys out window in high rise, etc.

01/06/95   Woke by a shrill "telephone" ring; thinking in dream about symbol of key dropping in last night's dream; about dropping key information.

01/07/95   Dream: Watching this baby go all over this kind of matrix model of life (?); climbing around on it; very weird; like the adult is switching to the baby model and watching; or the baby is shifting away from overly serious adult.

01/08/95   Telephone sound and word "Smead?" Smeed? Woke me up. Dream fragments.

01/09/95   Dreaming about how the sooner you eat meat after it is killed, the more life force you absorb; most meats we eat are very dead. RECEIVING lots of info about end-times; where to go; what to do; looks like sea—water—better than land; talking to Mom, showing her; a lot of governmental . . . seems an indication to move to Grand Junction . . .

01/10/95   Dream: ASIAN people; babies; toddlers; recording something on big screen TV; I'm worried about Asians bomb-
ing us; this being a trick; I call home; Mom says Dad,
brother there; they will pick me up at appointed time;
so I need to just relax, watch babies. Also dogs, cats.
And seems contact with higher beings, or holy men.

01/14/95

Lately every night about 10 minutes after I turn out
light, I hear a knock on a wall in dressing room. Too
coincidental to ignore.
Dream: A whole drama that included Sue, Keith . . .
about whales, history, prophesy . . . and the man I am going to meet . . . and the book I'm writing . . . children . . .
babies.

01/16/95

Laying down, felt strong tone/vibration in left ear;
something swept over my body; actually moving me;
swept up my body, AS IF TAKING HOLD OF ME, AL-
MOST LIFTING ME OFF THE BED.
Dream: Vivid dream . . . foxes, bobcat with yellow eyes,
accident on a mountain, etc.

01/26/95

3:49 A.M. Dreaming . . . noise like someone pounding
outside, woke me.

01/27/95

Turned out light at 2:30 A.M. Soon vibrations in feet. A
"soft light" explosion in head. Tinglings and vibrations
continue; a "spray" of tinglings, mid-body; 3:33 A.M.,
hearing lots of car traffic outdoors; can't sleep; tingling
continues; get up at 4:33, eat toast and milk; return to
bed, 5:13. This all happened the first night I wrote a
long time after weeks of flu/cold, etc. ALSO: Shortly
before I got up, felt very light, like I could have been
floating—opened my eyes to make sure I was still here!
Dream: Vague, but about Dr. Sprinkle; lost details, but
see his face.

01/28/95

A noise right on pillow—like snap of rubberband—woke
me! Dream fragments; also earlier, some vibrations,
spray-chills, but nothing to bother me.

01/29/95

Tinglings; noises on inner walls; bed vibrating gently; sharp vision, eyes closed; "spray" of tinglings like chills; I keep saying, thinking, "Well, God, I turned this over to you." Doesn't stop it! When I was meditating before I went to bed, saw some "rippled lights" flash, which I suspected was an announcement.
Dream got away. But impression of naked people.

01/30/95

Very mild tinglings in feet. Dream: Babies; children; feeding a baby. The feel of an alternate reality, much like this one.

01/31/95

Tinglings, like mild electrical impulses; all over lower body, and upper too; quite a bit last night for maybe 1-2 hours before I finally went to sleep. And some sensations when I lay there for an hour in a "half-nap" state in morning.

02/2/95

3:46 A.M. Wakened by a high shrill telephone ring; earlier some tinglings/vibrations, but light. And feeling that something was going on, a "lightness," a feeling in room.

02/3/95

Blatant popping sounds; rustlings; felt a presence/mild tinglings; a kind of explosion like at top of my forehead. (I wrote this note: I know something is "present" by the absence of such noises, etc. for weeks, as comparison.)
Dream: About a Russian defector, and Michael Lindemann.

02/04/95

A shrill phantom telephone ring at 3:08 A.M. just after drifted off; felt immediately a change in my body; very short gentle "treatment"; I was even moved once; moved like "straightened up."

02/08/95

Smart baby dream with an airplane crash.

02/10/95   Nap: Dream I see an airplane land on 5th West (south pointing); I exclaim (in dream) to one of my brothers—"I dreamed that!"

02/15/95   Some "chills," vibrations.

02/16/95   3:58 A.M. Strong tinglings over legs, thighs, hips; heard a "voice" like my "angelic voice," and then while laying down, eyes closed, felt like I lost equilibrium; disoriented; lost balance. Weird! I "swooned."

Dream: 4:47 A.M. This house but different; JS comes to talk; like I'm up against him, as if we were talking in cramped quarters; talked a lot; he asks if I'm of the Agarthas? Grogans? I tell him I'm a recluse; I write! He has to go; leaves. Then in closet (where I am), I hear a drill, and think I see two beams being drilled through the wall from laundry room. Can't be! Where am I? Suddenly realize I've got on brown boots; no wonder my feet were vibrating. Then I'm in this bed, FEELING MYSELF BEING PICKED UP AROUND SHOULDERS (my body felt like marshmallow; soft/rubbery). Bodily moved; I groan . . . "Oh, Lord . . . " or "Lord, God . . . " and instantly I awaken. Feeling sure I was taken somewhere; or about to be; very suspicious, and tinglings continue as I record this incident. Next dream includes babies . . . audience . . . etc.

02/17/95   Sound of soft chimes wakes me at 4:28 A.M

02/19/95   3:58 A.M. Tinglings/"electrical sprays."

Dream: I am part of a team that is up in remote village; we go up a mountain in cars; we're trying to interrupt; foil behavior of these people here; see some cats in one house; I think these people are environmentalists; very strange landscape; encounter these people who are resistant to our group; some fantastical stuff; like a CAR RISING? Darkish atmosphere; tunnels.

02/22/95

Tinglings, etc. gentle; a "shift," feeling of bed vibration.

02/23/95

Very light tinglings; prior to popping noises.
Dream: Looking at a globe; comparing a map to it; to see where this is—near Spain? Next day, found a red welt high on thigh near vagina; no explanation. Wrote this after dream: The brain is a receiver-transmitter for Divine mind. Some operate better as receivers/transmitters than others. Some are "shut down" in this capacity. They "recirculate" past ideas . . . and the information "stored" mutates for lack of new information. Meditation is an invitation, an offering up of our minds to the reception of Divine Mind, and then transmission in our own creative way.

02/25/95

Long session of gentle tinglings, subtle shifts, and noises.

02/27/95

Tonight and last night: Humming vibrations in my pillow; tonight, lots of sprays/tinglings.

02/28/95

Tonight, while writing to Karla Turner, two distinct sounds (same sound); a long hum-buzz-sizzle, second time, felt tinglings rush over my body; and stereo receiver "popped" as the sound ended.
Dream: about ML and a UFO field investigator, about working for them.

03/01/95

Heavy "sprays" of tinglings all over, especially arms, back, chest. Woke 5:08 A.M., was dreaming about "other side," but can't quite put into words; see some images; sky . . . looking out window . . . see some symbols . . . one I like (?) . . . in maybe a craft? Mummy dolls? Earlier I was awake, thinking about a dream, or just thinking, picturing a woman having a thought, and I sort of "revised," edited the thought, as if it were mine—and there was a "ping" sound . . . that looked like a big silver iridescent teardrop sound . . . like musical . . . And I said "Thank you" out loud . . . and I did not need to write this incident down, because I was AWAKE . . . not a dream!!! But a while later, I wake up and can't remember the details. But it was about how we can change experience by changing our thoughts . . . I think.

03/02/95 Some tinglings; some major body "sprays"

Dream: About a green closet door . . . get a letter from a woman regarding UFO experiences.

03/03/95 Tail-end of dream . . . remembered that I was working on understanding how the soul works, like I'm seeing something; about how soul relates to a person? . . .

03/04/95 Earlier in dream, I drew a heart around some water, like a pool . . . a man I love . . . (was too tired to write this down earlier.)

03/07/95 Long siege of tinglings; insomnia; was thinking before I turned out light how tinglings may be over (!) (Not.) Strongest in feet; other weird sensations; lightness; was also trying to concentrate on remembering an important dream; giving myself an instruction to remember, though I know it was about 4 or later before I finally went to sleep; woke at 7:30 A.M., feeling pretty rested.

The dream that follows . . . WROTE THIS DREAM UP SEPARATELY, SIGNIFICANT . . . ONE WITH M. SCOTT PECK, and UFO sighting . . . .

03/08/95 Heard a bee-buzzing-hum sound earlier.

03/09/95 Lots of "sprays"/tinglings; looked up and saw mesh pattern over archway; faded quickly; closed my eyes; saw a zillion dots; took a long time to go to sleep. A woman's voice said, "TALK!" woke me up. When I saw the mesh (gray color) over archway, then dots . . . immediately my body felt different; suddenly felt "floaty" and vibrations like I would lift . . . only lasted a minute or so and hands felt "thick."

Dream: Features a strange Nordic child . . .

03/11/95 Dream: I saw a woman on ground, laying down; I got right down with her, lay my face on pavement and began to talk to her; telling who I was, why I was here; she told me the word . . . (town name?) was Apache . . . not what people think. But when I mention to an Apache man in a store, a barber shop, he scoffs.
A baby. I am to babysit while parents, others go for several days; I do something; talk to it, to let it know I'm okay; seems like it communicates with me too. Baby is in sleepers; a TV show is going, one of those classes like OZ or Wonderland . . . ? Seems parents/others leave and this baby and I are getting along fine. Impression of a cat, and something about language.

03/12/95 Dream: Something about flying . . . I'm in a small airplane; a man I know is pilot; talking about wingless airplanes . . . for a minute I'm thinking this one is wingless . . . but no, It has these fixed wings . . . but shaped like this . . . Nose I see is long, angular, like a sausage.

03/13/95 Tinglings/vibrations/strong and feelings of lightness, floatiness, FEEL I WILL FLOAT AWAY . . . or some of me did.

03/14/95 Heard some popping sounds . . . like circling the room.

03/16/95 Last night . . . before I fell asleep, I had clear, vivid image of a hummingbird with bright green feathers, a red/white underside; it was faced the other way . . . just a "snap" image, but so vivid, so colorful.

03/17/95 Tinglings . . . sprays . . . but nothing else weird.

03/19/95 More tinglings . . . mild

03/20/95 Unusual, distinct popping sounds in living room as soon

as I opened blinds, turned out lights and began to meditate (common). And Monday night/Tuesday morning, I have seen this before . . . a kind of light flash. I am looking down and as I raise my eyes, I see a very quick ripple of light. So brief, and like in another dimension; and earlier, walking into the living room from entrance-way, I think I saw a flash near TV (off).

03/22/95 3:30 A.M. Gentle tinglings for about 30 minutes, then begin to feel "light," then I see behind my eyes like tunnels

of spirals . . . then bed gently vibrating, then I can hear distinct tones in my pillow, bed? Octave tones, low, high, etc. Like a kind of song; I am wide awake; is this some sort of METHOD OF CONTACT—of reinforcement? Does it go on while I sleep? Oh . . . while I was seeing this tunnel-spiral thing, I felt pressure all over, inside my head. The tones came and went and came and then was a definite tingling pressure applied to one side of body; soon I fell asleep. Maybe 4:30.
Dream: A man at the window . . . and a dog . . . I'm like in kitchen, trying to do dishes; this dog—a small doberman . . . won't leave me alone, keeps jumping up on me; I feel pretty helpless and my brothers aren't helping. Afraid to whack the dog down; afraid it will attack; seems my whole family is around. Somehow I get rid of dog or it's diverted . . . Dog annoys me; why does it persist? Like it's out to get me, like it knows I don't like it, so it's hassling me; almost a sexual connotation; maybe I wonder if I should try to give it attention, pretend. I am told something about this dog, why it behaves this way. Half-awake, earlier thought I had it figured out. Why is this happening to me? LIKE I WAS BEING DIRECTED BY REMOTE CONTROL, OR SOMETHING WAS INSTALLED IN ME LIKE A COMPUTER CHIP PROGRAM; but it was something at once more sensible and more wild; and like other

times, I was *positive* I would write it down later, after all I
was awake! But must have been a dream because I
think I remember telling Mom . . . being quite matter of
fact about something that sounds pretty wild. About the
time I was thinking/realizing this, earlier, I turned on left
side . . . and was dizzy/disoriented. Amazing how at 5:15
A.M., I feel so wide awake and fine . . . and then a few
hours later I am totally whacked. Does not compute.

03/23/95   Some tinglings; dizziness, turning over this morning.

Dream: Dreamt I found the back door slightly open;
did I leave? Or was I visited? I wondered in dream.
Or did I forget to lock? Don't think so! *The back door
was unlocked this A.M.*

03/24/95   Dream: Trying to write a message . . . a letter that will
convey my situation without exposing who I am; *trying
to get help without bringing attention to myself . . .*

03/25/95   Two hours of strongest vibrations ever; THOUGHT I

MIGHT FLY AWAY; lay down my head at 1:17 A.M.;
heard tones right away; strong; can feel the vibrations
in my ear; a kind of song, like electronic bass/cello; can
hear by pressing ear to mattress too, but not as strong;
only lasts a few minutes, then begins to fade.

03/26/95   Felt a "buzz" in my head, then tones; but I refused to

pay them attention! Was determined to go to sleep,
and sleep long and well. Worked! Dream not clear;
but wrote a bunch of stuff afterward.

03/28/95   Dream: Imagery—ASIAN/Japanese landlady; my manuscript . . .

03/29/95   Strong hums in right ear/pillow; !asts only a few minutes.

03/30/95   Dream: Interrogation; I fill out lengthy questionnaire,
about 7 sections . . . Summation can be rolled to a band
I wrap around my forehead/face; call it a "snood."

03/31/95   I was dreaming about the argument as to whether or

not to "go public" about abductions . . . impression of
An image of snakes entwined in my head where mem
ories are . . . .

04/01/95   About 3:25 A.M. heard like a chorus, very strange
music, very distinctive, like nothing I've ever heard
before; quick, then I was "swept over" with sensations;
4:23— heard a door knock—seems like front of
house, like a reminder to write this down; also lots of
sounds. When I first lay down, popping and the "tic tic
tic . . . " at my ear. Also I was JOLTED, like you do sometimes half-asleep.

04/02/95 No nocturnal strangeness, but I woke with back sore
at center; very unusual to wake with a back ache; very
sore all day and I was depressed.

04/03/95   (The "ATTACK dream") Not long after I lay down,
between 2:22 and 2:45 A.M., the vibrations started in
the bed, gentle, then the humming sounds. Also saw a
red light behind my eyes. Then, much tingling, sprays,
vibrations, noises, etc. And I decided to try and project
a "golden shield," then woke at 4:43 A.M. with disturbing dream. (This is a dream about an entity that grabbed
and paralyzed me. TYPED UP THIS DREAM. Since
this 4/03 "dream," I began to feel a new sensation in
my body, a kind of gentle surge of energy throughout
lower portion of body, occurring many times during
day. *This condition lasted for many months.*

04/05/95 This weirdness again; I swear the clock said 10:30 A.M.
when I got up; was miffed that coffee was not on—and
now I look at clock and its says 9:59! Heard some suspicious noises; some feet tingling. Said, "I'm going to
sleep!" sternly. Then did.
Dream: About a tall lanky blond-haired man . . . a lecture
in a hall, folding chairs, I go sit down among various scientists; then my friend and the blond man come in; I feel
guilty for taking a chair; I'm not a scientist; but enjoy
these lectures; the men sit along a back row; so okay,
they do have seats . . .

04/06/95

Found bright red mark near left knee . . . but no other funny stuff.

04/09/95

Tones—heard through pillow (since this date, I discovered I was hearing these tones in ears . . . when I was meditating in living room . . .) Anyway . . . heard a kind of song being played, like the thumping/humming of electronic bass viol strings . . . I KNOW this is directed by something intelligent; I smiled; was so glad for the contact after 6-7 days of nothing; the last incident felt so negative (4/03) hated to end on that.

04/10/95

Sprays, tingles, also have been hearing "rings" in ear, special "one message" kind. Felt pressure on my hip, something pressing down. There was a code word, some kind of water and the phrase was incredibly descriptive . . . like burnt water . . . but not. Word that perfectly invokes image of burnt water/brown water/ old water . . . might be a control word.

Dream: Some sense of being aboard a spacecraft, but humans in charge; a man, a professor . . . slender, tall, dark curly hair . . . his daughter is privileged . . . etc.

04/11/95

Tinglings were mild, but overall feeling of same old stuff; more "meaningful" rings in ears at times; shrill "telephone" ring woke me at 4:51 A.M.

Dream . . . some imagery . . . four movies shown, but all Seem cartoon like . . . Mom and I at this university; I'm On upper campus and there's one farther up; I'm remarking how I used to know most everyone out on the lawn; over three years, almost complete turnover; a woman dressed in a huge cape of feathers (almost engulfs whole parking lot); sweeps past me. I enjoy her flamboyance; also saw a college-aged ASIAN man.

04/14/95

At some point in night, awakened by a loud voice— called my name? Did not write down dream because I was sure I would remember; do remember I laughed and said—"That was blatant!" Dream in morning, a secret facility, like Martin-Marietta; see a man I know;

beds close together; Annie with me next day; we hear there will be a crackdown on secrecy, etc; I'm not worried about getting caught; "What did I do wrong?" I ask Annie; we go to fast-food restaurant; out in main area . . . like underground? Or enclosed area; see lots of military coming, going, not worried about seeing me as a spy; I'm just visiting.

04/16/95

Tingles, etc. Quite strong; noises . . . there are always these popping noises in room during these sessions; like there's a charge in the air; at one point, something jerked my arm up; not like anything has happened before; a spontaneous jerk; before this session began, I could sense something in air; like air pressure changes; I can feel something "brushing" past my face.

Dream in A.M . . . .vague, something to do with secrets, spying, somewhere I work; walking in dark, cold, with boy or young man; like we're going to school; but it's dark, all is silent, like walking in an Alaskan village before sun is up; I have done this alone, but now I can walk with this friend; we seem to be kids, not adults.

04/18/95

Last night; there was a "shift," pressure; not so much like tingling all over as a kind of intense pressure through body; like I would burst from my skin; not pleasant. Awoke this morning, ear feels funny, kind of plugged up; feel pressure inside my head; to the left of brain stem.

04/19/95

2:38-3:07 A.M. Felt/heard something. Happening now . . . the vibrations, etc. . . . . saw many rippled lines in the air, turned on light. 3:28—tingling session; then something new; sound; lightning swift high-pitched whistle. And a singing session . . . and when I awoke after dream below, face feels like swollen on right side; ear; this radical difference between one side and other (I have experienced before).

Dream, 4:44 A.M. I'm staying at this house with others; like a conference; I've done my presentation . . . later I'm out in a main room/den . . . see that this baby has crawled up on lawn chairs? To get in a buggy kind of bed; this baby is so smart; saw it earlier; now I'm watching it; asleep (night), like an angel. Later, more activity in house; baby wakes up; I go out to be near her? him? She's sitting up; she says to me, "Don't call me Jezebel." Saw pattern of light, dancing of energy . . . precious cargo; something must be packed carefully.

04/21/95

Horn/bell/whistle sound jarred me alert, 2:28 A.M. And I can see the bed shuddering again; again, right side of head, ear feels distorted, large, sore.
No dream recall, but SEE THIS IMAGE OF ME RISING UP OUT OF BED TOWARD CEILING.

04/22/95

Tonight in living room; lots of popping sounds, a change in air and could see like spots of light and occasional flashes; very subtle, but definitely this is not ordinary experience . . . mild tinglings later. Fragmented dream later.

04/24/95

Tonight is when I first heard the humming tones *in my ears when I was meditating*; and *felt* them; like a loosening of earwax, vibrations; and thought I detected a couple of subtle light flashes; gentle tinglings; I could hear hums in bed too; went to sleep quickly; also meditating . . . saw a flash of rippling light behind eyelids.

04/25/95

About midnight, while I was in living room—I was buzzed! Something like an electronic bee buzzed my head (after I heard popping sounds in corner); I took it humorously; heard the humming sound again tonight in living room; but this time seems far away, even though some pressure/vibrations in ears, especially right. Wrote waking up in the morning: It's not that I'm seeing into the future; there is a *lag* in perception; my perception is sluggish; but Stuff a few days ahead is in progress; all I need to do is to relax, tune in . . . (Many times in "messages" and in dreams, I am told to relax.)

04/26/95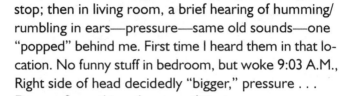

Felt pressure in ears again, while typing—like a signal to stop; then in living room, a brief hearing of humming/ rumbling in ears—pressure—same old sounds—one "popped" behind me. First time I heard them in that location. No funny stuff in bedroom, but woke 9:03 A.M., Right side of head decidedly "bigger," pressure . . . Dream: Something about a militia group.

04/27/95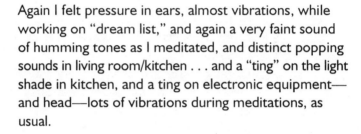

Again I felt pressure in ears, almost vibrations, while working on "dream list," and again a very faint sound of humming tones as I meditated, and distinct popping sounds in living room/kitchen . . . and a "ting" on the light shade in kitchen, and a ting on electronic equipment— and head—lots of vibrations during meditations, as usual.

04/28/95

Heard humming in ears, while meditating, and very clear, but distant sound, a kind of song. Some noises in bedroom, felt they were here—but no strong ting- ling sensations, etc.

04/29/95

Some auditory stuff in living room, then in bed I was "tingled" and heard subtle sounds—on lamp shade and around. I felt I was "shifted"—looked up and saw light show in archway. They know how much I like those. A complex pattern of light.

04/30/95

Mild tinglings in feet, but no other funny stuff. No dream, but recorded a long message about the wisdom or feasibility of getting hypnotic regressions done. A lot about "memory," screens, etc.

05/02/95

After meditation, could hear faint humming music and then in the bedroom, briefly, the buzzing sound. Felt "electrical" stroke—to inner leg. Just one. Neat dream that included being on a boat in water.

05/04/95

About 6:30 A.M. I jolted straight up. I've experienced this before. Impossible to explain. Maybe the direct opposite of feeling like you will burst from your skin. Inside—which slams you upright. Maybe a return from OBE? Not like other times I thought were, like the rushing in my head. I did feel last night a bit "light" and floaty, the shifts . . . like I was spreading out . . . but only briefly.

Dream: Some interesting imagery, a baby, etc. Then wrote in dream journal some "bizarre" thoughts . . . about them CREATING ALTERNATE BODIES FOR US. And maybe a channeled message.

05/05/95

Saw swirls of light in the archway . . . sometime (?) last night. Telling myself to remember dreams . . . Waking up yesterday, my star map on the wall was undulating. I felt heavy going to sleep . . . that strange "thick" feeling. Had a "hyper-real" dream, but I did not sleep deeply . . . a nap. A sound like "water drop music sound," then the "phantom" telephone, but was not fully asleep, so sounds were less loud, but real.

Dream: Neighbors come into the bedroom, just make themselves at home; part of me wants to wake up and talk to them, part of me wants to continue the dream to see what happens.

05/08/95

This evening, felt the strangeness in my legs more than usual. Strong tinglings . . . so the strangeness is a kind of mild tingling . . . because the sensation after lying down was a considerable intensification; new, not exactly like old tingling sensation; more an "all over at once" with some "wand passes" (some sensations zinging up inner legs, too). Sort of wanted to stay awake and observe, but went to sleep fairly quickly.

05/13/95 Tonight in living room, experienced that "sound laser" effect—as if sweeping through my ears, from right to left—like a needle of light that pierces, then during meditation, stronger than usual pressure on head— image of hands—healing—and AWARENESS THAT "DIRECT CONTACT" WOULD BE TOO MUCH— TOO MUCH POWER—MUST BE ABLE TO WITH- STAND, BEAR. In bedroom, first several "shifts" . . . getting lighter . . . not quite asleep heard distinct phantom telephone sound . . . dream images..then significant ting- lings and feelings of floatiness, lightening up . . .
Dream: I'm out in a parking lot (dark) . . . TALKING TO A DOG WHO LOOKS LIKE A MAN; blond-haired; I understand what he's feeling and tell him so; he's very impressed. Others—a man wants to hug me because I hugged the dog man. No, I tell him and move away, because haven't met this one, and don't like his leer, manner—very tall slender man. Like we were going to walk out in field to see UFO?

05/16/95 Suspicious sounds last night; mild tinglings, but dream quickly faded. Imagery: Monkeys? training? travel? lab? Head felt lopsided. Note: Lately I am feeling every evening this pressure in ears and "hums" difficult to describe but ongoing, like other recent change . . . which I will call "light infusions" from my own center. This is weird: As I was writing the above . . . dream symbols kept flashing . . . but too fleeting to capture . . . like the word is an umbilical cord . . . light cord . . . connection.

05/17/95 At 3:00 A.M. I was writing . . . I was BUZZED in left ear —STRONG, and heard faint buzzing all around. Saw LIGHT SHOW . . . ripples of light in archway; tinglings all over feet/legs; no suspicious dream remembered. Woke up with sore right ear and noticed around 5:00 P.M. that both ears are bright red!

05/18/95 Some noises, tinglings, mild, went to sleep. Either

OBE or dream about all-mind . . . how you have to be in physical form to experience/see. Some imagery—a resort in the sky . . . flashing night lights . . . Dream had flavor of traveling, vacation, but also purposeful—a learning experience.

05/24/95 No funny stuff before, but a dream . . . something about UFOs. Near end of dream, visualizing a dog—STANDS UP LIKE A DOBERMAN, BUT A DIFFERENT HEAD (I SKETCHED), NO MOUTH? A GREENISH-GRAY LUMINOUS COLOR; I AM THINKING . . . "WELL, THIS HAS ET CONNOTATIONS. THIS IS REALLY NO DOG" . . . but seems more a mental exercise than part of dream sequence. Ah—maybe they do look like this? Also at tail-end of dream, I'm telling a friend something about me and UFOs; maybe I tell her I'm not sure it's really UFOs/aliens; she sounds very relieved; I say "But something was visiting me—the experiences are/were real."

05/25/95 Tinglings on feet/legs, etc.; noises, very strong tonight . . . almost a voice . . . a presence. A light show—swirls of lines.

Dream: Newspaper; big headlines—UFOs, a page or longer article . . . I certainly expected something significant to happen . . . maybe finally I would see something consciously . . . but I fell asleep fairly quickly. Amazing I would have only fragments . . . I FELT ALMOST PICKED UP—MOVED AT ONE POINT. There WAS a presence! For sure! I was not afraid. I prayed and meditated more than usual this day.

05/26/95 Tinglings, and a light show.

05/29/95 Tinglings (Note: I'm not listing every night I feel tinglings, because rarely do I *not* feel them anymore.)

06/02/95 Lots of strong tinglings last night and "shifts." Red streak on right leg near knee; woke feeling new energy and better attitude.

Dream: I have this baby; I'm like in a hotel lobby, people around here know me; a nude baby looks about 18 months old; but intelligent; understands what I tell it; a feeling some of these people don't think I know how to take care of this baby; but I am showing them I do.

06/03/95   Mild tinglings; felt "shifts," very light, floaty . . . Dream . . .

includes an "angel"—very tall, completely white; she like "rolls" something white in like energy rolls—up the face of a mountain—then she rises up with these "rolls" —and then all evaporates. Both Michael and I saw it— I'm awestruck; we both go "Wow!"

06/06/95   To bed 2:32 A.M., wrote this 3:28 A.M.: Buzzed my ear earlier; much strong tingling; feel very floaty; distinct noises; feel presence; bed is vibrating like jelly.

Dreaming: At some point aware I am looking at concepts I can't understand on Earth; frustration; trying to

get, absorb, explain; feeling I am real amazed at what

I'm seeing. Later see a map; the ground from the air— California; FM has this land; from air looks very green and brown; vividly see this dirt road through the green part; a location away cities . . .

06/07/95   Feeling of presence during meditation; distinct noises all around; also could hear distantly but inwardly—the

"music." Phantom telephone ring jerks me awake at 8:30 A.M.

06/08/95   Tinglings . . . some kind of subtle noise woke me; dream

fleeing . . . I was working on words to describe something, separation, connection . . .

06/09/95   Dream about what goes on between here and other side; interactions; memories? Are some of our dream memories about other lives? Images of people, scenarios, but just didn't catch them.

06/15/95

Hum tones loud in my ear, in pillow. When I lay down last night, definitely felt this is something transmitted by something intelligent; there is a pattern to music, movement, etc.

06/17/95

Subtle noises in living room earlier; I flashed on a couple of round white lights, golf-ball sized; faint, pale but there; also need to mention that the "loose ear wax" feeling—vibration-wise is still going on; as are the "surges" of subtle energy in my legs.

06/18/95

Noises/tinglings; about 6:10 A.M., awakened by a shrill whistle sound; went back to sleep . . . awareness later something earlier I should have recorded.

06/19/95

Distinct "popping" sounds in living room; strong tingles on legs; feeling of a presence; but no dream memory.

06/20/95

Living room, one of those swift around the room "sparkings" when I was writing to Carla McCarty, and other "pops." Dream.

06/21/95

Loud ring wakes me 5 minutes before I thought I should get up.
Dream: KT . . . water component..of a system or packet, psychic/spiritual . . . I see like this roll of something . . . silver . . . can't let it dry out, but mistakes were made.

06/24/95

Mild tinglings; a funny "brush" sound wakes me up.

06/25/95

Strong tinglings—kundalini? Feeling of presence but intelligence (not a body); felt floaty, light, experienced "shifts"—saw a WEBBED MATRIX of LIGHT. A dream, then woke at 6:13 A.M . . . seemed like I had awakened several times to clock radio music—but how could that be?

06/26/95   A "shift", subtle change, mild tinglings. Dream.

06/27/95   Again I think I keep waking and seeing clock in 10:00 position—then finally see it's only 9:00—but so real! (Slight shift/tinglings.)
Dream . . . a cat on floor of closet?

06/28/95   Felt whole rash of tinglings/vibrations all over left side/hip—why not whole length of body? Mainly knee to chest part; then shortly after lying down I heard the phantom phone ring. Dream fragments . . . could sort of see the dream material moving away from my head like radar spreading out . . . Want to say fish/water, maybe a swamp; men with short-wave radios; in boats/canoes, messages to shore; then in a house? . . .

07/03/95   Strong tinglings/noises outside, on walls, windows; lift my head to look for light display but none; when I lay head back down, the tones (music) began very strong and noises in the house. Federal Express man banging On the door kept me from getting dream. This is the morning I woke with the strong urge to go to Denver.

07/06/95   (In Denver, Colorado.) Woke to "noise" (pressure/head/ noise)—light show on Annie's curtain. Dreamt later— rearranging letter/words, about me and my work/ success; maybe I eliminate word "fledgling" or maybe this is included; I sense this is in preparation for regression session today.

07/07/95

Still in Denver; various popping sounds, I felt the "shift," I felt "they" were around; mild tinglings. Vivid sensual dream.

07/08/95

Denver: Woke about 3:30 with a very loud sound—like HAICK! Very strange dream, underground, about Virginia preparing papers to transport a dead body, etc. Her husband Bill is, in real life, dying. Died the next morning, but I did not find out until that night (Sunday) at 10:30 P.M.

07/09/95

Denver: Woke to a very loud sound about 5:30 A.M., but no dream, nothing else; went back to sleep. Learned at 10:30 P.M. that Bill had died at 5:30 A.M. Since I had spoken to him about life after death, I believe he must have "saluted" me as he crossed over.

07/13/95

(Back in Moab.) Last few days, some tinglings, some hummings. Awakened this A.M. by a noise that jerked me awake. Noise so weird, like a loud rattling in my ear; beads on a string shook very hard; at the end: "Love is a sword that cuts the soul."

07/14/95

Most definitely felt a presence; noises in room, clicks, etc., faint hums in both ears; tinglings, but more like an electrical charge in air and behind my closed eyelids I was seeing lights jump around; a feeling something big could happen; I could fly away or something could suddenly appear; but went to sleep quickly. Waking up, my head is very "lopsided," pressure in right ear; soreness in left side of head/neck.

07/15/95   "Poppings" in LR/kitchen earlier; then a light show, a kind of symmetrical net pattern.

07/16/95   Very loud tones in my ears while I wrote to Carla.

07/17/95   Tonight during meditation flashed (eyes closed) on a fox or coyote; he wagged his tail very fast, to my left. Before this I "glimpsed" a room, very vivid, so real I took for granted, then suddenly realized my eyes were closed! This was not ordinary mental imagery that occurs during thinking/meditation, but starkly vivid/ real flashes.

07/22/95   Tinglings/shifts; some flashes of light behind my eyelids—this is new lately.

07/23/95   Popping/snapping sounds in house. Jerked awake/upright at 5:22 A.M. Images fled quickly.

07/24/95   Today during nap (didn't really sleep), very strong tinglings in feet/lower legs; night: light out 2:53 A.M., moderate tinglings and snapping noises and feeling of a presence and a sound—a quick toot of harmonica or car horn, but no light show.

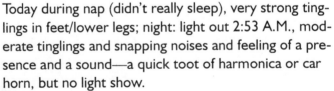

07/25/95   Tones, musical, when I was sitting in chair; could not tell where they were coming from, sort of connected to my ears, but not. Not music from outdoors, but like previous tonings, but different too; also, some very loud snappings/poppings. Noise (?) Awakens me in morning.

07/26/95

Loud popping sounds in living room/kitchen; also earlier a kind of bee-buzzy sound; tinglings/feet/legs. 2:57 A.M.: The most intense scary thing: I was drifting off, going to sleep, had dream-like thoughts of standing, on phone, talking to KK; suddenly I lost balance, was falling, couldn't talk. I moaned (in reality) loudly, which woke me and I was having the most intense "electrical" shaking-up experience thus far; my whole body, but most intense through hips and legs; vibrating like a huge fluttering of wings. Did I catch myself going or coming out of body? It was INTENSE! Like WIND. Like huge butterfly wings flapping; like I was this and would fly, or come apart. Then I felt oddly wide a-wake. Finally went to sleep.

Dream . . . I'm showing the sky to KM . . . image of a boy telling us that we are going to have to stop eating foods; A boy-genius type, giving this message. And something about UFOs.

07/27/95

Nap: I'm somewhere, like the house in Casper. Suddenly I feel so light, like I could lift off the ground, so I do; I spring upward and then I just start flying all over the place; I'm wondering what people are thinking about this; feels so free and fun; the point is, I could just feel this ability to fly, so I just went with it; and was so surprised, yet it seemed to me it had always been possible and we had not yet discovered how easy it is.

07/28/95

4:16 A.M., wake up, see a "leafy" pattern of light on ceiling; I say so, out loud—turning to tell MC, who I believe is next to me in bed, but seeing he's not, I jump up and run out into the hall, calling "Michael?" Suddenly I realize (though I am conscious) that I'm dreaming. Michael was not over here. But I have vivid "memory" of him going to sleep beside me. Of me telling him some new secrets about me and these events. He was just "here," so "real" I actually got up, looking for him. Before going to sleep, the usual "soft" tinglings and subtle shifts and feeling of presence; various noises, nothing blatant. The significance of certain sounds is in their absence other nights; i.e. I have learned to identify by what else happens in relationship.

07/30/95   Saw a bright red spot on the ceiling.

07/31/95   Channeled message tonight (personal); very mild sensational stuff, no significant noises. I see, as I wake, up a red light splotch. Dream, university/tower-like buildings, etc.

08/01/95   Tonight while talking with Annie on phone, emotionally, about abduction stuff, about me getting to truth and telling my story—there were noises at the window and at a point when I said "And I will tell—" Something hit the front door, so hard and loud, Annie could hear it on the phone; simultaneously some snapping noises at back door. Unnerved me; I fully expected I would be in for it in bed, but nothing significant. However, I awoke the next morning, in despair.

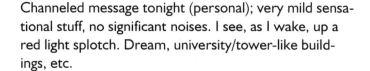

08/02/95   Some noises in living room; kind of a one-tone hum, left ear. In bed, felt internal knocking inside my head—twice. Mild tinglings/subtle shifts/body. Dreaming something about UFO discussions, etc.

08/03/95   Heard the "one-tone" hum again in my ears, especially left, while meditating. A "pop" at a certain moment/_thought. Bee-buzzy sound. In bedroom, bee-buzz sound continued. I hear a kind of "snap/click" (electrical/insectile) at the window, then same instant tinglings begin on legs in earnest. Before this moment I was hearing crickets outdoors, annoyed at how loud they sounded. The instant this "shift" occurred—the cricket sound was suddenly distant—like the whole room was shifted somehow. Rustling sounds in room. But later heard crickets again. Dozed. Snapped conscious to see a light design, like a cluster of grapes moving toward me . . . then design dissolved, looking like water, moving toward me. Bed then going to jelly, vibrating. Tinglings change and noises continue, here and there; I'm talking, asking to be shown, to see, etc. Sitting here 2:05 A.M., can hear the bee-buzzy sound. I might as well go to sleep. In the past, staying up does not stop it. It goes on and on and on. Then when I fall asleep, "it" happens. I turn out light; more tinglings, singing tones in ears and more bed vibrations. Finally I fall asleep. I awoke at some point and observed robed figures on the curtains; said to myself, well, that's an hallucination; but after waking up and recording, I feel this was rather bizarre and suspicious.

08/07/95   Popping sounds, pressure around head. Found today a BRUISE on my right eyelid! Not sore, no idea how . . .

08/08/95   Faint bee-buzzy sound, about 1:32 A.M.

08/09/95   During meditation, a long "zing" tone in left ear. Sort of feel rumbling in left ear, 1:37 A.M. At 2:47 A.M., was awakened . . . up earlier too . . . tingling, vibrations, feeling of a presence.

08/10/95   I was "sung" to, right ear. Mild tinglings. Noises. Door slams—two inside my head—one "out there." Something veered close to my left ear. I sat up, said, "That was a bit close!" Continues . . . about 7:45 A.M . . . twice an "ethereal voice" says "MOAB!" or something . . . wakes me up.

08/12/95

Definite visitation or alteration . . . 2:22 to 3:17 A.M. Feeling of pressure in head, and then feeling it all . . . think I'm dreaming (thinking I'm awake) . . . that my sister Sue is right here beside me . . . when I do come awake (feeling vibrations all over), I realize this was a dream, Sue was never here. 4:12 A.M.: I just got "tweaked" by a "blue moth." A real noise, then saw a blue light in corner of dream (??), then a moth flew in and the light was like paint . . . I was somewhere in dream like a conference . . . I heard this "click/snap," which woke me. After I wake I discover my legs are very weak and sore way up . . .

08/13/95

(On my way to Scottsdale, Arizona.) Something wrong with my legs, at upper joints—woke up with it yesterday, on left side; then by evening "wrenched" my right side and now I'm hobbling around. (This happened on trip down to get regression with Ruth Hover. Happened in Camp Verde motel.) About 11:32 P.M., feet tinglings the instant I lie down. 12:44: Was dreaming something that I was telling myself to wake up and record. But when I did, I sat up, thought someone was in the bathroom . . . went to investigate—lost the dream.
5:25 A.M.: Very loud horn noise jars me awake. Like a "bobby" (police) whistle.

08/14/95

(In Scottsdale) I lay down about 10:08 P.M., feeling very tired. I had heard distinct loud noises at door and around. The moment I lay down I heard/felt vibrating tones in right ear—a sustaining note, then a jump down an octave, etc. I heard more noises and felt something was going to happen. I relaxed and fell asleep. Awoke about 10:55—seeing a face dissolve on the ceiling. It was a man's face, fair . . . balding blond hair, and I Thought: "Oh, that's_____" (my dreamself knew the man, but my awake self did not), and his face certainly is not really on the ceiling. As soon as I moved over to the sofa, I forgot the name of this man, who had seemed so familiar. Meditation about 1:00 A.M . . . could hear chimes/xylophone . . . faint—wind chimes? But when I first placed crystals against my ears, for an instant the chime sound increased, then peaked—a kind of song—and for an instant a deep rumble tone in left ear . . . Some "pops" in the room.

Dream (later): I'm at this big long factory like place—maybe they make airplanes? I see/speak with all these people at different sections, up, down this . . . Colonnade? Like a huge hangar . . . seems outdoors, behind or to north of the place.

08/19/95

(In Tuba City, Arizona motel.) Discovered a bruise on underside of lower left leg. No idea how . . . Light out about 11:33 P.M. Felt tinglings, heard a couple of "snap" sounds, and bee-buzzy sound. I feel a "shift" occur. Feel other strangeness . . . drifting. At 12:34 A.M., wake up, fully, to sound of water . . . gushing, trickling . . . not sure . . . Drifting off, saw these eyes . . . cat eyes, or reptilian eyes . . . yellow and green. Dreamed I am involved with an Indian woman, trying to figure out . . . seeing a new way to look at things. She says . . . need to question more statements, such as "we all know deep down what's up." Which implies that when I say I don't know about (what goes on during) nocturnal events, I'm lying. Was there a cat in the dream?

08/21/95

Bee-buzzy sound, loud . . . very light tingling. This morning, heard a "drill" sound that I recognized as having heard before, as an ethereal wake-up call. Busy dreams. Bee-buzzing and snaps/pops. Maybe different visitors? Covers all messed up on bed, like whole cover was taken off and thrown haphazardly back on.

08/22/95

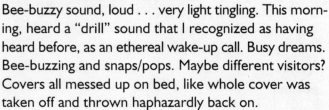

4:48 A.M. I WAS JUST VISITED. Made to think it was Ruth (Hover), but I saw her/it fade/disappear, as she dissolved into the mattress . . . I jumped up quickly. Earlier in night, soon after turning off light, I could hear like a couple of "explosions" of sound . . . and voices . . . I was buzzed at the right ear, but remember no more.

08/23/95

Stronger "energy" feelings in legs. A few loud "pops" in kitchen, during meditation. A buzzing sound in bedroom. Turn out light at 2:11 A.M. I felt the "shift," felt myself go rubbery all over. Dozed. Looked up and saw faint curtain of light. But no dream images. Got a call from S. (mother of boy who was abducted). She heard a "buzz-hum" sound, loud, went outside and saw a blue/white globe of light, (size bigger than a human head) above roof-line of house.

08/25/95

Missing time? 12:30 A.M., buzzing twice out in living room; I went out and sat under stars; came in to that special kind of silence. My right ear itched; I scratched, lay down my head, and the singing/toning started. But so far (12:54 A.M.), no funny noises in room, and tinglings on feet are mild. Very strange effects. I awake around 3:30 A.M., get up to go to the bathroom. A strong feeling that I've been somewhere, etc. It's like at these time I have knowledge that later my logic can argue with . . . . Then it seemed I just lay there awhile (after 3:30), but when I turn on the light—it's 5:45! Dream: Auditorium—I know lots of people here. Lots are internationals. But all seem Caucasian, or Nordic . . . some young men quite charming; people get up and share their stories? Something in the air over my bed . . . like a deer? I'm reaching up (literally) to touch it.

08/27/95

(In Woodland Park, Colorado.) A nightmare about a dangerous man being in my house. And this I wrote: "I am on the run. This man is not safe! I must leave, disappear, keep changing identities—my only hope. Saw him in my house and he may have tampered with my car.

08/28/95

(In Gunnison, Colorado motel.) Woke to find a rash mark, on my right thigh, like ringworm. A rough circle . . . see if it stays. (And this evening, July 9, 1996, I showed this mark to my roommate D: so yes, it stayed.) Woke around 4:16 A.M. After dream, tingles, feet/all over; strange feelings; sounds like I'm picking up traffic hum in my ears. Seems I could mentally hear someone say something about stopping by again and seems without light on, I could see this black box, up by lamp shade (nothing really there). Dream . . . about JS, a brief conversation about UFOs. (Months later I would actually have this conversation.) The place where we are talking in the dream—seems like a place (want to say Boulder City, Nevada—the dam works), a resort place, built up sides of pinkish rocks. I was talking with this other man, about UFO stuff. Seems also a place of experimentation, a "UFO place." Talking with this man, seems some question about authenticity of my experiences, but I don't seem threatened. Geez, this is like a futuristic city, like those "highways" that loop around, vehicles are more like roller-coaster cars.

08/29/95

One loud pop, one small pop, very mild feet tingling. Someone told me in dream that we were going to be learning more through pictures in near future. All part of greater changes. Was up in the night—what woke me? I think I was told something about coming events.

08/30/95

Rumbles in left ear today; especially this evening. Right eye twitches; "special silence" in room tonight. Mild tinglings and the "shift." 12:06, lights out. 12:30, after large popping sounds, looked up in dressing room and saw a new design (drew it in my journal). And then later SAW TWO SMALL DISCS IN THE ROOM. One a turquoise color, the other orange . . . about size of a dinner plate or basketball—just appeared in dressing room, then faded. I said "WOW!!" out loud. The blue one "flew" briefly.

Dream: Suspicious. "Interactions" with a boy who comes "out of a book." Sexual antics. See Journal.

08/31/95   Dream: Message: Being told, shown, how way above there's this thing going on . . . but down here, it looks very different. So don't over-react. You can't judge. Nothing that happens is exactly as it appears. (I knew that.) I'm sitting here, having strange feelings . . . about who I am, who we are, almost seeing the "extension" . . .

how I am but this finger on a hand . . . which is to say, if the finger were "intracted," I would then experience at the whole-hand level, not just the finger end. So, when I feel shut off, I have lost the feeling of a finger connected. No need to ever feel shut off, because it isn't true. Even if the fingers all got cut off, the essence would flee into the hand.

09/01/95

Some pretty loud popping sounds in living room, earlier; and some "moving light" activity behind my lids when I meditated. But went right to sleep.
Dream: Image of a naked body stretched out, face down. Like this is a border or something.

09/03/95

Tingling, feet.

09/04/95

Heard phantom phone—saw it, and thought: Oh, this is the phone that wakes me up. This morning, *smell of sulphur* strong in my room. Also saw a pink light up near ceiling, as I woke up. Size of grapefruit.

09/05/95

Tinglings, popping sounds, weird feelings, floaty, but went to sleep quickly. Lately falling off to sleep I hear voices, but nothing coherent.

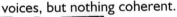

09/06/95

Heard the tonal singing out in living room; not loud, but there. Now here in bedroom . . . that eerie kind of silence. 4:25 A.M., a whistle wakes me up. Sitting up, feel everything expanded. Earlier: Was wakened . . . noise, etc. Felt this was "it," the "big change," whatever that means.
Dream: ASIANS around here; a young man dies; a shrine is built; down in a cave. The body is displayed

naked (preserved, I assume); sort of draped on side of this structure built; see poles, ropes, like it's "roped off," and stairs going down, etc. I say to several people— "But how long will he be left alone? Because this is America, kids will steal the body—vandals will come," etc. Much more.

09/07/95

Faint tonal vibration again in living room. Faint buzzing sound. Tinglings. The "shift," the "oz effect." A feeling of a presence before I went to sleep.

Dream: Active . . . lost details, but something about living with this thing, understanding that it is real, and important that I accept as real before we can go further. Thoughts about clones, how we're all clones, really. All bodies are clones, copies of other bodies, but yes, there are small distinctions. So thoughts about spirit in matter, and ego and personality, essence, etc.

09/08/95 Very busy dreams. Thoughts about UFO reality.

09/09/95

Tinglings, gentle shifting movements. Shrill telephone sound.

09/11/95

Strong tingling in feet; floaty feeling, etc. At 5:44 A.M. NOISE very loud! Wakes me up. Ethereal? Too high-pitched to be a voice, but sort of like a "voice-like explosion." A thunderclap voice? 7:00 A.M., I'm asking, was that a coming back into body noise? *Before going to bed, CD player started playing of its own accord,* and the coffee maker which I had set for morning, came on and started to brew coffee. Discovered the time had changed to 7:00 A.M.!

09/12/95

(In Woodland Park, Colorado.) Mild, brief tinglings, couple of "pops." Woke at 4:54 A.M. thinking—Hey I woke up earlier but clock said later! (huh?)

09/13/95 About 3:37 A.M., sleeping lightly, heard a loud tone, like a bass violin, then kind of vibrations ringing on air conditioner unit.

09/15/95   Some tinglings and gentle sounds . . . and I felt I heard some tones, but not sure. 1:35 A.M.—dreaming something I recognized as previous dream. Observing all this. Now seeing bigger meaning . . . something about . . . how we learn how to travel by air . . . a contraption (?) on our backs as if we are "in" bubbles.

09/17/95 Tinglings, then about 20-30 minutes later, loud telephone ring at top of my head.

09/20/95 Lots of dreams; waking up this morning, for a moment, I heard tones being sung!

09/22/95 Pops, noises, loud slam . . . inside my head. A presence. Dream: 2:29 A.M. Barely fell asleep, then this dream. I am somewhere with others, a party down the hall in a room; the door opens; I see people; looks like they're enjoying; someone says there's a psychic for 75 cents; I want to go get my purse; I am flying down the hall; not fast; a man with me grabs hold; he's flying with me; I pass a man who seems kind of half in/half out of a locker; doesn't want to go to party; when I realized I was flying (so easy, like swimming, so natural)—I woke up.

09/26/95 Strong feet tinglings; dream.

09/28/95 Loud telephone ring before I was asleep, about 2:00 A.M. Dream: Strange locale; like I'm going up this tunnel-like walkway (open) to places where people live and work; again I want to say a kind of tree house construction

with many branches. I go into water and get something a woman left on floor of pool . . . etc.

09/29/95   Heard noises and felt a presence.

10/03/95   Heard tones sung distinctly, as I lay down my head.
     Lasted a while.

10/03/95   Mild foot tinglings.
     Dream: Encounter with beings in white robes (small
beings with round heads, white robes). All to do with
     my dream self trying to move in/adjust to next environ-
ment.

10/09/95   Felt the "shift," body sensations; mild tinglings.

10/14/95   (Back in Moab.)Lots of vibrations/tinglings.

10/18/95   Strong feet tinglings; a hum in the air.

10/19/95   Hyper-real "dream," strong foot tinglings; shifts, etc.
     First woke to soft "explosions," rapid static at back of
head. Like tones in pillow, then I was "out." Definitely
felt a presence (dark). "Real" time I woke up, 1:41 A.M.
     Dream: Very strange . . . I come awake to some "explos-
ions" in back of my head, like frequency problems on a
radio; physical; wakes me up. Also, while I was "dream-
     ing," I heard someone walk across a wooden floor
above my head, slow and even steps.

10/24/95   About 10:30 P.M., aware of subtle bee-buzzing sound.

10/25/95   Before going to bed, some loud pops and other blatant noises; subtle body shifts.
Dream: Seems like I'm kind of a hostage or we all are; I'm with others; trying to figure out how to go somewhere? Something about big white rats; pets; seems I like them, but think I shouldn't, because they're rats—something about end of world information.

10/26/95   Shrill phone sound wakes me at 5:40 A.M.

10/27/95   Tinglings; noises.

11/01/95   Early Tuesday, during meditation; as soon as I set crystals on my body, the floor "moved" beneath me. Then there was a crash near/inside closet, like an explosion; then later on east wall . . . a coincidence? Not neighbors slamming door; that's a different kind of sound. 12:59: gentle knocking on wall above my head; I open my eyes—see some black spots dancing; felt a presence.

11/05/95   Dream: I'm moving into a trailer . . . with Michelle who is about 4 or 5 . . . a dog around . . .

11/10/95   Phantom telephone wakes me at 12:30 A.M.

11/12/95   Mild tinglings on feet. Gentle double knock on walls wakes up around 9 P.M.

11/13/95   Felt the tingling in my legs today . . . like I used to.

11/14/95   Classroom dream in an old place.

11/15/95   Strong tinglings, feet/legs; noises in room.

11/16/95   Tinglings/sprays on body, very loud pop-click! sound, also when I closed my eyes, saw some wavy colored lines.

11/18/95   Very strong tinglings all over body; LOUD popping noises.

11/20/95   Very strong tinglings, "sprays," electrical-like sprays all over mid-section, and I felt the "lightness" like I would float away . . . and some blatant noises in room.

11/21/95   Auditorium dream, seeing presentation of five things That were "the best . . . " Five books . . . academy awards for books? Then . . . I'm at home (not here), waiting for Dr. Walker . . . I'm in a semi-truck?

11/23/95   Tinglings, feet/legs; one loud pop, then floaty feeling.

11/26/95   VERY ACTIVE . . . intense . . . tingling . . . bed vibrations . . . multiple snapping/clicking noises . . . I was vibrated . . . Intense pressure . . . the "swimmy" feeling . . . Awoke later with something I saw . . . light on ceiling? But slow to fall asleep with all this stuff going on, then wake early (second time) with dream I think suspicious.

Dream: Seems I have this baby . . . it was like in smallest container in one of those Chinese puzzle things . . . I take it out, it's all furry, and small. All I do is keep it around, pay attention to it. I think MC says something like "Who you giving that to?" "No one! I'm keeping this one. I want to watch every stage of growth."

12/01/95

Felt a presence; funny stuff in my ear; and heard a male voice—very deep say ROWAH! I felt a bit swimmy, floaty, just for a passing moment, and noises in room in connection with ear sounds and feelings, and a feeling of being gently pressed down on bed.

Dream: Something we are doing beneath the ground; I'm part of this community; and there's a hole, a formed hole, men go down to work on something . . . etc. Another part . . . about going to live in a community in Arizona; to teach ASIAN youth our language. I observe a session and this turns me on; I want to do this; so I tell the woman, who can help me . . . we can go in together, live in temporary quarters; but this interferes with another journey for me.

12/02/95

Tinglings.

12/03/95

Woke to gentle telephone sound.

12/04/95

EXTREMELY INTENSE, virtual reality dream, wrote up as EL-4; began with feeling of pressure as I lie on my side; this happens sometimes and I realize it is associated with an event . . . this intense pressure, especially in head, and a feeling of kind of swelling, as if I will explode; so I shift, and immediately tinglings begin in my feet. This continues for a while. A couple of noises in the house, but nothing major. I remember being awakened by a phantom phone ring in morning and wonder if this was an announcement of what was to come at night. The tinglings continued; I moved a-round, watching, waiting . . . feeling the overall "some-thing"? . . . don't know when I went out, but later I saw on the wall a bright two-tone spider web . . . half was bright purple, and I knew they shined this for me, to let me know, yes, we did something, we were here. There was another light, but I forget; all I recall is seeing another light, maybe the familiar round spot on ceiling? Two dreams: A meeting with "aerospace" people, talking to a man in a kind of conference . . . we may have discussed production of a kind of rocket or flying saucer. All seems quite scientific . . . dry discussion.

12/05/95 Sound wakes me up . . . like a metal lid sitting down on a metal dish . . . last night, mild tinglings on feet. Dream about helping a child brush her teeth.

12/07/95 Dream—vivid image of a white wolf dog. My head had that "huge feeling" . . . half hammered, one side numb feeling. NOTE: lately my watch is getting warm. (Went on for over a year.)

12/08/95 Today felt a surge of heat in left ear; tonight while meditating, a lot of loud pops around LR and kitchen. 2:22 A.M., then 2:39 A.M. . . . phantom telephone ring, then I feel the head pressure and feet tingling begin; I turn on my back; I ask to remain conscious; I lie there until 3:07 . . . feeling the sensations, tinglings in-crease; "sprays" from waist down; then upper body; behind my eyes I see strange patterns, a zillion pinpoint black dots, like in a cartoon background; I catch images, too vague to call "real." At some point I go to sleep, or shift . . . Then a dream . . . vivid . . . Suddenly I awake and see the distinct red flower with black/yellow center float across the ceiling. I've seen this flower before. (And saw it a lot after this date.)

12/09/95

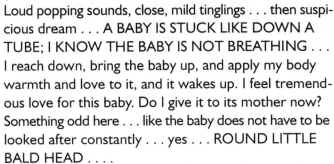

Loud popping sounds, close, mild tinglings . . . then suspicious dream . . . A BABY IS STUCK LIKE DOWN A TUBE; I KNOW THE BABY IS NOT BREATHING . . . I reach down, bring the baby up, and apply my body warmth and love to it, and it wakes up. I feel tremendous love for this baby. Do I give it to its mother now? Something odd here . . . like the baby does not have to be looked after constantly . . . yes . . . ROUND LITTLE BALD HEAD . . . .

12/10/95

Definitely strong tinglings all over lower body, then a noise and the pressure and the floaty feelings . . . went pretty fast . . . no dream recall. But this morning when I awake, the red flower on the wall, faint. Dream about being over in Germany. Nap: Tinglings, a loud pop when I was thinking about twelve tribes . . .

12/11/95

Mild tinglings and other signs, and I awoke later and saw something in the corner, like a silver dot network spiral?

12/12/95

Tinglings . . . again I don't recall dreams, but do recall seeing those red flowers on walls/ceiling . . . like I kept seeing it, a return, like I could make it rerun . . .

12/14/95

Strong tinglings and sprays, but not for long, and I woke later and saw that the air all around and above was "swirling," like energy swirls; I wondered if it's like this all the time and just don't see, or if I'm seeing what happens when I'm tingling, like the vibrations are turned up, and when I woke this morning, earlier, that round pink/red spot . . .

More of the same continued throughout 1996 and 1997, with a decrease of both phenomena and UFO-related dreams, when I moved to Virginia in April 1997. Two abduction-like events happened in 1996, and one in 1997, which I considered to be the last of that kind to date. Certain phenomena continue—tinglings, vibrations, humming tones, an occasional light display, and the "ethereal" telephone ring.

The mystery continues.

ABOUT THE AUTHOR

Summoned is Dana Redfield's first published work of nonfiction.

Redfield was born in California and raised in Utah, Wyoming, Texas, and Oklahoma. She attended Northeastern State College in Oklahoma and Brigham Young University in Utah.

Redfield lives and writes in southeastern Utah. She is currently working to complete a modern-day Jonah tale, scheduled for publication by Hampton Roads in the near future.

Hampton Roads Publishing Company

. . . for the evolving human spirit

Hampton Roads Publishing Company
publishes books on a variety of subjects including
metaphysics, health, complementary medicine,
visionary fiction, and other related topics.

For a copy of our latest catalog,
call toll-free, 800-766-8009,
or send your name and address to:

Hampton Roads Publishing Company
134 Burgess Lane
Charlottesville, VA 22902
e-mail: hrpc@hrpub.com
www.hrpub.com